ANOTHER ARABESQUE

ANOTHER ARABESQUE

Syrian–Lebanese Ethnicity
in Neoliberal Brazil

JOHN TOFIK KARAM

TEMPLE UNIVERSITY PRESS
Philadelphia

Temple University Press
1601 North Broad Street
Philadelphia PA 19122
www.temple.edu/tempress

∞

The paper used in this publication meets the requirements
of the American National Standard for Information Sciences—
Permanence of Paper for Printed Library Materials, ANSI Z39.48-1992

Library of Congress Cataloging-in-Publication Data

Karam, John Tofik.
Another arabesque : Syrian–Lebanese ethnicity in neoliberal Brazil /
John Tofik Karam.
    p.   cm.
Includes bibliographical references and index.
ISBN 13: 978-1-59213-539-4   ISBN 10: 1-59213-539-0 (hardcover : alk. paper)
  ISBN 13: 978-1-59213-540-0   ISBN 10: 1-59213-540-4 (pbk. : alk. paper)
  1. Lebanese—Ethnic identity—Brazil.   2. Syrians—Ethnic identity—Brazil.
3. Ethnicity—Economic aspects—Brazil.   4. Ethnicity—Social aspects—Brazil.
        5. Brazil—Civilization—Arabic influences.   I. Title.

F2659.L42K37 2007
305.892'75692081—dc22   2006015346

2   4   6   8   9   7   5   3   1

To the memory of my grandmother, Tamar Ghosn Sfeir,
meus olhos.

To the memory of my grandfather, Tofik Sfeir,
ya ʿaiuni.

To my mother, Amelia Therese Karam,
ya ruhi.

To my father, Maron Joseph Karam,
ya ʿalbi.

CONTENTS

ACKNOWLEDGMENTS

WHILE VISITING LEBANESE RELATIVES in Rio de Janeiro in 1992, my brother and I accompanied our Brazilian-born cousin to a local arts-and-crafts fair. Among tourists and national artisans, my brother set his eyes on an elaborate bottle decorated with fake stones. With a client in his midst, the vendor declared, "Forty thousand cruzeiros." Appalled at the inflated price, my cousin and I countered that it was not worth more than twenty. Lowering his initial offer by almost half, the dealer grew impatient as I demanded another *descontinho* (little discount). "Twenty or nothing," I repeated. Tired of my haggling, the vendor met my demands but then commented to me, "You don't have the face of a Brazilian. You're *turco* [Turk]!" He proceeded to raise his clenched fist into the air to signify my tightfisted character, concluding, in a tone of defeat, "*Pão duro!* [fig., cheapskate]." Walking away from the successful transaction, we all laughed. Our cousin was afforded free entertainment. My brother acquired the uniquely decorated bottle. And, as a third-generation Lebanese American from upstate New York, I received my first lesson in being recognized as Arab in Brazil, at no further cost.

Notwithstanding this penchant for bargaining associated with Arabs in Brazil, I have incurred innumerable debts in the almost fifteen years that have passed since that exchange. To John Burdick, Arlene Dávila, Jeff Lesser, Karin Rosemblatt, Caroline Tauxe, and Hans Buechler, I am indebted for the countless number of detailed commentaries and critiques of what began as a dissertation project at Syracuse University. I can only hope that this book is worthy of all the time and effort that you all have spent on it. To Bob Foster, I am indebted to you for taking me under your collegial and intellectual wings ever since I took my first anthropology course with you at the University of Rochester in 1992. To William Hammell, Laura Nader, Eugene Nassar, and two anonymous reviewers at Temple University Press, I am indebted to you for crucial suggestions and energizing words of encouragement that brought this manuscript to fruition. Any shortcomings in the coming pages are of my own doing.

I am also thankful for the financial support that I received from several institutions. My graduate studies were made possible by a University Fellowship from Syracuse University. A Maxwell School Summer Fellowship Grant and Roscoe Martin Fund Grant helped me to begin research in Brazil and Lebanon. A Fulbright-Hays Doctoral Dissertation Research Award from the U.S. Department of Education was crucial for the bulk of research undertaken in Brazil. A library travel grant from the Center for Latin American Studies at the University of Florida, Gainesville, enabled me to consult primary and secondary sources on Middle Easterners across Latin America and the Caribbean. Finally, the Sultan bin AbdulAziz Al-Saud Postdoctoral Fellowship at the Center for Middle Eastern Studies (CMES) at the University of California, Berkeley, provided me with a marvelous space and wonderful colleagues to complete this book project. I am especially indebted to Nezar AlSayyad, Emily Gottreich, and the CMES staff.

This book would never have been possible if it were not for Arab Brazilian friends and colleagues. Words cannot express my gratitude to so many of you who shared your experiences and thoughts on what it is like to be, and be seen as, Arab and Brazilian. Except in the cases of public or well-known figures, I decided to use fictitious names throughout this book, because I did not want to compromise anyone's position or opinions that were often conveyed to me in confidence. But I will here extend my deepest appreciation to many of you. In particular, I thank Magali Abbud, Samir Abdul-Hak, Michel Alaby, Dr. Sami Arap, Valéria Aron, Dr. Samoel Atlas, Adel Auada, Dr. Sarkis Joud Bayeh, Sílvio Bussab, Sílvia Tonetti Bussab, Maurice Costim, Teresa Salemi Cury, Eduardo Daher, Chaker Ussama Al-Debes, Roberto Duailibi, Paulo Daniel Farah, Luiz Fernando Furlan, Miguel Gantus Júnior, Eli Ghanem, Dr. Claude Fahd Hajjar, Dr. Alfredo Salim Helito, Sadik Kassis, Adhemar Khachef, Georges Fayez Khouri, Mauro Fadul Kurban, Regina Helena Kury, Khaled Fayez Mahassen, Bernando Badra Maluhy, Vera Kattini Mattar, Dr. Antônio Moucachen, Dr. Ismail Rajab, Nassar Rajab, Jean Risk, Chaalita Saad, Nicolau Saad Filho, Roberto Safady, Jorge Sarhan Salomão, Gilberto Afif Sarruf, Omar Atique Sobhie, Omar Sleiman, Áddil Wansa, Sahak Varteresian,

Suzana Yazbeck, and Dr. Riad N. Younes. I am also indebted to many political leaders of Syrian–Lebanese descent: City Councilor Abdo Mazloum from the Municipal Council of Guarulhos; City Councilors Nabil Bonduki, Salim Curiati, and Mohamad Said Mourad from the Municipal Council of São Paulo; State Deputies Salvador Khuriyeh and Jamil Murad from the Legislative Assembly of São Paulo; and Federal Deputy Ricardo Izar in Brasília.

Several colleagues played a crucial role in my research, not only imparting to me their reflections about Arabness and _brasilidade_, but also connecting me into their social, religious, charity, medical, and commercial associations. In particular, I profoundly thank Wilson Haddad of Clube Atlético Monte Líbano, Rubens Anauate of Club Homs, Dr. Samer Farhoud of Clube Marjeyoun, Eduardo Elias and Rezkalla Tuma of the Federation of Arab Entities in the Americas (Fearab), Roberto Cabariti of the Esporte Clube Sírio, Hafez Mograbi of the Lar Sírio Pró-Infância, Nailize Kaba of the Sociedade Beneficente "A Mão Branca," Hassan Ali Sharis of the Associação Beneficente Islâmica do Brasil, Walid Shukair of the Sociedade Beneficente Muçulmana and its publication _al-Urubat_, Dr. Fares Abdulmassih of the Grupo Hakim, Dr. Raul Cutait of the Hospital SírioLibanês, Fadley A. A. Fattah of the Câmara de Comércio Árabe Brasileira, Fouad Naime of _Carta do Líbano_, Carlos and Marcello Moufarrege of _Orient Express_ magazine, George Thame of _Jornal do Brás_, and Rosa Saposnic Chut of _O Hebreu_. To Maurice Saad Jr. of Univinco, I am extremely grateful to you for bringing me into the world of Rua 25 de Março. To Jorge Hamuche, thank you for welcoming me into Brás. To Raul Fajuri of _Revista Chams_, I am forever indebted to you for being my first introduction to the Arab experience in Brazil. An enormous debt is especially owed to Leila Chamaa, who continuously went out of her way to arrange for me to be invited to the most varied events in and outside the _colônia sírio-libanesa_. Leila not only made my research possible; she also made it thoroughly enjoyable.

As part of my research in Brazil, I partook in a tourist excursion with other youth of Lebanese descent for one month in Lebanon. Called the Emigrant Youth Camp, the program is sponsored by the General Directorate of Emigrants in the Ministry of Foreign Affairs of the Lebanese government. For giving me the opportunity to participate (and enjoy myself), I am indebted to Mahmood Joumaa, general director; Ahmed Assi, public-relations director; Ranya Maalouf, public-relations assistant director; Elie Khachan, also of the public-relations department; and the staff hired for the camp, including Fatima Ayoub, Fadi El-Far, and William El-Ghajar. I also thank Boushra Haffar and Claudia Karam in the publications department at the Ministry of Tourism. During the trip, I made close friendships with participants that I continue to cherish. Our _turma_ of more than sixty Brazilians of Lebanese descent made for a memorable time. To Aron, Alex, Daniel, Gabriel, Leandro, Lucas, Maurício, Michel, Pedro Paulo, and many others, *valeu!* Special thanks go to Eduardo Chaalan Bittar, too.

Some of my largest debts are owed to relatives and family friends across Rio de Janeiro and São Paulo. Without meaning to sound like a greeting card, it has been my honor and privilege to be related to you by blood, marriage, or fate. To my cousins in Rio de Janeiro—especially Antônio and Nazaré Bichara, Bichara Neto and Ana Paula Abidão, Isabella and Jeff Hooker, and Felipe Bichara—I owe you all for giving me a second home, literally. When I am with you, I feel closer to *siti* and the world that she, her brothers, and her parents, experienced. *Ya 'aili habibi, kila bil 'albi para sempre.* Close friends and relatives in São Paulo—especially Sérgio, Diana, Daniela, Fabiana, and Sandro Lex; Helô and Geds Machado; Adonis Oliveira; Felipe and Carol Machado de Oliveira; Fernando and Natália Machado de Oliveira; and Saed, Isabel, and João Khoury—have been a constant source of strength and exhilaration. Ever since my first stay in São Paulo as a high-school exchange student in 1991, you have always been there for me. *Talvez vocês não sejam de sangue, mas sem dúvida compartilhamos a alma.*

All of these debts are far beyond excessive, but I owe an even greater amount than can ever be repaid to my late grandparents Tamar and Tofik Sfeir; my parents, Amelia and Maron Karam; my sister, Mary Therese Karam McKey; my brother, Joseph Karam; my uncle, George Sfeir; my brother-in-law, John McKey; and my sister-in-law, Marianne Skau. The love and sustenance that you all have given me has been unconditional, total, and automatic. When I was (and still seem to be) lost in my thoughts, buried under articles or books, and glued to the computer keyboard, you have continuously, and often defiantly, pulled me back from this iron cage of academic abstractions to a world where I am a grandson, a son, a younger brother, a nephew, and a brother-in-law. In view of the indefatigable support that you have unconditionally granted me, I cannot help but wonder whether I was "sized up" correctly by the street vendor in Rio de Janeiro. Am I a tightfisted character who receives far more than he gives? In the case of our family, it could not be closer to the truth.

ANOTHER ARABESQUE

The Politics of Privilege

N EARING AVENIDA PAULISTA (Paulista Avenue) in uptown São Paulo on a cool evening in 2001, I follow the public signs of Arabness. I first come across Habib's Arab fast-food restaurant. Preparing almost half of the estimated 1.2 million esfihas ("Arab" meat pies) sold daily in the city, the chain is ignored by professionals who drive in the direction of posh Syrian–Lebanese restaurants up the street. I proceed toward Club Homs on the main avenue. Hailed as "the house of Arabs," it is one of a half-dozen Middle Eastern country clubs in the area. On this night, the club is hosting a chic commemoration of the National Day of Syria. Passing through the security gate, I join a cadre of mostly Arab and some non-Arab Brazilians. Among the eminent businessmen in attendance is a third-generation Syrian–Lebanese who has been praised by President Cardoso for training Brazilian executives in how to export to the Arab world. The Arab Brazilian Chamber of Commerce over which he presides is located just across the avenue. Also present are dozens of foreign dignitaries and national politicians, such as a second-generation Lebanese city councilor who leads the annual Lebanese independence day event in the São Paulo city government. Her honored guests the previous year included physicians of Lebanese descent who practice at the award-winning Syrian–Lebanese Hospital just two blocks off the main avenue.

That such an arabesque winds through and beyond Avenida Paulista may seem puzzling. After all, Avenida Paulista is hardly an Arab space. Considered the "postcard of São Paulo," it guides the country's current neoliberal experiment. Attracting increased flows of foreign capital since the 1970s, Avenida

Paulista today is home to headquarters of national and transnational groups in industry, trade, and finance, such as the Federation of the Industries of the State of São Paulo, Banco Itaú, Citibank, and the Bank of Boston. State and business elites from Brazil and the world pass through the many blocks of high-rise buildings that line the eight-lane avenue. Alongside traders and statesmen, prosperous doctors, lawyers, engineers, and other professionals meet in the upscale cosmopolitan restaurants and bars in the adjacent "noble" neighborhoods of os Jardins (the Gardens). How have apparent Arab elements and events attained such a marked visibility amid such dominant interests on Avenida Paulista? What does this say about the place of Middle Eastern descendants today in this Brazilian city and nation?

Nearly a half-century after the last major waves of immigration, Middle Easterners have attained an unprecedented kind of privilege throughout Brazil. They oversee multimillion-dollar business ventures, constitute an estimated 10 percent of both the City Council in São Paulo and the federal congress in Brasília, own advertising and television enterprises, star in the top-rated soap opera *O Clone* (*The Clone*), and run some of the most envied country clubs among national elites. This book focuses on the greater recognition of Brazilians of Syrian–Lebanese descent during the neoliberal "transition." Through the 1970s to today, neoliberal initiatives—such as market liberalization, government downsizing, and consumer diversification—further linked Brazil into the world system. At this crossroads, second- and third-generation Syrian–Lebanese have ethnically projected themselves as export partners, ethical politicians, and diverse connoisseurs, shaping and reflecting the Brazilian nation-state in the late twentieth and early twenty-first centuries.

Drawing on the work of Michael Omi and Howard Winant (1986), my wider contention is that Syrian–Lebanese ethnicity has intensified as a project in Brazil. "Every project," writes Winant (1994: 139), "is necessarily both a discursive or cultural initiative, an attempt at ... identity formation on the one hand; and a political initiative, an attempt at organisation ... on the other." I show that second- and third-generation Syrian–Lebanese have articulated an "ethnic project" about the meaning and place of Arab business, politics, family life, social mobility, and leisure. Layered with contradictions and ambivalences, the Arab ethnic project is evident not necessarily in daily situations, but in "marked frames" of action for the "public sphere" (Habermas 1989; Lewis 1999), such as business seminars, political celebrations, dinner banquets, and heritage vacations. Represented in newspapers, television, advertising, or other media, these institutional practices guide my analysis of Arab ethnic recognition in Brazil. Throughout my book, "arabesque" is used to express this privileged design of Arabness today.

The Arab ethnic project is intricately part of Brazil's neoliberal experiment. In the open economy, Syrian–Lebanese descendants have fashioned themselves as Arab promoters of Brazilian exports to the Persian Gulf market. During a World Bank anticorruption program in the São Paulo city government, politicians of Lebanese descent have sponsored an ethical celebration of Lebanese independence day. In consumer diversification, Syrian–Lebanese socialites have used the mainstream marketing appeal of "Arab food" to build social capital with non-Arab guests in their country clubs. Brazilians of Syrian–Lebanese descent have even been targeted as a market for homeland tourism in Syria and Lebanon. In short, Arab ethnicity has gained a novel force in the turn toward economic openness, state transparency, and consumer diversity. This focus on the novel formation of Arabness in Brazil is what I mean by "another" arabesque in the book's title. While attentive to its continuities with the past, I suggest, Syrian–Lebanese ethnicity has also undergone significant change in neoliberal Brazil.

ETHNICITY, THE NATION, AND NEOLIBERALISM

By framing the Arab project in such terms, my work builds on and advances a recent turn in the anthropology of ethnicity. Since Frederik Barth's (1969) constructivist approach to ethnic boundaries, anthropologists have traced the historical production of ethnic difference from colonialism through nationalism (Alonso 1994; Friedlander 1975; Munasinghe 2001; Stutzman 1981; Warren 1989 [1978]). In the most sophisticated way, Brackette Williams (1989, 1991) has explored how the colonial order of ethnicity was later reproduced by subordinate groups in the making of nation, despite the formal end of colonialism itself. Recently, however, more nuanced questions have been raised about the greater recognition of ethnicity in the nation through advertising agencies (Dávila 2001), free-market reforms (Schein 2001), and human-rights campaigns (Warren 1998). While addressing the shifting ways that ethnicity has been marginalized in the past and present, these authors have turned their attention to the increased visibility of ethnicity in the nation through globalizing images and networks.

A parallel shift can be traced through scholarship on the nation and nationalism. For the past two decades, Benedict Anderson's seminal theory of the nation as an "imagined community" has sparked much critical work across disciplines (Anderson 1991 [1983]). The nation, Anderson has shown, was created in the New World of the Americas and became a model transplanted first to Europe and later to Africa and Asia (Anderson 1991 [1983]: 4). In an early debate, Partha Chatterjee (1993) contended that the idea of nation was not merely transplanted by Western powers to South Asia but had been autonomously defined by elites under colonialism. More recently, however, anthropologists have focused on how nations are imagined through global commodities such as Coca-Cola or Budweiser (Dávila 1999; Foster 2002), television (Abu-Lughod 2005; Mankekar 1999; Wilk 1995), and migratory networks (Basch et al. 1994; Duany 2002; Glick-Schiller 2001). These studies raise a fresh set of questions about the imaginative construction of the nation in global political economy today.

Following these lines of inquiry, my work pushes beyond colonial and postcolonial histories of ethnicity and nation-making. As Aihwa Ong (1999: 35) has asserted, "We must move beyond an analysis based on colonial nostalgia or colonial legacies to appreciate how economic and ideological modes of domination have been transformed ... as well as how ... countries' positioning in relation to the global political economy has also been transformed." With this in mind, my book asks: How have the hierarchical relations between ethnicity and the nation reorganized in the world system today? Ethnicity, I contend, is no longer only peripheral to the nation but also privileged in ways that reflect and shape wider political-economic trends. I explore this transformation by tracing the ways that ethnicity was primarily marginalized in earlier times and gained greater recognition in the late twentieth and early twenty-first centuries.

The current phenomenon of neoliberalism in Latin America foregrounds the need for this approach. Its origins lay in the 1776 oeuvre of Adam Smith, *The Wealth of Nations*. Coining the "the invisible hand" metaphor (Smith 1976 [1776]: 1:477), Smith has been construed as a champion of the free market and a critic of big government. His nineteenth-century successor David Ricardo added that trade and wage contracts "should be left to the fair and free competition of the market" (1951 [1815]: 1:105). Through World War I, their ideas gained wide acceptance among Latin American elites in the paradigm of progress and positivism. Ironically, liberalism was used to "reject imperial hierarchies and assert sovereignty" as well as to emphasize whiteness and masculinity as ideal qualities of the national citizenry (Appelbaum et al. 2003: 4).

With the effects of the Great Depression, this free-market orientation was reversed across Latin America. To reduce external exposure and ensure stability, high tariffs were placed on imports, public companies were established, and the state gained control over exchange rates. Though part of political discourse since 1919, John Keynes published *The General Theory of Employment, Interest, and Money* in 1936. Challenging the free-market ideal in classic liberalism, Keynes promoted state-led development. His blueprint took the form of the Import Substituting Industrialization (ISI) program implemented in many Latin American countries at this time. While the ISI paradigm protected and bolstered the domestic market, political projects sought to incorporate groups along lines of race, class, and gender into the nation. Across Latin America, protectionist policies developed alongside nationalist ideologies.

By the 1970s, most of the continent had begun to experience significant economic growth (Gwynne 1999: 72; Kay 1989). Such expansion, though, was partly due to large capital inflows that "peaked at US $22 billion in 1978" (Gwynne 1999: 76). Banking institutions were eager to lend to Latin American states because of their increased capital holdings from oil-price hikes. In 1982, however, this credit dried up when Mexico declared that it could not meet scheduled repayments. Similar moratoria were announced by other countries in and beyond Latin America in the 1980s. A world financial crisis tantamount to the 1930s seemed to be on the horizon. In this milieu, two institutions founded under the aegis of post–World War II U.S. power—the International Monetary Fund (IMF) and the World Bank—provided funds necessary to protect bank lenders and took charge of debt restructuring in Latin America, with strings attached.

Viewing the ISI program and Keynesian economics as manufacturing only inefficiency, the IMF and World Bank disbursed loans to indebted states contingent on their adoption of an economic program outlined by Smith, Ricardo, and their twentieth-century heir, Milton Friedman. Dubbed "the Washington Consensus," the set of policies has included stabilization by reducing inflation and fiscal deficits; opening the economy and privatizing public companies; and adopting an outward, export orientation (Williamson 1993: 1329). These so-named neoliberal reforms were initially supported by middle classes dismayed by state-led development policies that seemed to shelter corrupt national industries and civil servants. In what has been called a "silent revolution" (Green 1995: 2), several Latin American governments have downsized, sold public companies, and opened national markets from the mid-1980s until today.

Welcomed by some, bemoaned by others, this new instance of liberalism has been primarily treated as a structural phenomenon in Latin American Studies. Some have seen it as crucial to reform states and markets (Kingstone 1999; Oxhorn and Ducantenzeiler 1998; Weyland 1996, 1998). Others have argued that it exacerbates gender inequality (Babb 2001), social exclusion (Chase 2002), and political-economic vulnerability (Gwynne and Kay 1999). Making a critical contribution in this line of inquiry, Charles Hale (2002, 2005) has recently shown that neoliberal policies do not negate but selectively recognize ethnic claims in order to safeguard dominant relations in the nation. In a similar fashion, I demonstrate that the increased recognition of Brazilians of Middle Eastern descent not only signals their greater privilege but also reveals certain limits to ethnic claims within the neoliberal order.

In significant ways, however, this book diverges from scholarship that has approached neoliberalism from a structural and policy-based standpoint. Instead, my work builds on what Jean Comaroff and John Comaroff have called "the culture of neoliberalism" (2000: 304). The provocative phrase is part of the Comaroffs' aim to highlight "less remarked" aspects of the current moment, such as "the odd coupling … of the legalistic with the libertarian," as well as their connection to "more mundane features," such as "the increasing relevance of consumption … in shaping selfhood, society, identity" (Comaroff and Comaroff 2000: 292–93). In a similar manner, I grasp neoliberalism in cultural and discursive terms of market openness, government transparency, and consumer diversity. The open-market model required by the IMF and the Washington Consensus has given newfound significance to national exportation and its interlopers. The defense of the "efficient state" headed by the World Bank has overtly politicized the struggles against corruption and for ethics or transparency.[1] Marketing has commodified ethnic culture, while target marketing has made ethnic groups into consumer niches. By attending to the culture of neoliberalism, my work is able to better capture its embeddedness in specific national contexts.[2]

My approach to ethnicity, the nation, and neoliberalism thus engages with Arjun Appadurai's seminal interpretation of ethnic intensification in globalization. Appadurai has reflected that "ethnicity, once a genie contained in the bottle of some sort of locality (however large), has now become a global force, forever slipping in and through the cracks between states and borders" (Appadurai 1996: 41). Whereas Appadurai has understood the increasing force of ethnicity as reflecting and contributing to the crisis of the nation-state, my work, to a degree of contrast, maintains that the greater recognition of ethnicity remains linked to the still hegemonic framework of the nation. I show that Arab ethnicity has gained privilege in Brazil today, but such acknowledgment ultimately ties into the Brazilian national context.

ETHNICITY AND NATION IN NEOLIBERAL BRAZIL

Though gaining popularity among exporters, politicians, and marketers today in Brazil, the labels *étnico* (ethnic) and *etnicidade* (ethnicity) would seem esoteric to most lay citizens. Much more common are the terms *descendente* (descendant) and *descendência* (descent). In this idiom, the typical ethnic question is: *Você é descendente de quê* (What are you a descendant of)? It is often heard in this country made up of citizens who trace their origins to more than 8 million immigrants from Europe, East Asia, and the Middle East (Fausto 1999). In relation to an ethnic group, the standard designation is *colônia* (literally, "colony," and figuratively, "community"). In particular, Brazilians of Syrian–Lebanese descent consider co-ethnic persons and institutions as part of *a colônia sírio-libanesa* (the Syrian–Lebanese colony).

As a unit of analysis, ethnicity has been increasingly employed in immigration studies in Brazil, especially in the 1990s (Fausto 1993; Grün 1999; Hall 1979; Martins 1989; Reichl 1995; Seyferth 1990; Truzzi 1997). Focusing on immigrants as *colonos* (tenant farmers), *operários* (factory workers), or *mascates* (peddlers), these authors have limited their study of ethnicity to the socioeconomic and structural realm. Recently, however, ethnicity has also been explored in relation to the cultural politics of nation-making. In *Negotiating National Identity* (1999), Jeffrey Lesser has asked how non-European and non-African immigrants forged a hyphenated ethnicity through symbolic means in the nation. Focusing on the period between the mid-nineteenth century and the 1960s, Lesser has reflected that ethnicity is a "hidden hyphen"—"predominant yet unacknowledged"—in modern Brazil (Lesser 1999: 4). My work is indebted to, and builds on, Lesser's historical analysis by exploring how the hyphen has become more visible today.

Ethnicity has gained acknowledgment during what I call the neoliberal moment or experiment. In Brazil, the structure of neoliberalism began to be implemented in the 1970s, but its culture became evident only in the 1980s. At that time, business elites founded neoliberal think tanks, called "liberal institutes" (Gros 2004; Nylen 1993). State immigration policy was also revamped for transnational executives and cheap labor (Galetti 1996; Sales e Salles 2002). By the 1989 elections, the term *neoliberalismo* entered into public debate. The then parochial Fernando Collor de Mello championed it as an antidote for the corruption allegedly resulting from past decades of big government. Framing a presidential bid on a "platform in favor of neoliberalism" (O'Dougherty 2002: 117), he promised to fire corrupted civil servants and end protectionist policies that sheltered praetorian domestic industries. As a "hunter of mahajaras," Collor assumed the presidency in 1990, slashed trade tariffs in 1991, and then fled under charges of corruption and impeachment in 1992. Presidents Fernando Henrique Cardoso (1994–2002) and Luiz Inácio "Lula" da Silva (2003–), as well as the mayor of São Paulo, Marta Suplicy (2001–2004), have since maintained, renewed, or sealed accords with the IMF and World Bank upholding the free-market model and transparent governance programs in Brazil.[3]

My book shows that Arab ethnicity was primarily devalued in earlier times but gained greater recognition during the contemporary moment. In the first half of the twentieth century, for instance, Luso-Brazilian elites disparaged Middle Easterners as innately cunning traders who accumulated vast sums of wealth yet produced nothing for the nation (Campos 1987; Karam 2004; Lesser 1999). Today, however, the commonly held notion of an inborn Arab commercial shrewdness has been praised by Brazilian exporters in the "free" market. Moreover, the ethical image sought by politicians of Lebanese descent has been officially celebrated in the São Paulo City Council during an anticorruption media campaign. Respectively explored in Chapters 1 and 2, Arab ethnicity has gained greater public power through the novel significance of exportation and ethical accountability in Brazil's open economy and transparent state.

Indeed, most Brazilians of Middle Eastern origin allege the near absence of discrimination in their lives and their "integration" into the country. Such claims, however, must be understood in relation to Brazilian nationalist ideas of *mestiçagem* (mixture) and *democracia racial* (racial democracy), first celebrated by Gilberto Freyre in *Casa grande e senzala* (1977 [1933]).[4] Freyre claimed that miscegenation among Indians, Africans, and Portuguese in Brazil created a mixed society that "balanced racial antagonisms" (Freyre 1977: 126). Although scholars since the 1950s have documented racism in Brazil (Cardoso and Ianni 1960; Hasenbalg 1979; Wagley 1952), the idea of the slight existence of racism remains prevalent today. Since the early 1990s, social scientists have disagreed over whether this situation is specific to Brazilian history (Bourdieu and Wacquant 1999; Fry 1995) or serves racial hegemony (Andrews 1991; Goldstein 2003; Hanchard 1994). Disrupting this debate, Chapter 3 suggests that the nationalist idea of racial democracy has been reconstructed today in a market model: either undermined by the statistical imagery of the economic disparity between "blacks" and "whites" or confirmed by anecdotes of the economic mobility of "ethnics" (such as Arabs). Likewise, Chapter 4 shows that the nationalist idea of mixture has remained important in the public sphere but has been removed from the state immigration policy of economic productivity. In both cases, market representations have not replaced but remodeled national belonging.

The current reorganization of race and ethnicity is most evident in the Brazilian cultural industry. In *A moderna tradição brasileira* (1988), Renato Ortiz has explored how Brazilian national identity took shape through the expansion of broadcast and print media from the 1940s through the 1970s. His observation that "something changed" in Brazil during this period could easily characterize related developments in the 1990s until today. To a degree of contrast, though, the culture industries now have helped produce not only national, but also racial and ethnic, identities. Along these lines, scholarly work has just started on Brazilian racial and ethnic formations vis-à-vis the cultural commodities of blackness—including funk music and hip hop—flowing from Europe and the United States (Pardue 2004; Sansone 2003), as well as commercial media in Brazil, such as the U.S. African American-inspired magazine *Raça* and the blonde pop star Xuxa (Kofes et al. 1996; Simpson 1993). In some contrast to these works' emphasis on the reproduction of past hierarchies, however, Chapters 5 and 6 of this book direct attention to how the conventional order between Arab ethnicity and the Brazilian nation has been partially rearranged as "Arab culture" is commodified, and the "Arab community" is made into a consumer niche in the Brazilian market of culture today.

ANOTHER ARABESQUE AS ETHNOGRAPHY WITHOUT QUALIFIERS

My work also speaks to the two-decade debate over anthropological writing. During the "crisis of representation" that formally started in 1986 and continued through the 1990s, seminal critiques were made of the reification of culture and the naturalization of the authority of the researcher/author. In this milieu, ethnography was in need of qualification. George Marcus and Michael Fischer (1986) first probed an "experimental ethnography." Dorinne Kondo (1990) then crafted a "postmodern ethnography." Charlotte Aull Davies (1999) also ruminated over a "reflexive ethnography." Though few at that time wanted to abandon it, anthropologists were trying to reformulate ethnography to go beyond conventional parameters, beyond a naïve writing of culture.

Meanwhile, James Clifford and George Marcus, the editors of *Writing Culture* (1986), the volume that inaugurated the critique, moved from being postmodern savants to diasporic and transnational canonizers. Clifford published a seminal essay on diaspora (Clifford 1994) and later included it in *Routes* (1997). Marcus came out with a piece on transnational research methods (1995) and later inserted it in his volume *Ethnography through Thick and Thin* (2000). In retrospect, it seems only fitting that the critique of anthropological conventions that reified "peoples and cultures" led to transnational and global studies. Consequently, by the 1990s ethnography had become less about "writing culture" than following peoples and things in wider processes.

But this current direction has been invariably criticized for its inattentiveness to the anthropological tradition of holism. As a post-revisionist move, I have arranged this book's six body chapters to express the varied facets of Arab Brazilian lives as an interconnected whole, addressing business, politics, liberal professions, marriage, leisure clubs, and tourism. But since my goal is to chart the intensification of Arabness in Brazil, the content of each chapter shifts between historical and current Arab Brazilian self-understandings and institutional practices, changing paradigms of the Brazilian nation and state, and the shifting flows and models of the world system. In so doing, my book aims to be an ethnography without qualifiers. It points to the greater intensity of ethnicity in the nation today by engaging with people in their public struggles, alliances, and ambivalences.

NUMBERS AND NAMES IN THE ARAB AMERICAS

Addressing the construction of Arabness in nationalist ideologies and political-economic agendas on the Brazilian periphery of the world system, a corollary aim in this work is to redirect the study of Arabness outside the Middle East, Europe, and the United States. My focus on Brazilians of Syrian–Lebanese descent aims to call attention to another arabesque in the world today. But to highlight the particularity of this Brazilian formation of Arabness, my book makes brief comparisons with Arabs in the Americas, especially in the United States.

Mostly departing from present-day Syria and Lebanon, Middle Eastern immigrants in the Americas have been estimated at more than 300,000 between the 1870s and the 1930s (Himadeh 1936; Issawi 1966; Karpat 1985). Spreading evenly across Argentina, Brazil, and the United States,[5] these immigrants attained a striking presence as peddlers by the 1890s and were popularly caricatured as such for the next several decades.[6] In Brazil in 1945, the poet Carlos Drummond de Andrade rhymed: "The *turcos* [Turks] were born to sell / colorful knick-knacks in canisters / door-to-door. / … If they open the canister, who resists / the impulse to buy? / It's cheap! Cheap! Buy now! / Pay later! But buy!" (cited in Gattaz 2001: 15). Likewise, in the United States a Syrian peddler appears in Lynn Riggs's play *Green Grow the Lilacs* (Riggs 1931).[7] When Rodgers and Hammerstein turned the play into the musical *Oklahoma* in 1943, the figure became "the Persian" Ali Hakem (Baringer 1998: 452). Today, this peddling past remains striking in the public construction of Arabness in Brazil, but it has been replaced by the "reel bad Arab" stereotype in the United States (Shaheen 1984).

Historians agree that the vast majority of Middle Eastern immigrants to Brazil arrived in the early twentieth century (Gattaz 2001; Lesser 1999; Nunes 1993; Truzzi 1997). Mostly stemming from present-day Syria and Lebanon, 140,464 Middle Easterners immigrated to Brazil from 1880 to 1969 (Lesser 1999: 8). From the 1970s onward, however, it appears that only 500 to 700 immigrants from mostly south Lebanon and Palestine arrived annually.[8] Despite such small numbers, news reportage and immigration museums have estimated that there are 6 million to 10 million Syrian and Lebanese descendants in present-day Brazil.[9] How could an ethnic group that totaled fewer than 200,000 grow to upward of 6 million within a century?

Such statistics must not be dismissed as misrepresentations but probed as social facts. Take, for example, an article published on Middle Easterners in the newsweekly *Veja* (Varella 2000). It "estimated" that 7 million citizens of Syrian–Lebanese origin now live in Brazil.[10] Within a month of its publication, a second-generation Lebanese (who owns an advertising agency) asked if I had read it. He then added, "It was me who gave much of the information." I suspect that he and others introduced such estimates in interviews for news reportage or academic research.[11] Maintaining a privileged presence in business and political circles, Middle Easterners have overestimated themselves as a way to strengthen their place in the Brazilian nation.

These numerical claims have gained greater legitimacy in public circulation, as made evident in the social life of an article from *Folha de S. Paulo*'s Sunday magazine in 2001, "O Nosso Lado Árabe [Our Arab Side]." It "estimated" that "10 million immigrants and descendants live in Brazil" who "are basically of the nationalities Lebanese (7 million) and Syrian (3 million)." Citing the article as a source, the São Paulo state immigration museum, Memorial do Imigrante, publicized the statistics in an exposition about Lebanese immigration in 2002. Reflecting the intensification of Arab ethnicity, these figures have depicted Middle Eastern descendants as nearly 5 percent of the Brazilian national population.

In comparison, a brief look at the numbers of Middle Easterners in the United States is revealing. From the 1870s through the 1930s, roughly 130,000 immigrants from present-day Syria and Lebanon went to the United States (Suleiman 1999: 2). Since 1967, however, more than 250,000 Middle Easterners have immigrated to the United States (Orfalea 1988), mostly from the Arabian Gulf, Egypt, Iraq, Jordan, Lebanon, and Palestine. But census and similar estimates for U.S. Americans of Middle Eastern heritage have been criticized as "low" by activists and researchers during the past two decades (Schopmeyer 2000; Zogby 1990). A more accurate, if unsubstantiated, estimate today is 2.5 million (Suleiman 1999: 2). That Middle Easterners have been under-represented in the United States and over-represented in Brazil speaks to the historic "invisibility" of Arabs in the United States (Naber 2000; Saliba 1999) and what I suggest is their growing visibility in Brazil.

"Middle Easterners" are identified by many labels in Brazil: *turco* (Turk), *sírio* (Syrian), *libanês* (Lebanese), *sírio-libanês* (Syrian-Lebanese), *árabe* (Arab), and *árabe brasileiro* (Arab Brazilian). What must be stressed is the degree of ambiguity and fluidity between them, like other racial and ethnic terminology in Brazil.[12] As a Middle Eastern descendant, for instance, I am regularly called a "Turk," "Lebanese," "Syrian–Lebanese," and "Arab." Historically, the *turco* designation was coined by Brazilian statesmen to classify sojourners who carried travel documents of the Ottoman Sultanate from the late nineteenth century until World War I.[13] After Syria and Lebanon were created as geopolitical entities under the French colonial mandate in the 1920s, the categories of *sírio* and *libanês* were added to Brazilian immigration rosters (Lesser 1999: 8). Yet, from the late nineteenth century to the present, *turco* has been commonly used by Brazilian elites and masses in reference to people of Middle Eastern origin. In earlier times, the label was seen as derogatory. But today, Middle Easterners claim that *turco* is not discriminatory but a "joking" or "caring" term of reference, thus reflecting the nationalist ideology of racial democracy.

Conventionally, "Syrian–Lebanese" has been the term crafted and used by Middle Easterners themselves, which "included an implicit notion of Brazilianness" (Lesser 1999: 42). But the designation of "Arab" has gained increasing usage as well. Brazilians of Syrian–Lebanese descent who oversee the Arab Brazilian Chamber of Commerce (CCAB), for instance, have stressed an explicitly Arab identity to (non-Arab) Brazilian clients interested in exporting to primarily Arabian Gulf markets. Likewise, Habib's, the "Arab" fast-food chain, has been represented to consumers with an overt *apelo árabe* (Arab appeal), notwithstanding the fact that most of its menu is derived from "Syrian–Lebanese" cuisine. Even the *colônia árabe* (Arab community) has become a "target market" in airline advertising. Such currency of the Arab label reflects the culture of economic openness and consumer diversity in Brazil.

The politics of naming Middle Easterners in U.S. history is instructive here, too. Like their counterparts in Brazil, Middle Eastern immigrants to the late nineteenth-century United States were classified as "Turks" (Samhan 1999: 216).[14] The term continued to be used to insult "Syrian–Lebanese" until midcentury. But today, this etymological past has been forgotten. U.S. Americans of Middle Eastern origin are generally identified by themselves and others as "Arab American" or "Middle Eastern," as well as by nationalities of origin (such as "Lebanese"). Yet scholars have pointed out that labels like "Arab" and "Palestinian" are invariably constructed in a discursive relation to European Jews (Massad 1993; Saliba 1999). In the United States, one must speak of "Arabs" in reference to European Jews. Unlike the usage of the "Arab" designation in Brazilian racial and national economies, the U.S. politics of identifying "Arabs" reflects the racial ideology of U.S. nationalism and the historical privilege of European Jewish colonialism in U.S. foreign policy.

In this book, "Brazilian of Middle Eastern descent," "Middle Eastern descendant," and "Middle Easterner" are etic, blanket terms used in instances involving variably identified "Middle Easterners." Syrian, Lebanese, Syrian–Lebanese, Arab, and Turk labels are employed according to the empirical text or context.

I also use the terms *árabe* (Arab) and *árabe brasileiro* (Arab Brazilian). My editorial decision stems from the fact that such language has been employed in magazines published by and for Arabs themselves, including *al-Urubat*,[15] *al-Nur*, *Carta do Líbano*,[16] *Chams*, and *Orient Express*. Envisioning my work as one more publication about Arabs in Brazil, I take my privileged, accountable, and limited place alongside other writers and editors who document, engage, and represent the *colônia*.

ARAB BRAZILIANNESS, SEPTEMBER 11
NOTWITHSTANDING

But, one may rightly ask, are the contrasts between Arabs in Brazil and the United States still relevant in a post–September 11 world? Entering the final months of research in São Paulo in September 2001, I watched with incredulity news reportage of Arabs and Muslims being scrutinized and held incommunicado in the United States. Given the past discrimination against Middle Easterners and Muslims in the United States, such violence was tragic but predictable. But I was really shocked by news coverage of the alleged terrorist transnational connections of Middle Easterners in the Brazilian city of Foz do Iguaçu, located near Paraguay and Argentina in the so-called tri-border region (*tríplice fronteira*). Within weeks after September 11, the BBC, *New York Times*, and other global news agencies claimed that international and local authorities were monitoring tri-border Middle Eastern communities for terrorist suspects.[17] By late September, these imaginary links had made prime-time news on the Globo television network in Brazil. Drawing special interest was the U.S. military forces' discovery of a photograph of Brazil's famous Foz do Iguaçu waterfalls in an al-Qaeda training camp in Afghanistan.[18] With global and national media spotlights on this purported "proof," it seemed that Arabs across national borders in the Americas could become subsumed by the U.S. American "war on terror."

In the first weeks of uncertainty in São Paulo following the September 11 attacks, the Arab Brazilian Chamber of Commerce (as well as the Syrian consulate, in the same building) received a bomb threat. An official government event honoring Arab immigration and culture in the nearby city of Guarulhos was postponed. Recent Lebanese migrants who operate stores on Rua 25 de Março (March 25 Street) in the city center were interviewed about the September 11 attacks on the eight o'clock news. Even a close friend, Leila, kept her daughter home from school for two days, fearing reprisals from classmates or even teachers. After more than a year of research with Arabs in Brazil, I harbored fears that the *colônia sírio-libanesa* was being abruptly reorganized according to U.S. American national representations of Middle Easterners. Were Brazilians of Syrian–Lebanese descent, I anxiously wondered, experiencing a break with historical and current patterns of Arab ethnicity in Brazil? Had they been suddenly encompassed by the politics of Middle Easternness endemic to, and established before, the September 11 attacks in the United States?

As a reminder against any hasty prediction of a post–September 11 world, Leila herself stated, "I was really worried, but then the soap opera started." Already slotted to begin on the Globo TV network in September 2001, *O Clone* (*The Clone*) hit the airwaves as scheduled but in a context that its financiers, cast, and audience could never have imagined. As will be discussed in Chapter 4, its storyline was the "forbidden love" between a Brazilian boy, Lucas, and a Brazilian-raised Muslim Moroccan woman, Jade. Filmed and set between Brazil and Morocco, the first of three parts was lengthened from under 100 *capítulos* (episodes) to nearly 200. Capitalizing on tumultuous world events (including reprisals against Arabs in the United States), Globo media moguls reinvented the soap opera as a way to educate the Brazilian public about the Muslim Arab world. During the soap opera's premiere, the screenwriter Glória Perez was cited as saying: "We need to say no to prejudice, to stop feeding this ignorance, showing common people. There is terrorism in all countries and between all peoples, and the Muslims are people like us."[19] Despite such claims, however, *O Clone* touched off a consumption frenzy of "Middle Eastern" cultural commodities. As examined in Chapter 5, belly-dancing classes and "Moroccan" clothing accessories, among other products, gained popularity in the Brazilian public sphere. In such terms, the September 11 attacks provoked initial concern among Arab Brazilians, but—as Leila remarked—"then the soap opera started."[20]

Within weeks, on September 23, 2001, *Folha de S. Paulo*'s Sunday magazine published "Brasil das arábias [Brazil of the Arabias]," a cover story about Arab culture and immigration to Brazil. The magazine's caption began: "Our Arab Side: Portuguese legacy and Syrian–Lebanese immigration inscribed the influence of Arab culture in the Brazilian quotidian." It continued: "The strong influence of Arab culture [is] in cuisine, music, architecture, fashion, and the Portuguese language." A half dozen articles explained the reach of Islam across Brazil and the world, the Koran's central tenets, and Arab contributions to Brazil. One article spoke of Arab culture as "literally consumed" in the state of São Paulo: "According to the Syndicate of Hotels, Restaurants, Bars, and Equivalents of São Paulo, ... almost 25 percent of the meals served daily in São Paulo city restaurants come out of Arab cuisine" (Yuri 2001: 8). Other news columns described the Moorish style of architecture in the city of

São Paulo, the Moorish origins of many words in the Portuguese language, the "children of 25 de Março" who became international fashion designers, as well as the presence of Arab descendants in MPB (música popular brasileira, or Brazilian popular music]). In the last editorial on cuisine, the food critic Josimar Melo evoked the words of Gilberto Freyre from *Casa grande e senzala*: "Much of what is in the Brazilian is not European, nor indigenous, nor even the result of direct contact with black Africa. ... [I]t is still much of the Moor which persists in the intimate life of Brazilians through colonial times." In emphasizing "arabisms" in this nationalist narrative of a post–September 11 Brazil, Melo concluded, "*Ou seja, somos todos um pouco árabes* [In other words, we are all a bit Arab])."

These subtle references to the "mixture" of Arabness in Brazil were accompanied by explicit public claims of racial democracy. A "March for Peace" had been carried out in the SAARA, an acronym for a downtown commercial district (and association) in Rio de Janeiro. It was organized in response to both the September 11 attacks and the continuing violence between Israelis and Palestinians. Making the eight o'clock Globo news on September 25, the march was said to have been purposefully held in the SAARA, a "traditional" area of Arab and Jewish commerce in Rio de Janeiro. The Globo news anchors explained that since the early twentieth century, Arabs and Jews "have lived together" in the same neighborhood, and that the only *briga* (fight) was over prices and customers. Showing images of middle-aged merchants grasping each other's hands and torsos, the television anchors concluded: "Brazil is a country of tolerance." In a world of violent acts and retaliations, the Brazilian notion of racial democracy has taken on a novel ideological, and potentially progressive, purpose.

A different scenario unfolded in the U.S. American context. Amid the real fear that anyone perceived as Arab or Muslim would be made scapegoats for September 11, mass media embarked on a campaign to educate the public at large about Islam and the Arab world, including television documentaries on the Public Broadcasting System (Howell and Shryock 2004: 455), one hundred questions and answers about "Arab Americans" on the *Detroit Free Press* website, and an op-ed piece in the *New Yorker* (Shryock 2002: 918), among others. Headed by John Ashcroft, the U.S. Attorney General's Office also issued several calls to respect Muslims, Arabs, and South Asians. Made just two days after September 11, one such announcement declared that "any threats of violence or discrimination against Arab or Muslim Americans or Americans of South Asian descent ... are not just wrong and un-American, but also are unlawful and will be treated as such" (U.S. Department of Justice, cited in Howell and Shryock 2004: 447). At the same time that actual Arabs and Muslims were monitored and targeted by the Federal Bureau of Investigation and Central Intelligence Agency in the United States, Arab and Islamic differences were encompassed by U.S. American multiculturalist ideology.

This anecdotal comparison between Arabs in Brazil and the United States should suggest that September 11, 2001, and later events are *not* a homogenizing force whereby Arabs across the Americas have been encompassed by the U.S. American "war on terror" and similar politics. While Arabs and Muslims in the United States continue to be identified, and separated out, by U.S. American multiculturalism, Arabs and Muslims in Brazil remain acknowledged within the Brazilian nationalist ideas of "mixture" and "racial democracy." This not only suggests that Arabs have been contained by national projects (Howell and Shryock 2004: 455). It also demonstrates that September 11 and its after-effects have reinforced—at least for now—the historically specific formations of Arabness in U.S. American and Brazilian nationalist frameworks.

DIASPORIC NOTES ON LEARNING TO BE ARAB IN SÃO PAULO

This book is based on eighteen months of study in the city of São Paulo, from June to August 1999 and from September 2000 to December 2001. Just over half of the Middle Eastern immigrants to Brazil through post–World War II times came to settle in the state (Mott 2000: 190),[21] and today their descendants make up highly influential circles in the city itself.[22] I carried out eighty-five formal interviews: sixty-four with men and twenty-one with women. The gender disparity was due to male predominance in professional networks. One-fifth of interviews (19 of 85) were conducted with non-Arabs (who self-identified as descendants of Germans, Italians, Jews, Portuguese, and Spanish; a *mistura*, or mix, of them; or *morenos*, brown-skinned).[23] As gleaned from my business-card binder, I had contact with almost 250 individuals in what Renato Rosaldo has called "deep hanging out" (cited in Clifford 1997: 56).

In the São Paulo city center, my research focused on two spaces: Rua 25 de Março, which came to be home to Arab merchants in the late nineteenth century and northeastern Brazilian migrants in the late twentieth century, and the "Anchieta Palace," which houses the legislative branch of city government. Heading uptown to Avenida Paulista and the neighborhoods of Jardins, Paraíso, and Moema, my research centered on multiple locales: the Arab Brazilian Chamber of Commerce and nearby export enterprises; the medical, legal, and engineering offices of Middle Eastern professionals; four Syrian–Lebanese country clubs; and restaurants featuring "Arab culture." In June 2001, I accompanied Brazilians of Lebanese descent on a tourist excursion to Lebanon, building on previous surveys in four homeland travel agencies. These events and advertisements were covered or featured in four Arab-run magazines or newspapers, which I collected from October 2000 until December 2003.

Learning what it means to be Arab in Brazil began when I departed for pre-dissertation research in São Paulo in June 1999. I remember the second day after my arrival when I called contacts from a friend's high-rise building near the city center. One person agreed to meet with me: the editor-in-chief of an Arab community magazine, *Chams*. In that first week, he offered his thoughts on the *colônia*, mentioned upcoming club events, and arranged for me to speak with business executives. These reflections, rendezvous, and referrals became my formal introduction to the Arab experience in Brazil. In those days, and in subsequent months, I was occasionally mistaken and came to feel like a journalist, interviewing or making small talk with professionals and covering their meetings and soirées. With a notepad tucked in my pockets, I more than once found myself beside other journalists—both the ethnic and national varieties—jotting down excerpts from long speeches and partaking in intriguing conversations.

In the first months of research, I found myself frequenting institutional events on a weekly basis, not just business meetings and commercial seminars, but political celebrations and cultural gatherings as well. Initially, I thought these public performances would serve as a methodological tool, providing the opportunity to meet and build rapport with Middle Easterners. This turned out to be the case. But by the fourth month of keeping up with three to four formal weekly gatherings, it dawned on me that these "marked frames of social interaction" were important in and of themselves (Lewis 1999: 717). Middle Easterners expended much time and energy in scheduling and frequenting formal gatherings. The bulk of my work is thus based in descriptions of these public events, how and by whom they were organized, and what was said and done about them in the *colônia* and the Brazilian public sphere.

Yet I took a position not only as an anthropologist *cum* paparazzo in São Paulo. My personal intentions began back in 1997 while visiting relatives in Belém do Pará. Through stories told by family in the United States and Brazil, I had known that *siti* (my grandmother) was born and raised in northern Brazil, the daughter of a migrant Lebanese couple. But I did not know that her father (my great-grandfather) died and was buried there. A much loved affinal uncle took my brother and me to his resting place. Under the hot midday sun, we entered the cemetery of majestic gravestones, each adorned with black-and-white photographs of defunct souls. Abruptly, our uncle pointed to a blackened tomb with a small oval-shaped portrait set in porcelain. The image startled my brother and me on the broken concrete. It was a small copy of a large picture that sits on top of our grandmother's bedroom dresser in upstate New York: It was her father. We stared at the image that was so intimate and in such a seemingly distant place.

This story is one of the autobiographical accounts that I used during research in 2000–2001. As a third-generation descendant in a Lebanese American family that maintains closer ties with relatives in Rio de Janeiro than in the official homeland of Lebanon, my own intention in telling the graveside tale was to make a claim to Brazil. In retrospect, however, my narrative provoked only stories of movement across the Americas and the Middle East.[24] Colleagues recounted their own family dispersion, re-encounters with relatives through unexpected calls and letters, as well as the power of *'asl* (origins, in Arabic). As an older second-generation woman put it, *as raízes falam alto* (roots speak loudly). For counterparts, my story substantiated a claim not to Brazilianness but to diasporic Arabness. Somewhat unintentionally, then, my place as a researcher became that of an *ibn 'arab* (Arab descendant) in the Americas.[25]

But recognition as a *patrício* (countryman) or *primo* (cousin) was nationally specified. Perhaps due to my surname (and, I suspect, my pronounced brow and off-white complexion), the issue that mattered most was not my Arabness but my status as U.S. born and educated.[26] *Ele é americano* (He's American), emphasized friends and relatives who introduced me to others in intimate and formal encounters. Invariably I added, *infelizmente* (unfortunately) in a sardonic effort to clarify my politics, especially since the sound of *americano* suggests chauvinism.[27] In response, my new acquaintances often queried, "Why?" Though I usually made a diatribe of U.S. American foreign policy, it occurred to me that upper and middle classes who knew the United States through tourism were not that turned off. In fact, my U.S. Americanness was often most crucial to gain the confidence of business and liberal professionals. Initial access to interviews and events, for instance, was granted only after my affiliation with a U.S. university was substantiated through a business card or letter with college insignia in English. "Say you're American," advised close friends, "because Americans have a way of doing everything right." In a hegemonic way, U.S. Americanness was respected in the high ranks of Brazilian society.

Yet these "strands of identification … tugged into the open or stuffed out of sight" at any given moment (Narayan 1993: 673) represented just one aspect of research. Another dimension concerned what Laura Nader (1972) has called "studying up." The tendency to *ficar alinhado* (dress up) and *aproximar-se às costas largas* (rub elbows) weighed heavily in Arab livelihood and leisure circles (which is the rule, not the exception, in Brazil). Early on, it became evident that my collared shirt, slacks, and standard shoes would not suffice, for I was irremediably outdone by other men in dark blue suits and ties, as well as matching belts and footwear.[28] I responded by trying to make myself over with similar clothing and accessories. Also compulsory were business cards (*cartāozinhos*). I ordered some from my university in upstate New York and eventually learned how to introduce myself and query into exchanging them with a given interloper. "Always keep *cartāozinhos* in your blazer," advised one friend.

As suggested by this struggle with dress and décor, my encounter with the culture of class in Brazil was far more challenging than ethnic or national politics. In contrast to anthropologists who take up socioeconomically dominant positions vis-à-vis subaltern research subjects, my status as an *antropólogo* marked me as part of the insecure middle class, and hence expendable to bourgeois Brazilians of diverse backgrounds. This personal experience of class subordination led me to sharpen my wit and presentation among more well-to-do ethnographic subjects in the most varied informal and formal settings. Unable to benefit from the material power used by other anthropologists who "study down," I was forced to rely on my own symbolic capital and, most important, the good graces of colleagues who took time from their busy work schedules to meet with me for many hours. Upscale research, in this sense, served as a much needed lesson for a young anthropologist in the world of professionals and socialites. This will be evident in the high-powered Arab export promotional seminars to which I now turn.

PART I

Imagining
Political Economy

ONE

Pariahs to Partners in the Export Nation

DOZEN OR SO powerful industrialists of Syrian–Lebanese descent founded a chamber of commerce together in 1952. Financed by their family fortunes from the Brazilian textile market, the chamber originally served their high-society pretensions in Brazil and with the homeland. Yet, under its present-day name of the Câmara de Comércio Árabe Brasileira (Arab Brazilian Chamber of Commerce, or CCAB), this coterie of Syrian–Lebanese elites has been charged with the task of promoting Brazilian exports and exporters in the "Arab world."

Regularly appearing in financial news coverage, the chamber even received praise from Brazilian President Fernando Henrique Cardoso (1994–2002). In 2001, Cardoso thanked the chamber—still run by Syrian–Lebanese descendants—for bringing about a "very large increase in the commerce of Brazil with the Arab world." Focusing on the historical formation and current project of CCAB, this chapter explores the association between Syrian–Lebanese and commerce in two paradigms of Brazilian national economy: protectionism (1930s–1970s) and liberalization (1970s–present). Though used by Brazilian elites to question Arab ethnicity in the earlier model, Middle Easterners' alleged commercial propensity has won greater recognition today in Brazil, as long as it is exercised in exportation. While Middle Easterners who engage in importation continue to be questioned in the Brazilian nation, the ethnic directors of CCAB have gained greater recognition as Brazil's export partners to the "Arab world."

As noted in the introduction, the virtues of exportation trumpeted by the "Washington Consensus" have been adopted by national and state elites in Brazil. For the latter, exportation attracts a secure flow of external capital, which can free the country from speculative trade and counterbalance the imports needed for development.[1] Though not a novel phenomenon in Brazilian history, exportation today has been redirected beyond Europe and the United States, toward "non-traditional" or "emergent" markets, such as the Middle East.[2] In this context, Brazilian business and state elites have turned to the chamber of commerce run by Syrian–Lebanese descendants to help promote Brazilian exports not to the latter's Syrian and Lebanese homelands, but to the more lucrative Arabian Gulf and North African markets.

Examining exportation as a cultural idiom and social fact, this chapter follows a recent turn in transnational studies. Early theorists analytically opposed national and transnational formations, arguing for *either* the downfall or the persistence of the nation-state (Appadurai 1996; Basch et al. 1994). In contrast, later work has investigated the mutual constitution of state, national, and transnational forces (Cheah and Robbins 1998; Ong 1999; Sassen 2001). This line of inquiry has asked how state constructs and nationalist ideologies "condition the activities that constitute transnationalism, both propelling and molding the latter without necessarily dampening them" (Schein 1998: 164). This chapter's focus on exportation reveals how ethnic, state, and national formations shape and strengthen transnational processes.

This convergence between ethnic, state, and national forces in and beyond Brazil has been regularly described as a *parceria* (partnership) by CCAB directors and Brazilian state officials, as well as Brazilian business and media professionals. While the notion of "partnership" has been explored vis-à-vis the recent shift toward the private corporate funding of state programs for artistic production in the United States (Yúdice 1995, 1999), this chapter seeks to examine it in the changing hierarchical relations between ethnicity and the nation in contemporary Brazil. Once disparaged as economic pariahs and still questioned as sly store owners, Middle Easterners have also gained recognition as the *parceiros* (partners) of national and state elites in Brazil. They have collaborated in the forging of a novel economic paradigm for the nation: *O Brasil Exportador* (the Exporting Brazil). In this remodeling, the alleged commercial propensity of Arabs—an element that historically marked their peripheral place in the country—has been welcomed under certain circumstances by export-eager Brazilian elites.

ETHNIC COMMERCE AND PROTECTING
THE NATIONAL ECONOMY

Imagining the earliest currents of Syrian and Lebanese immigration, many descendants today recount the story of two Syrians, Assad Abdalla and Najib Salem, who disembarked in São Paulo in the early 1890s. They established a "resale entrepôt" on the present-day Rua 25 de Março in the city center. A similar immigration story is that of the Jafet brothers, who arrived in the same decade and opened textile factories as early as the 1910s. In their respective prosperous undertakings, the Abdalla, Salem, and Jafet family enterprises supplied goods to fellow *patrícios* (countrymen) who peddled them on urban and rural peripheries alike.

As early as 1893, Middle Easterners made up 90 percent of the *mascates* (peddlers) in the São Paulo city almanac (Knowlton 1961: 23; Truzzi 1997: 49). In 1907, 315 Middle Eastern–owned businesses were listed, most specializing in clothing and dry goods. By 1920, their small-scale factories numbered ninety-one in São Paulo. For the sociologist Clark Knowlton, Syrian and Lebanese entered into "industries that required a minimum amount of capital. One could install a small factory with four or five workers in a rented room, using second hand sewing machines" (Knowlton 1961: 143). Middle Easterners' eventual forte, however, was wholesale trade. In 1930, Syrian–Lebanese owned "468 of the listed 800 retail stores and 67 of the 136 wholesale" throughout the city (Knowlton 1961: 143). This Middle Eastern–driven commerce was especially concentrated on the Rua 25 de Março in downtown São Paulo.

In 1913, figures from the Abdalla, Salim, and Jafet families convened the "preparatory meeting" of the Câmara Síria de Comércio (Syrian Chamber of Commerce). The main speaker at the event was the eldest Jafet brother, Nami. "Commerce," he began, "is the greatest realization of man, the most important of factors that he created for the growth, robustness, and progress of the social corpus" (Jafet 1947: 302). This glorification of commerce was self-congratulatory, especially in view of Jafet family–owned businesses. But it was also expressed in efforts to raise the then lowly status of commerce, as well as the reputation of the *turcos* who were viewed as epitomizing it. "The Chamber," he concluded, "will be a lighthouse that will illuminate and orient each Syrian merchant, from the peddler with a box to the wholesaler. ... In this way, we will have a base of operations for large and small and we will be able to progress" (Jafet 1947: 304). As a precursor of the "Arab Brazilian" entity today, the Syrian Chamber of Commerce was conceived as a private entity to benefit Arab-run commerce in early twentieth-century Brazil.

Jafet's praise of commerce, however, fell on deaf ears. Brazilian elites regarded the country as an agricultural plantation that could supply rubber, cacao, and mostly coffee to North America and Europe (Dean 1969; Holloway 1980; Stolcke 1988; Weinstein 1983). In their vision, he and other Middle Easterners were innately shrewd *turcos* who accumulated considerable sums of wealth through petty commerce. In this regard, the famous writer João do Rio commented, "Every Oriental brain has a Potosí in the circumvolutions" (Rio 1928: 168).[3] Alfredo Ellis Junior also spoke of the "*syrio*" as a "merchant by ... inheritance ... [who] is able to barter his own life, swearing to have not earned a penny" (Ellis 1934: 65–66).[4] Similarly, Guilherme de Almeida, a commentator in the 1930s, reflected, "What's the recipe for a Turk? Take the 25 de Março street cocktail shaker and put in a Syrian, an Arab, an Armenian, a Persian, an Egyptian, a Kurd. Shake it up really well and—boom—out comes a Turk" (as cited in Lesser 1996: 58).[5] Especially evident on Rua 25 de Março, *turcos* were thought to possess an inherent propensity to be peddlers and merchants.

Arabs were also assumed to use their innate business acumen for personal enrichment at the expense of the agriculturally imagined Brazilian nation. Take, for instance, a participant in the 1926 National Society of Agriculture meeting who commented, "We should also do everything to make difficult the immigration of Syrian elements which, far from benefiting agriculture, parasitically exploit it in the[ir] profession of false businessmen" (Sociedade Nacional de Agricultura 1926: 359). One of the most outspoken critics of Syrian immigration, Herbert Levy, wrote that "the type of immigration required by the country's needs is that of agricultural workers and the Syrians are not classified in this category," being rather "dedicated to commerce and speculative activities." He pointed out that "Syrians are not present" among the 700,000 agricultural workers tallied in São Paulo (cited in Junior 1935: 39, 41–42). Middle Eastern peddling was also criticized by a well-known ethnologist and statesman, Edgar Roquette-Pinto (partially cited in Lesser 1999: 53). Deviating from the subject matter of his book on the natural history of the Greater Amazon region, he surmised:

> *Turcos* peddle in all parts. They entrench themselves, seeking clients in all corners. From the thousands of them that Brazil annually receives, there is not even a hundred [agricultural] producers. Here, there does not exist rural *turco* workers; and still there is not a foreign element more spread out in the whole country. In the heart of Mato Grosso, in the Amazon, in Minas Gerais, in the nation's capital, there live great masses of *turco* merchants. Although, by the condition of their habitual mystery, they are obligated to

enter into relation with the Brazilians, they live perfectly segregated in their race, in their norms, in their way of doing things [*feitio*]. No one really knows for sure how they call themselves, where they are from, what religion they profess. They live among one another, practically ignored by the Brazilians. ... It would be unjust to deny the basic services that these peddlers provide for the populations in the hinterlands. It is an immigration that fulfills at the present time a mission of utility; it has not brought with it, however, a single germ of progress. (Roquette-Pinto 1935: 81)

Although Roquette-Pinto recognized the "elementary utility" of *turcos*, itinerant commerce clearly did not hold the currency that could guarantee their place in the agricultural Brazilian nation. In this vision, *turco* merchants were pariahs.

In the next few decades, however, trade and industry experienced extraordinary growth in Brazil. Accounting for 21 percent of the gross national product (GNP) in 1907 and again in 1919, industrial production expanded to 43 percent of the Brazilian GNP in 1939 (Leopoldi 2000: 69). While agricultural growth rates hovered between .5 percent and 3 percent per year in the 1940s and '50s, industrial output expanded by annual increases of more than 10 percent in the 1930s, falling slightly to 5 percent in the early 1940s, and again rising to nearly 10 percent through 1961 (Baer 1995: 49, 81; Leopoldi 2000: 231). Symbolizing the dawn of a nation of industrialists and proletariats was the construction of the Volta Redonda steel complex between São Paulo and Rio de Janeiro. Fully operational in 1943, Volta Redonda served as a metaphor for a Brazilian nation imagined no longer as a mere plantation but as a bustling factory writ large.

In this historic turn, Syrian–Lebanese continued their ascension from peddlers to proprietors in São Paulo. In 1945, Brazilians with Middle Eastern surnames accounted for 27 percent of the firms in the spinning and weaving segments of cotton, silk, rayon, wool, and linen fabrics (112 of 413). They represented 40 percent of the rayon-weaving segment alone (90 of 215). Almost without exception, these enterprises opened in the mid-1930s, due in part to the trade and industrial incentives of Getúlio Vargas (Stein 1957). Catering to urban commercial and industrial classes (mostly composed of immigrants), Vargas instituted a protectionist policy that placed high tariffs on imports. This benefited the national textile industry from the 1930s onward. "Protected by extremely high tariffs against imported textiles" that reached almost 280 percent as late as the 1960s (Bergsman 1970: 137; Evans 1979: 133), textile industrialists, wholesalers, and garment makers grew in numbers and networks. They developed a chain of production and distribution wherein textile rolls were purchased by wholesalers who then sold them to garment producers. Through the 1960s, the hundreds of store owners on 25 de Março accounted for an estimated 60 percent of wholesale profits from textiles in Brazil.[6]

By way of this network, *turcos* gained an ambivalent respectability in the nation. On the one hand, media elites congratulated them for making 25 de Março into a "public thoroughfare of a distinguished commercial function."[7] For the urban chronicler Gabriel Marques, the street "should be called *rua Sírio-Libanesa* ... which merges well in São Paulo's roadway conjuncture ... and its agitated economic milieu."[8] Marques later noted that the "Old Road of Raw Kibe" marks "Paulista prosperity" and "symbolizes the power of a people united and strong."[9] However, on the other hand, the region began to make news as a hotbed for irregular fiscal activities. One article recounted how a team of forty tax inspectors "conferred thousands of fiscal receipts, opened hundreds of packages, and apprehended a sizeable quantity of goods in an operation ... dubbed 'taking the pulse of trade.'"[10] *Sírio-libaneses* and the 25 de Março, in this light, were praised for their "commercial functions" and mistrusted in view of questionable fiscal activities.

Much had changed for Brazilians of Middle Eastern origins from the late nineteenth century to the 1960s. While immigrant peddlers were disparaged as economic pariahs in the agriculturally imagined nation until the 1930s, they had gained an ambivalent respectability by midcentury, not only because of their social mobility as proprietors and industrialists, but also due to the commercial and industrial turn of the Brazilian national economy. Despite such changes, however, Middle Easterners' alleged commercial propensity continued to be regularly used by elite commentators to question the place of Arab ethnicity in the Brazilian nation.

FAMILY REGIMES FOUNDING THE CHAMBER

In 1952, a dozen or so businessmen who attained wealth in the 25 de Março environs and the then thriving textile market came together to (re)establish the Syrian and Lebanese Chamber of Commerce. The founding took place at the headquarters of a Jafet family business, the Mineração Geral do Brasil. In the original statute, the chamber's objectives were to strengthen the commercial ties between Brazil and the Middle East and the "union and cooperation between 'elements of production and consumption among [CCAB] members spread all over the immense [Brazilian] national territory'" (as cited in Câmara de Comércio Árabe Brasileira 1998: 30). For the next few decades, the chamber's presidency and board of directors predominantly lay with members from three influential Syrian–Lebanese families: the Jafets, the Abdallas, and the Chohfis.

Two second-generation members of the Jafet family, Nagib and Eduardo, served as the first and second presidents in three mandates from 1953 until 1958. Materially and symbolically, their prestige derived from the grand capitalist success of the preceding immigrant generation. As mentioned briefly above, the Jafets arrived in late nineteenth-century Brazil. They opened a wholesale textile outlet, Nami Jafet e Irmãos (in deference to the eldest brother). While investing in imports, the five Jafet brothers entered the industrial sector, founding the Fiação, Tecelagem e Estamparia Ypiranga Jafet in 1906. Expanding in the following decades, the Jafet family's industrial complex came to employ more than 3,000 workers by the mid-1930s (Jafet 1935: 11). As the richest family of the *colônia* in the first half of the twentieth century, the Jafets founded an entire neighborhood, Ipiranga, home to their factory complexes and residential mansions. But it appears that some of the Jafet brothers' initial capital "came from a windfall in importing: an order for aniline dye placed by their firm before ... World War I contained two ciphers too many, so that one hundred times more dye arrived than was needed, at the moment that the price of anilines soared" (Dean 1969: 31). In the next few decades, Jafet family investments and enterprises vertically expanded into mining, banking, transportation, and other sectors of the Brazilian economy. Perhaps emblematic of the Jafets' declaration of bankruptcy in the 1960s, no Jafet family members led the CCAB's board of directors after that time.

The Jafets were succeeded by descendants of the famed Assad Abdalla, who had immigrated to Brazil in 1895. Three second-generation members of the Abdalla family, in fact, presided over the chamber through five terms between 1959 and 1964, as well as between 1977 and 1980. As mentioned earlier, their progenitor, Assad Abdalla, peddled on the outskirts of São Paulo in the late nineteenth century, opened a wholesale entrepôt with his cousin Nagib Salem in the early twentieth century, and eventually came to own and construct an entire neighborhood in the city of São Paulo, Parque São Jorge. The son, Nabih Assad Abdalla (CCAB president in 1959–60), related that his father "religiously" transferred half of his textile firm's profits to real estate from 1912 onward, especially in downtown São Paulo. The father was said to have once jestingly rationalized to one of his partners, "*Primo*, a meter of German ribbon ... imported costs $300 [and] a meter of this property $240; [and] it doesn't run out or fringe and better still is on the trolley-car route in front of Celso Garcia" avenue in downtown São Paulo (Greiber et al. 1998: 38). In the first half of the twentieth century, this investment approach helped the Abdalla family to own the nearly 1 million square meters of the Parque São Jorge, whose sports square was later sold to the present-day Brazilian professional soccer organization, the Corinthians. Albeit on a smaller scale, this strategy of investing in real estate was exercised by many Syrian–Lebanese merchants and industrialists (see Karam 2004).

Following the Assads, Ragueb Chohfi served as the chamber's president for three terms from 1965 to 1970, and his son, Lourenço Chohfi, rose to the post for two mandates between 1983 and 1986. Having also immigrated from Homs, the father founded and developed the Ragueb Chohfi Textile Company. But it was the son, Lourenço, who made the company into Brazil's largest textile wholesale chain from the late 1970s to the early 1990s. The secret of his success lay in stockpiling large quantities of merchandise from manufacturers as the wholesale profit margin widened with the soaring inflation of that period. For instance, the Chohfis would purchase thousands of meters of fabric from national industries. Stored in their warehouses, the textiles gained greater value as general price indexes were marked up each month due to inflation rates that ranged from 100 to 2,700 percent a year (O'Dougherty 2002: 63). By the time the fabric was sold to retailers months later, it was worth several times what the Chohfis had originally paid for it. On a smaller scale, this strategy of *ganhar em cima do estoque* (earning on top of stockpiles) was a common practice among merchants during that era.

But with the 1991 economic opening and the 1994 monetary stabilization, the Chohfis' textiles ceased to appreciate in value and began to be undersold by both Asian imports and national manufacturers who sold directly to retailers. Having lost close to $17 million in 1997 alone, Chohfi Textiles shut its doors. All was not lost, however. The family-run business had invested two decades of profits into real estate across the city and country. Selling lots that have fetched tens of millions of dollars, as well as renting out storefronts with less resale value (around 25 de Março), the Chohfis no longer look to textile wholesaling, but to the real-estate market, as the source of family wealth. Their continuing influence can be gleaned from the fact that Lourenço Chohfi's son-in-law, Paulo Atallah, has served as president of the chamber between 1998 and 2002.[11]

Directed by these three wealthy families of Syrian–Lebanese descent, the chamber depended almost solely on their generosity to finance its high-society activities in the 1950s and 1960s. During that time, a present-day director explained, the chamber had "more cultural activities. They'd receive ambassadors. They'd promote conferences. It was really attached to society." With directors whose lives were interwoven with the textile market and the Brazilian economy, the Syrian and Lebanese Chamber of Commerce provided successful businessmen of Syrian–Lebanese descent with an institution through which to network with Arab community associations in São Paulo, Brazilian social and business groups, as well as diplomats and visiting dignitaries from the Arab world. In 1966 alone, the chamber was visited by state officials from Lebanon, Jordan, Egypt, and Syria (Câmara de Comércio Árabe Brasileira 1998: 38).

Alterations in the actual name of the chamber speak to the increasing role of Arab state powers. The 1958 union between Syria and Egypt in the United Arab Republic (UAR) and the joining of their respective diplomatic corps in Brazil caught the attention of the chamber's directors—still overwhelmingly of Syrian–Lebanese descent—who were interested in widening "relations with Arab countries." In the same year, they met with the General Consul of the United Arab Republic in Brazil and adopted the name Arab Brazilian Chamber of Commerce (Câmara de Comércio Árabe Brasileira 1998: 37). But when the Syrian Arab Republic was proclaimed with the breakup of the UAR in 1961, the official name Syrian Brazilian Chamber of Commerce was adopted (Câmara de Comércio Árabe Brasileira 1998: 37–38). This language was not fortuitous. Ties with the Syrian government were so close that when the chamber purchased and moved to its present location on Avenida Paulista in 1965, the chamber's president, Ragueb Chohfi, donated office space for the General Consul of Syria in the same building. Only in 1975 was the name finalized as Câmara de Comércio Árabe Brasileira. At the time, CCAB's directors sought ties with embassies from the Arab world in Brazil, including Libya, Iraq, Algeria, Egypt, Saudi Arabia, and Morocco (Câmara de Comércio Árabe Brasileira 1998: 41–42). The Chamber hoped to lend future diplomatic services and intermediate in Arab and Brazilian commerce.

Directed by these Syrian–Lebanese textile magnates from 1952 through the next several decades, the Arab Brazilian Chamber of Commerce had been primarily financed by their family wealth in the then thriving textile industry in Brazil and mainly served their own social and cultural purposes in Brazil and with the Arab world.

CCAB, 25 DE MARÇO, AND
TRANSNATIONAL FLOWS

After the oil crisis in 1973, Brazilian state and business elites increasingly sought the chamber to assist in diplomatic and exportation matters with Arab countries. The Brazilian government inquired into how to reduce the trade deficit between Brazil and the oil-producing Arab world. Brazilian chief executives asked how to export to the Arab world. With such interest, the CCAB itself underwent major financial and organizational restructuring. In 1974, it began levying fees for the services requested by Brazilian and Arab governments and enterprises. At the same time, it gained official status as a "not-for-profit" institution from the Brazilian state. Materially supported by past directors of Syrian–Lebanese descent, the chamber had now become indirectly financed by the capital and goods flowing between Brazilian and Arab governments and businesses. The CCAB coffers and activities have not stopped growing since.

In the 1990s, roughly three-quarters of several billion dollars of annual Brazilian exports to Arab countries have consisted of food staples (such as frozen chicken meat), iron minerals, sugar, aluminum fibers, and raw coffee beans. Most of the revenue earned by the chamber stems from the certification of these Brazilian exports to the Middle East. As a current CCAB pamphlet reads, "Arab embassies in Brasília only concede the consular legalization of export documents after the certification realized by CCAB." Before it is sent to Arab embassies in Brasília, export documentation must pass through the high-rise offices of the CCAB. By increasing Brazilian exports to Arab countries, the CCAB provides the conditions for its very own existence. Indeed, its Brazilian clients justify that the chamber "needs earnings in order to survive," and this certification procedure for exported goods provides more than enough capital to bankroll its activities and agendas, such as Brazilian business missions to the Arab world, as well as "How to Export to Arab Countries" seminars for potential Brazilian exporters (discussed later).

In my casual jaunts within the chamber, I vividly recall the CCAB's secretary-general, Pierre, signing the certificates of origin for Brazilian exports to the Middle East. With a pen clenched in his hand to sign documentation, a burning cigarette hanging from his mouth, a telephone receiver braced between his chin and shoulder as he awaited an important phone call, and an avid anthropologist sitting before him, Pierre proved a master at serving the most diverse clientele. "What the chamber earns," he explained, "it earns from certification, the documents that I'm signing here." This exercise in paperwork ensured the CCAB's existence and reinforced its image as a "partner" of Brazilian exporters themselves. The latter reflected that the regulations in medical and food merchandise are complex, and the CCAB provides the technical support needed to meet them. "All the documentation for exports," a (non-Arab) client likewise explained, "passes through the chamber to be verified, and it gives you all the support in translation and necessary legislation. ... It's important work." As will be more fully explored later, Syrian–Lebanese descendants in the CCAB have gained greater acknowledgment through the transnational circulation of capital and goods between Brazil and the Arab world.

But their counterparts in the wholesale textile market on 25 de Março have undergone a very different experience in the neoliberalizing Brazilian market. Born within the protectionist period of the national economy, the chain of production and distribution that developed between manufacturers, wholesaler distributors, and garment producers/retailers had begun to break down in the early 1970s. At that time, domestic textile manufacturers started to sell directly to garment makers and retailers, passing over the wholesalers who made up the majority of businesses on 25 de Março. This cost-reduction move greatly accelerated with the *abertura econômica* (economic opening) in the early 1990s.[12] While enabling the recovery, if not survival, of the domestic textile industry, it dealt a severe blow to national textile wholesalers.

Having once led the wholesale distribution of textiles in the entire country, only six textile wholesalers, one pessimistic merchant estimated, have survived on 25 de Março.[13] Announcing this transition, a 1993 news article reported that "stores from the traditional region of 25 de Março are turning into big clients of Italian, North American, Korean, Chinese enterprises."[14] As president of the commercial association of the 25 de Março district, Beto is well aware of this increasing tide of imports. He is a third-generation Syrian–Lebanese who opened a textile-import firm just after the 1991 economic opening. His Lebanese father provided the start-up capital and a small office in the family-owned building in the 25 de Março environs. Today, Beto's firm imports most of its textiles from South Korea, manages twenty employees in its 25 de Março warehouse, and oversees forty commissioned sellers throughout the country. In addition, Beto's family owns five or six entire buildings (with many store spaces) in the region. Given this family business background, Beto commented that on 25 de Março, "any store that you enter today has ... half imported products, not less than that." He continued:

> The local economy is supplied with a lot of stuff from abroad. You have many stores that sell articles from abroad, from Asia, from China. Gifts, toys, and such. ... You enter, for example, a costume-jewelry store, there is a lot of stuff that comes from abroad. You enter a toy store, there's a lot of stuff from abroad. You enter a garment store, the same thing. So today, the commerce here is really dependent on importation.

Many merchants in the 25 de Março environs have switched from carrying national textiles and accessories to stocking their shelves with imported textiles, tennis shoes, costume jewelry, toys, and even electronic goods.

A firm owned by second-generation Syrian–Lebanese cousins, called King of Accessories, illustrates the transition from wholesale to retail commerce on

25 de Março. One of the cousins, Rodolfo, reflected that profits from whole-saling ribbons, buttons, and other goods decreased in the 1970s and bottomed out in the early 1990s. Having once supplied Rodolfo's business, the national manufacturers of such material now sell directly to customers. In response, Rodolfo imports 80 percent of his stock from Italy, China, the United States, and other countries. He and his partners have even renovated their four-story complex as a retail space. Originally a warehouse for textile wholesaling, their building now caters to lower- and middle-class shoppers.

His father's and uncle's office was located on the second floor. During the renovation, Rodolfo transformed it into the Memorial da 25 de Março (25 de Março Memorial) to "preserve the memory of Syrian and Lebanese immigrants in the 25 de Março region." It has two spacious rooms that ele-gantly exhibit black-and-white photographs, antique furniture, and office-equipment memorabilia. Textual banners lining the walls recount in prose and verse the shared histories of 25 de Março and Syrian–Lebanese com-merce. Having fled the Ottoman Empire "with 5 millennia of history to give and sell," Syrian–Lebanese are celebrated as peddlers of "a pioneering civi-lization" in Brazil. "The Syrian–Lebanese went through backlands, found-ing stores of commerce in each settlement," one banner reads. They trans-formed the Rua 25 de Março into "the great center of … wholesale textiles, clothing, and accessories." Omitting their marginal status in earlier times, descendants have displayed and extolled this memory only in the late 1990s, specifically when an old wholesale warehouse was renovated as a shopper-friendly store. In this light, the construction of the Syrian–Lebanese pioneer-ing past has reflected the region's shift to imported retail commerce in the open Brazilian economy.[15]

Despite this project, which tries to fix the Middle Eastern past of petty commerce to the region, 25 de Março has become well known—many would say infamous—for cheap imports, falsified name-brand goods, and even sweatshops. In fact, the sweatshops are often associated with immigrants from China, Taiwan, and Korea. Brazilian news reportage estimated that "there were 2,500 Korean commercial establishments in São Paulo, of which 90 percent were garment workshops" (Buechler 2002: 349). Opening at the same time that national textile factories scaled down, Korean-owned sweatshops allegedly produced "one out of every three" clothing items retailed in Brazil by 1998. This situation is further exacerbated by the nearly 7,000 street vendors, called camelôs, in downtown São Paulo.[16] Setting up tables with the most diverse items—garments, fake jewelry, pirated music CDs, and other knickknacks—street vendors frequently establish themselves in front of busy stores that spe-cialize in the same merchandise.

Whether they trace their origins to the Middle East, East Asia, or north-eastern Brazil, street vendors and store owners on 25 de Março are supplied through importation. Such merchandise, however, is often deemed "irregular" by Brazilian customers and state fiscal agents, allegedly smuggled into Brazil through Paraguay. Indeed, when the borders between Brazil and Paraguay were temporarily closed in early 2001, store owners and street vendors both were found to be lacking goods on stands and shelves.[17] Given these imagined and real linkages between imports and 25 de Março, several surprise inspection, or search-and-seizure, operations—called *blitzes*—have been carried out regularly from 1999 to 2001.[18] At times weighing more than a ton, goods without proper tax receipts and documentation were apprehended, not only from street vendors, but also from store owners. At one point, even Beto was paid a visit by a team of inspectors, much to the contentment of street vendors and his Asian tenants. Notwithstanding the display of a mythic Syrian–Lebanese pioneering past, there are limits to the ethnic recognition of 25 de Março today in the neoliberal nation.

Respectively associated with exportation and importation in the Brazilian national economy, the CCAB and 25 de Março have become linked to transnational flows of capital and goods in the current moment. While the economic shift beginning in the 1970s has benefited CCAB directors, it has carried greater ambivalence for 25 de Março merchants. This dissonance among Brazilians of Syrian–Lebanese descent suggests not just continuity, but also change in the hierarchy between ethnicity and nation in contemporary Brazil.

NATIONAL, STATE, AND ETHNIC PARTNERS IN "THE EXPORTING BRAZIL"

Ending a sixty-year period of protectionism, Brazil's economic opening lowered import tariffs and trade barriers, but in such a dramatic way that manufacturers have described it as "traumatic" and "shocking." Whether in cosmetics, medical supplies, or food staples, they have recounted similar experiences of suddenly confronting global competition in the early 1990s. Daniella, a cosmetics executive, explained that her company's three competitors bloomed into nineteen in 1992 alone. By importing brand-name products from East Asian outsourcers, several upstart import-oriented firms in Brazil were easily able to undersell her company's product lines. "With the economic opening, a lot of market was lost inside here," Daniella reflected, "so you have to export and look for more markets." Eduardo, a hospital-equipment executive, also explained that *grandes players mundiais* (big world players) from the United States and Europe entered the domestic market with cheaper products of higher technology. Although the experience was "traumatic," he said, "our sector is looking to prospect potential markets at the world level to also globalize." Having survived the flood of cheap and competitive imports brought on by the economic opening, Brazilian business executives have adopted export-oriented and "globalizing" strategies.

Striving to *incentivar* (motivate) the national bourgeois to sell a significant percentage of their goods or services abroad, the Brazilian state established several agencies and programs in the late 1990s. Garnering cryptic acronyms such as APEX (Agency of Export Promotion) and PROEX (Export Incentives Program), these export-oriented state entities have been welcomed in business circles. Reflecting on how they "awaken" the "exporting spirit" of Brazilian industrial elites, the president of Sadia, Luiz Furlan, stated:

> Traditionally, Brazil was not export-oriented. So, these agencies have as [their] reason of being *to awaken* the exporting spirit in small and medium-size companies and, at the same time, to educate, assist, and give access to information: What are the countries that buy? What kind of product?[19]

Hardly concealing his joy in the prospects of an export-driven national industry honed by state agencies, this important business executive subsequently praised President Fernando Henrique Cardoso for making Brazil into an export nation.

Furlan also emphasized the *parcerias* (partnerships) between export-oriented state agencies and international chambers of commerce. In present-day São Paulo, there are roughly twenty "international" chambers of commerce that often garner institutional support from state and business powers in their respective nations of origin. Run mostly by immigrants or descendants, the most prominent are the American, Arab, Italian, and Russian entities. For Furlan, these chambers "lend services to interested enterprises ... and, at the same time, have an integration [*entronsamento*] with Brazilian authorities looking to increase the flux of business between countries." In major newspaper headlines, these export partnerships between Brazilian public and private sectors have been acknowledged in positive terms. They have been generally perceived to generate a secure flow of external capital, thus providing a stable basis for national development in the world economy.

As one of these "international chambers of commerce," the CCAB honed its image as a not-for-profit and export-driven entity in the 1990s. Today, it issues "certificates of origin" for Brazilian exports to the Middle East, plans commercial missions for Brazilian state and business elites to the Arab world, represents Brazil in Arab-sponsored international fairs, and organizes seminars that train Brazilian elites in how to do business with Arab countries. Unlike chambers of commerce that aim to open the Brazilian market for the importation of goods and services from their own countries of origin, the CCAB has attempted to distinguish itself as an entity devoted primarily (but not solely) to the exportation of Brazilian goods and services to the Middle East:

> The Chamber, instead of representing foreign interests in Brazil, performs in a fully independent manner, turned mainly to exportation, in perfect consonance with the goals of the government and of the Brazilian economy. (Câmara de Comércio Árabe Brasileira 1998: 50)

Ostensibly, the CCAB has (re)presented itself as a chamber that primarily works toward increasing Brazilian exports to the Middle East. It has sought to secure its role as an ethnic partner in the export-driven Brazilian national economy.

Institutionally, the CCAB has been said to serve as a "bridge" between Brazil and the Arab world. In 1992, it was officially recognized as an economic promoter by the Arab League of States and later by similar chambers of commerce throughout the Middle East. Only in 2000, however, were the CCAB's institutional relations sealed with the Brazilian state in the form of a *parceria* (partnership) to further *conscientizar* (make conscientious) Brazil's cadre of business elites to export to the "Arab world." The CCAB has joined specifically with the Brazilian federal government's Agency of Export Promotion (APEX). Their partnership has enabled the CCAB to publicize its varied activities—whether commercial missions, international fairs, or export seminars—as "Brazilian state-sponsored." As is more fully examined later in this chapter, an APEX official has hailed the "how to export to the Arab world" seminars as *treinando* (training) Brazilian executives in the economic and cultural modes of the Arab world. Even the CCAB logo—a crescent moon colored by the green, yellow, and blue of the Brazilian flag—is displayed alongside the emblems of Brazilian federal agencies.

Serving as Brazil's link to the "Arab world," CCAB directors have underscored their Syrian and Lebanese origins as a broad Arabness. Take, for instance, the explanation given by Pierre, a third-generation Syrian Brazilian who has served as the CCAB's secretary-general since 1998: "I am Syrian, a Syrian descendant, but I am Arab. When they ask if I'm Lebanese, I say no, I am Arab, I am an Arab descendant. So, there isn't this ... idea of individual nations. It is the collective nation [*pause*] of Arabs." This general Arabness has served as the very stuff of the CCAB's institutional linkages with governmental and commercial organizations in the Arab world. Official ties with the Arab League of States, for example, are contingent on the CCAB's executive directory being *de ascendência árabe* (of Arab ascendance) stipulated in the chamber's revised charter in the 1980s (Câmara de Comércio Árabe Brasileira 1989: 15–18). In this regard, a long-time participant in the chamber has reflected that the "descent" of its presidents and directors *ganha espaço* (earns or wins space) for Brazilian executives in the "Arab world." Extended to the Arab world, this form of Arab Brazilianness has "opened" market space for Brazilian exporters.

Such Arabness, however, is distinct from its prior manifestation in the 1950s. At that time, the "Syrian and Lebanese" chamber had changed its name to "Arab Brazilian," reflecting the zenith of Arab nationalism in the three-year union between Syria and Egypt as the United Arab Republic. The chamber's current Arabness has more to do with socioeconomic changes in and beyond Brazil. Having displaced its early focus on Syria and Lebanon by the 1980s, the CCAB now interacts far more with the oil-rich nations of the Arabian Gulf. In fact, those states make up the major areas to which Brazilian exports and exporters are directed. Implicitly, the CCAB's reorientation was based on notions of "Arab petrodollars" in the global economy. In the 1980s and '90s, the Arabian Gulf accounted for more than half of Brazilian exports in the entire Middle East.[20] In manuals, seminars, and missions, the CCAB has directed Brazilian exporters to Arab countries referred to as "surplus states" (Câmara de Comércio Árabe Brasileira 1989: 28–30). Saudi Arabia, Kuwait, the United Arab Emirates (UAE), and others have been spoken of not as fellow Arab nations, but as markets that can "absorb" Brazilian exports. In this manner, Brazilians of Syrian–Lebanese descent have extended their Arabness toward the Gulf region with market logics, reflecting Brazilian—and not necessarily Syrian or Lebanese—national agendas.

This intensified Arabness has attracted some Brazilian clients of Middle Eastern origins. Shahid, for instance, is a second-generation Palestinian telecommunications businessman. Having lost revenue after 1991, he expressed interest in exporting to the Arab world. Shahid rationalized that importers in the Arab world would prefer the products of a fellow Arab in Brazil. Arabness, he stressed, was *alavancagem* (leverage). To Shahid's surprise, however, the chamber ignored him. He asked me to ask the CCAB why it had never attended to his inquiries. A CCAB director later confided to me that "Asian telecommunications" are strong throughout the Middle East and that Shahid would not get anywhere, even if the CCAB were to help him. I relayed the message to Shahid, who could not help but question the very purpose of the CCAB: "But shouldn't the chamber be helping us [Arabs]?" Shahid continues to frequent CCAB events and hopes for a future export opportunity.

In this light, Arab ethnicity has intensified but in ways that are potentially irrelevant to the actual interaction among self-identified Arabs themselves.

The CCAB's Arabness thus reflects market logics of belonging today. Despite the chamber's not-for-profit status, its directors have stakes in transnational flows between Brazil and the Middle East. Take, for instance, two Syrian–Lebanese participants from a 2000 commercial mission to the Arabian Gulf who were asked to join the CCAB's board of directors. While one deals in investment banking, the other works in the lactose industry. Sealing deals during the Gulf business mission, they have also secured directorships in the chamber. As another example, Bashar, the owner of a well-known tourist agency in São Paulo, joined the board of directors several years ago. Since then, he has mounted exhibits on Egyptian and Algerian tourism in Brazil. "Inside the chamber," Bashar explained to me, "this is my area." But in 2001, he formed part of a committee to publicize Brazilian tourism at an international travel fair, the Arabian Travel Market, in Dubai, UAE. A CCAB newsletter later noted that "the occasion was so propitious in the sealing of deals that one Brazilian tourist operator has already contracted four chartered flights [from the UAE to Brazil]."[21] The benefits of Arabness, in this light, have been earned by CCAB directors and the Brazilian national economy.

A brief point of contrast can be made with the American Arab Chamber of Commerce (AACC) in the United States. Founded in 1992 by a group of Arab American businessmen in the greater Detroit region, the chamber has sought to become a "hub of commerce between the Middle East and the United States, much as Miami is for trade with Central and South America."[22] In efforts to have a say in the estimated $55 billion of trade between U.S. and Arab markets, the AACC held the first-ever "U.S.–Arab Economic Forum" in Detroit in September 2003. Among the 1,000 participants who paid forum fees in the range of three thousand dollars were Colin Powell and U.S. state officials, Prince Saud al-Faisal and Arabian Gulf royalty, as well as U.S. American chief executives from Intel, Boeing, and ExxonMobil.[23] Receiving press coverage across the nation, the forum aimed to focus on the market relations among U.S. and Arab powers, but politics kept surfacing.[24] While the forum was criticized by grassroots Arab American activists as exclusionary and complicit with U.S. American interests, U.S. state authorities implied their goal to spread "democracy" through the "free-market economy." Arab American businesspeople have thus tried to project their ethnicity as a market logic in national and transnational scope, but they remain dogged by the U.S. American state agenda to spread "democracy" in the world. Like its Brazilian counterpart, the AACC seeks a partnership with U.S. and Arab states and businesses, but it cannot help but be complicit with U.S. American hegemony.

PERFORMING THE ARAB BRAZILIAN
PARTNERSHIP IN EXPORT(N)ATION

In contrast, in Brazil, the partnership between ethnic, state, and national elites has been performed in the CCAB seminars "How to Do Business with Arab Countries [*Como negociar com os países árabes*]" and "Exporting to Arab Countries [*Exportando para os países árabes*]." Begun in the mid-1990s, these structured seminars have been held bimonthly throughout Brazil, attracting between 50 and 120 businesspeople, overwhelmingly non-Arab, from Brazilian enterprises. Co-sponsored with APEX, the "Exporting to Arab Countries" seminars have gained visibility in the Brazilian business press, especially the *Gazeta Mercantil*.[25] What follows are descriptions of two "Exporting to Arab Countries" seminars in which I participated in 1999 and 2001.[26]

In the entrance to a seminar room packed with dark suits, the mostly male attendees fumbled with name tags handed out by female secretaries. Carefully placed on the one hundred and twenty seats were folders filled with pamphlets on upcoming international fairs and business missions. Participants perused them, adjusted name tags on lapels, and glanced at their gold watches as the seminar began. After panelists from the Arab chamber and the Brazilian federal government were introduced at the front table, a synopsis was given of their co-sponsored activities. "The role of the CCAB," began the chamber's president, Paulo Atallah, "is to increase trade between Brazil and Arab countries." For that purpose, he continued, the "Arab chamber" has national branches in Maranhão, Bahia, Goiás, Brasília, and southern Brazil, as well as international branches, such as the Dubai Brazilian Business Center in the UAE. Atallah made sure to point out that the Dubai business center was partly funded by the Brazilian state. The CCAB was thus introduced as an entity extending across Brazil toward the Arab world.

Atallah then introduced two officials from the Brazilian Ministry of Foreign Relations who stood beside him at the front of the seminar room. The first stressed that the Brazilian government planned to double the country's exports in 2000 through the recently created Agency of Export Promotion, or APEX. With a "very modern vision," APEX was said to represent one of the "principal points of advancement" in Fernando Henrique Cardoso's administration, which sought to transform Brazil into "a great exporting country in the global economy." One of the main "partners" in this objective has been the CCAB. "Few chambers have the background that this one does," boasted the state official. "It brings businessmen from Brazil to export to the Arab world." In concluding, he declared, "I salute this initiative of the CCAB in establishing a headquarters in Dubai." This was the very enactment of how the Arab chamber has gained recognition as a *parceiro* (partner) of the Brazilian state today.

In 2001, the state official's remarks were followed by a presentation by Pierre, the CCAB's secretary-general (himself a third-generation Syrian). Invited to take the floor, Pierre gave a twenty-minute talk on the characteristics of the "Arab market." After reviewing its major economic characteristics, including tariff barriers and growth rates, Pierre showed a map of the Middle East. "It's not precise," he qualified, "but it's only to give you an idea of the countries that compose the Arab market." Pointing to the "Mediterranean region" of Lebanon, Syria, and Palestine, Pierre noted that the "majority of immigrants in Brazil" stemmed "from these Arab countries," though later on he qualified that the area "has risks." Shifting to the Arabian Gulf, he explained that it "has the second-largest commercial movement, second only to Hong Kong." While Pierre pinpointed his own Syrian origin on the "Arab market" map, he highlighted the economic potential of another region. In this way, he conflated the ostensible Arabness of the chamber's Syrian–Lebanese directors, who had originated on the western edge of the "Arab market," with that market's eastern fringes, the Arabian Gulf. Shifting away from Syrian or Lebanese homelands toward the "larger commercial movement" in the Gulf, this extension of Arabness reflects the destination of Brazilian exportation in the Arab world.

A significant segment of the seminar was also dedicated to "Arab culture" in the hope of facilitating future business intercourse between Brazilian and Arab executives. At the 1999 and 2001 seminars, for instance, Pierre's discussion of the "cultural characteristics of the Arab businessman" provoked a flurry of note-taking in the Brazilian audience.[27] Particular emphasis was placed on the "importance of Arab culture." In 1999, Pierre specified that Arabs enjoy "interpersonal relations" in commercial deals, and "Arabs like to bargain, so it's good to give a little discount, to lower the price a little." In 2001, he offered a similar, but more polished, version of the profile of "the Arab importer": He "likes to feel important," Pierre explained. "He likes confiding in the partner and [is] really prepared to bargain. He likes to negotiate, to offer coffee and debate the price of the merchandise, … and he likes to feel victorious on the price issue." In these terms, CCAB directors projected the historically specific image of Arabs as shrewd traders in Brazil onto the Arab world itself. But in so doing, they strengthened their own role as *parceiros* for Brazilian executives, "partners" who ostensibly know how to negotiate and barter the way only Arabs do.

Such references to the bargaining ability of businessmen in the Arabian Gulf were not lost on the chamber's (non-Arab) Brazilian clients. As chief of the international relations division of FIESP (Federation of the Industries of the State of São Paulo), Maurice pointed out that an innate business acumen is common to Arabs not only in Brazil and the Middle East, but throughout Europe. Reflecting on the commercial adroitness of Arabs in his homeland of Romania, Maurice recounted a proverb that "an Arab is worth seven Romanians." Eduardo, the hospital equipment executive mentioned earlier, similarly noted that "the Arab has by nature a commercial way of being. It's in the roots to negotiate." Expressing admiration for the "highly qualified executives" that he met during the CCAB's business mission to the Arabian Gulf, Eduardo provided more detail about Arabs in Brazil:

> We always knew since childhood that the merchant had to be someone from the community, always in commerce, in garments, textiles, food stores. You always had the Arab community in this area. For us here in Brazil … this culture of the [Arab] immigrant is present in the day-to-day.

Taught "how to do business" in the Arabian Gulf, Brazilian executives found it only natural that the Arab commercial essence in Brazil was possessed by counterparts in the Arab world.

Daniella, the cosmetics executive, participated in the same commercial mission to the Arabian Gulf. She explained that she was prepared to "earn the confidence" of Arab executives and was armed with sample hairbrushes on whose handles was written, in Arabic, "For Your Baby." Expressing satisfaction with her cross-cultural business ploy, realized with translation assistance from the CCAB, Daniella related: "I'm getting into their culture." Yet she also reflected on the difficulty of doing business with Arab executives. Commenting on her experiences with "Arabs" both before and after the commercial mission, she explained:

> We hear a lot about how the Arab knows how to do business. You ask for a discount, but the Arab really holds out [*segura muito*]. He doesn't want to give in. People say, "Arabs will take everything they can from you." There on 25 de Março, the merchant speaks like this: "Oh, senhora! I'll give it to you cheap! I sell it cheap, senhora [said with an 'Arabic' accent, with hand in fist]." But when I saw that hospitality in Saudi Arabia, the lunches, the cars waiting at the airport, the clothes they wear. … So there it's another thing. It's a characteristic of Arabs to be hospitable. … But in spite of the hospitality, business is hard to make happen [*negócio é duro pra fazer*].

Hospitality notwithstanding, Daniella experienced difficulty in clinching deals with Arab executives who attended CCAB-sponsored trade fairs in the Middle East. Even if business dealings would not work out, she stressed that she had enjoyed her trip and learned that Middle Easterners are not just about "arduous work," but also about "hospitality." Far from dispelling the idea of the Arab commercial essence that Daniella came to know on Rua 25 de Março, her transnational business experience conflated it with the Middle East itself.

In the late 1990s, Eduardo and Daniella were just two of the several thousands of Brazilian businesspeople who partook in CCAB seminars on how to export to the Middle East. Having returned from a ten-day commercial mission in several Arabian Gulf countries, they were starry-eyed with potentially lucrative business deals.[28] And, like the six other participants interviewed, they expressed admiration for the CCAB's "role" in the commercial excursion. They found especially helpful the CCAB's distribution of an etiquette manual of cultural "dos and do nots" and its organization of trade fairs that "opened the doors" for Brazilian executives to meet and "deal" with Arab importers.[29] Eduardo explained:

> When you go to a country, it's important that you have someone who will open the doors for you. And the [Arab] chamber has this role. It has a relationship in these countries, since its part of the community. ... So it's able to fix up the channel of communication and facilitate transactions. ... It's an important agent that makes the channel between Brazil and countries of the Arab community.

Brazilian business executives situated the CCAB in the position of "opening the doors" to Arab markets. Forging a "channel of communication" between Brazil and the Middle East, the CCAB's "role"—as partner, not pariah—has been commended by Brazilian exporters.

Similarly seeking the assistance of the CCAB in his company's successful exportation of poultry products to the Middle East, Luiz Furlan, president of Sadia, reflected on the contemporary condition of the national economy and the place of the chamber therein:

> The Brazilian economy was always a very closed economy. ... It was very difficult [to export]. It was a science to export. And now with the opening, there has been a renewal of the role of chambers of commerce, and there are various ones that are very active. And one of the most active is the Arab chamber, which has brought together executives of many sectors

and, at the same time, has promoted missions abroad. ... It is admirable
the work that the Arab chamber has been doing in the last few years, in
the sense of uniting the interests of everyone, but at the same time having a pro-Brazil position, as well.

In the opening of a once closed economy, business elites have looked to "international" chambers of commerce to "facilitate" the flow of national goods
abroad. And, as a well-respected executive stated, the CCAB has been one of
the most "admirable" among them.

Extended to the far eastern gulf of the Arab world, the intensified ethnicity of the CCAB's directors has been recognized by state officials as well. In a
dinner commemorating the chamber's fiftieth anniversary in 2001, for
instance, President Cardoso thanked the CCAB for its role in the Brazilian
"exports [that] are continually increasing."[30] With some candor, he stated:

> There has been a very large increase in the commerce of Brazil with the
> Arab world. My government sees the community as an important and
> even indispensable ally in our efforts to augment and diversify our exports.
> ... I have to say that we owe much to the efforts that have been made by
> the Arab Brazilian Chamber of Commerce and by the community. It only
> remains for me to thank one more time the CCAB and, by its intermedi-
> ation, the Arab community for everything they have done to promote the
> good name of Brazil.[31]

Once disparaged as pariahs, "Arabs"—the CCAB and, implicitly, the "Arab
community"—are now considered an "indispensable ally" of the Brazilian
state and nation.

Likewise, Dorthea Werneck, director of APEX, commended the chamber
for its "leadership" among Brazilian executives.[32] With much ado, she stated
that "the project of the Arab chamber [Câmara Árabe] has been a success, not
only because of the concrete result in the increase of exports—more than 50
percent this year—but also for the ability to mobilize executives from very different sectors." Even the secretary-general of foreign relations under President Cardoso proclaimed, "I recognize as one of the Arab Brazilian Chamber
of Commerce's most laudable points the adoption of a pioneering stance that
consists in ... supporting, in an efficient way, Brazilian exporters in the con-
quest of Arab markets."[33] In the neoliberal restructuring of the national economy, the role of the CCAB and the "Arab community" has gained greater
acknowledgment as a "partner" in contemporary Brazil.

A LLEGEDLY EQUIPPED WITH an inborn bargaining ability, Middle Easterners have had their place in Brazil disparaged or questioned since the
late nineteenth century. Even today, importers of Syrian–Lebanese descent in
the 25 de Março district continue to be viewed with ambivalence about their
respectability by Brazilian elites and others. In counterdistinction, however,
the Arab Brazilian Chamber of Commerce has come to occupy a privileged
position. Conceived as a leisure institution for Syrian–Lebanese textile mag-
nets in the 1950s and '60s, the chamber was reinvented in the late twentieth
century. Its present-day second- and third-generation Syrian–Lebanese directors have striven to help Brazilian executives export to the Arabian Gulf and
North Africa. As such, these newfound export promoters of Syrian–Lebanese
descent have gained greater recognition as the literal partners of Brazilian
elites, not despite their alleged commercial propensity, but because of its perceived advantage for national exportation.

In this chapter, I have suggested that such a decided (but not definitive nor
seamless) shift in the hierarchical relations between Arab ethnicity and the
Brazilian nation began with the neoliberalization of the imagined national
economy in the 1970s and accelerated with the formal economic opening in
1991. During this time, exportation has been perceived as benefiting Brazil's
development and advancing its national agenda in the globalizing world. In
this paradigm shift, Brazilian national and state elites have allied with "shrewd"
Arab ethnics to spearhead the introduction of Brazilian exports not into their
Syrian and Lebanese countries of origin, but into the more lucrative markets
of the Arabian Gulf and North Africa.

~~~

Eth(n)ics and Transparent
State Reform

R EFERENCES TO THE ALLEGED shrewdness of Arabs also made headline news in a corruption scandal that mired the São Paulo city government in 1999 and 2000. As citizens from lay, business, and media
circles clamored for "more transparent" governance, city councilors of Middle
Eastern origin became the embodiment of corruption in mainstream media
reportage. In efforts to offset their image as corrupt ethnics, city councilors of
Middle Eastern descent carried out the second annual commemoration of
Lebanese independence day in São Paulo's city government. Clamoring for justice in the Middle East, these politicians expressed a righteous brand of Arab
ethnicity in a Brazilian government undergoing transparent reform today.

Exploring an ethical dimension of the Arab ethnic project, this chapter
focuses on politicians, media pundits, and lay people of Middle Eastern descent
in a São Paulo city government corruption scandal. My aim is to grasp how
Arab ethnicity has intensified through images of corruption in the Brazilian
media and the discourse of ethics from the World Bank. Attending to how
politicians of Middle Eastern descent have been charged with corruption in
the national media, I argue that they have used the official Lebanese independence day event in city government to gain ethical recognition as Arab ethnics in the public sphere. Serving as a platform to make righteous declarations,
the event has accentuated the accountability of Arab eth(n)ics in Brazil amid
an anticorruption program sponsored by the World Bank.

These ethical highlights of ethnicity are best grasped in what Akhil Gupta
calls the imagined state (Gupta 1995; see also Ferguson and Gupta 2003).

Exploring how the state is formed through representations of mass media and practices of low-level bureaucrats and villagers, Gupta argues that "the discourse of corruption turns out to be a key arena through which the state, citizens, and other organizations ... come to be imagined." He continues that "instead of treating corruption as a dysfunctional aspect of state organizations, I see it as a mechanism through which the state is discursively constituted" (Gupta 1995: 376). Far from invalidating state power, media and lay commentaries on corruption compose its discursive presence in the public sphere. In dialogue with his work, this chapter proposes another rhetorical way by which the state is imagined: transparency. As Todd Sanders and Harry West (2003) observe, transparency has gained a global currency among international organizations, governments, and media groups. In this milieu, the state, which historically secured power by persuading individuals to "see" how it bettered their lives (Scott 1998), can now do so only by claiming to be "seen through" by a host of global actors and entities. Expressed in relation to the discourse of corruption, demands for and claims to transparency both challenge and reconfigure state power today.

Although suspicions of corruption and declarations of transparency are nothing new in Brazil, their symbolic delineation grew more striking in the late twentieth-century imagined state. Reinaugurated with the country's democratic opening in the 1980s, the media—specifically, newspapers and television—have served as the very channel of electoral campaigns, political consciousness-raising, and government satire (Amaral 2002; Carvalho 1999; Guimarães and Amaral 1998). In the 1990s, press coverage focused on the seeming increase of corruption and hailed subsequent ethical probes in municipal, state, and federal government circles (Bezerra 1995; Cardozo 2000; Gois 2000). Covering the partnership between the World Bank and the seemingly "more transparent" São Paulo city government, mass media has been crucial in outlining the present-day contours of the imagined Brazilian state. Discursively, the state has been challenged by transparency claims and (re)composed through them.

Yet questioning "the very meaning of transparency," this chapter, in the words of Sanders and West, asks, "What after all, is claimed when the operation of power is described as transparent? What is *seen through*, and what, then, is *seen*?" (Sanders and West 2003: 28). "Seeing through" television or newsprint, elites have attested to the unprecedented rise in corruption. Leftists have regarded it as a result of the country's hurried neoliberalization. But conservatives have taken it as evidence of the efficacy of neoliberal reform. Despite opposing viewpoints, both sides "see" the "uncovering" of corruption as making the state "more transparent." But this chapter shows that only Middle Easterners were seen as corrupt in such transparency. Using

World Bank discourse, officials sought to make government more transparent but also needed to deflect accusations of corruption. Obfuscating the logics of power that worked as intended, the idiom of transparency has revealed the alleged Arabness of corruption in the public sphere.

This episode thus shows that, although Brazilians of Middle Eastern descent have gained greater visibility, there are limits to their claims within the shifting hierarchical relations of ethnicity and the national state. Bearing the brunt of ethical accountability in the media, city councilors of Lebanese descent did not hide their ethnicity but, rather, took charge of the city government's commemoration of Lebanese independence day. This and other events legislated for specific ethnic constituencies have become institutionalized in the São Paulo city administration. In fact, the Secretariat of International Relations in city government—founded in 2000 by Mayor Marta Suplicy—not only culls relations with global institutions such as the World Bank, but also sponsors official events of *colônias* in São Paulo, such as the Lebanese independence day celebration. Though part of a broader intensification of ethnicity in city government, Middle Eastern–marked events have served to deflect suspicions of corruption from the imagined state.

PAST POLITICAL CONNECTIONS AND THE CURRENT CONJUNCTURE OF CORRUPTION

Graduating from prestigious postsecondary institutions from the 1930s onward, the sons and grandsons of humble Syrian–Lebanese merchants were well positioned to rise into the political vacuum of the post–Estado Novo regime led by Getúlio Vargas. Called an "experiment in democracy" (Skidmore 1967), these later years of the Vargas era brought about the involvement of immigrants and their descendants amid the marginalization of "traditional political elites" (Fausto et al. 1995: 26). Oswaldo Truzzi found that forty-one "distinct politicians of Syrian–Lebanese origin" from São Paulo exercised eighty-eight mandates in municipal, state, and federal arenas from 1945 to 1966 (Truzzi 1995: 53–54). Most striking in 1962 and 1966, Syrian–Lebanese garnered 10 percent and 17 percent of the total number of state and federal deputies, respectively, elected in São Paulo (Truzzi 1995: 59).[1] Such an "overrepresentation" of Middle Easterners in midcentury politics continued through two decades of military rule and the return of democracy in late twentieth-century Brazil (Truzzi 1995: 59).[2]

Early electoral success was achieved as part of a liberal professional trajectory (as will be discussed in Chapter 3). As university graduates, Syrian–Lebanese gained footholds in the government through legal, medical, or media professions. Of the forty-one Arabs elected and reelected to city, state, and federal posts in São Paulo from 1945 to 1964, two-thirds were lawyers, radio announcers, or medical doctors (Truzzi 1995: 59). Anis Aidar, for instance, was elected to city- and state-level positions from 1940 to 1952, surmising that he was "basically elected for being the lawyer" of a pharmaceutical association (cited in Truzzi 1995: 39). Likewise elected to various posts from 1947 to 1968, Nicolau Tuma was assured a long political career due to his previous job as a sports announcer on Rádio Record through the 1930s and '40s (Truzzi 1995: 36–38). By engaging in liberal professions, midcentury ethnics made their historic entrance into municipal, state, and federal politics.

In this fashion, São Paulo State Deputy Antônio Salim Curiati initiated his public career in the 1960s. Originally, he operated a small medical practice with an ear, nose, and throat specialization in a rural São Paulo town. The (in)famous politician's son, himself a present-day councilman in the city of São Paulo, recounted that his father

> was the only ears, nose, and throat doctor in the entire region. So he attended to the biggest plantation owner of the area to the worst-off peasant of the area. He is used to telling the story that he has done well in life because he has a lot of "God will pay you" accumulated on his back. The [poor] people [would say]: "Doctor, I can't pay." [And he would respond]: "That's not a problem." [And they would say]: "God will pay you! God will pay you! God will pay you!" Since he received a lot of "God will pay you, God will pay you," he grew a lot in life [*pause*] and was the only doctor there, right? Everyone consulted him. He would operate on everyone.

Having accumulated various debts from elites and masses as a gregarious medical patron, Curiati was approached by a political big shot in the early 1960s. Asked to muster support for a candidate in the federal deputy elections, the Lebanese physician was ensured no fewer than two thousand votes. Within the same decade, Curiati decided to organize his own campaign for the state deputy chambers. He never looked back. In his thirty-year political career, alleged medical debts were transformed into political capital. Today, this social power has helped his son get elected to the City Council in São Paulo.

As the most infamous *patrício* in Brazilian politics, the second-generation Lebanese Paulo Salim Maluf shows a similar trajectory. Born in São Paulo to a Lebanese immigrant father and a mother from another wealthy Lebanese family, Maluf was educated at the Colégio São Luís and later attained his degree in civil engineering from the University of São Paulo. In *O Malufismo*

(2000), the journalist Mauricio Puls recounts that Maluf gained political clout through an amicable friendship struck with General Costa e Silva in horse-racing clubs during the 1950s. As chief of state in the early years of the dicta-torship (1967–69), General Costa e Silva appointed the young Maluf mayor of São Paulo. In the next thirty years, Maluf embarked on a career as a very resourceful—some would say sly—politician. He won special infamy in the race for the São Paulo governorship in 1978. At the time, President General Ernesto Geisel (1976–80) passed him over in choosing the candidate of Arena, the political party of the dictatorship. Meanwhile, Maluf personally visited the majority of the eight hundred Arena delegates who would choose the party candidate. "On the day of the convention," relates Puls, "Maluf greeted all the delegates of Arena by name … he knew their city and wives' and children's names," too (Puls 2000: 33). In late 1978, Maluf was made governor by the leg-islative assembly in São Paulo. Like Maluf, Arabs were assured of success by making political connections in authoritarian Brazil.

Still, Maluf has garnered much support among those who identify with his brand of populism, *malufismo*. Detractors and followers alike say that Maluf *rouba mas faz* (steals but gets things done). Puls suggests that Maluf con-tinued the populist tradition of Adhemar de Barros, a prominent figure in the country's first re-democratization process (1945–64). The expression *rouba mas faz* was originally coined in reference to Barros, specifically in his dispute with Jânio Quadros for the São Paulo governorship in 1954. While Barros was characterized by the popular mantra, *rouba mas faz*, Quadros won the elec-tion based on his promise to *varrer* (sweep out) corruption.[3] Historically, Maluf's image as a wily politician had been inherited from *adhemarismo*, Adhemar de Barros's style of populism.

In 1999 and 2000, these past dynamics gained a novel force in the so-called *máfia das propinas* (mafia of kickbacks), implicating past and present São Paulo city governments. In exchange for legislative deference to the mayor, city councilors were given the power to appoint directors of local administra-tive sub-units of the municipality (called Regional Administrations, or ARs). In the cases investigated, handpicked cronies had bribed constituencies by bypassing or providing government laws or services. The kickbacks collected from different groups—namely, street vendors and commercial enterprises—had been then rerouted back to city councilors who voted in accordance with the mayor and rightist establishment.[4] This quid pro quo provided the mayor with a council majority and city councilors with administrative machinery to cull election support and forward self-interests among voting publics. Once ensuring political success, this institutionalization of personal connections increasingly has been labeled "corruption" by the press.

The mafia of kickbacks erupted when a street vendor denounced a well-known Lebanese Brazilian politician in early 1999 and then turned into a drama of governance in newspaper articles and television reports through the year 2000. Exerting influence over the municipal administrative unit of Sé in downtown São Paulo (AR-Sé), City Councilman Hanna Garib (Brazilian Progressive Party, or PPB) allegedly ordered the murder of the street vendor who had made the damning accusations. Garib had a lot at stake. He had extracted bribes from street vendors in exchange for de facto permission to remain stationary on sidewalks and streets. Ironically, Garib also received payments from commercial establishments to remove the area's street vendors. The extortion scheme netted millions of dollars for Garib and other councilmen, but investigations were cut short by the rightist establishment, allowing the conviction of only three councilmen: Vicente Viscome, José Izar, and Hanna Garib. Only Izar and Garib had been ethnically marked by corruption in media headlines.

Suspicions of irregular machinations at City Hall continued to haunt members of the Brazilian Progressive Party (PPB). In fact, eighteen of the thirty city councilors who supported the mayor in exchange for control of the city's administrative units stemmed from the PPB. Even its "godfather," Paulo Maluf, had been implicated when accusations of corruption reached his hand-picked successor, Mayor Celso Pitta (1997–2000). As Maluf's one-time *apadrinhado* (political godchild), Pitta was elected mayor in 1996 due to Maluf's support.[5] At the time, the PPB political godfather promised in newspapers, on television, and in radio broadcasts, "If Pitta is not a good mayor, never again vote for me." Though bills were proposed to continue formal investigations of the mayor's office (and to impeach Pitta), they were defeated by the rightist old guard in City Council chambers.

The success of pro-establishment forces only accentuated media coverage. After the premature closure of formal investigations, radio stations distributed bumper stickers that read, "São Paulo doesn't deserve corrupt city councilors" and "I'm ashamed of the city councilors of São Paulo." Similarly, *Folha de S. Paulo* drew attention to the name, political affiliation, and legislative record of each city councilor who had voted against ethics investigations and impeachment hearings.[6] Other news reportage placed the São Paulo city government crisis in relation to the "world ranking of corruption" compiled by the nongovernmental organization (NGO) Transparency International.[7] Although one article noted that the country's ranking improved from 1995 onward, it qualified that "Brazil only doesn't appear in a worse position in the ranking because the survey was done before the scandals of the Municipal Council Chambers of São Paulo."[8] In publicizing city councilors' relation to corruption and the country's place in an international ranking of corruption, media images had both constituted and challenged the unethical São Paulo city government. Though suspicions of corruption had previously arisen in Brazilian history, they were met and magnified by the global idea of transparency.

The second-generation Lebanese Councilwoman Myryam Athie had a significant presence in this media coverage of city government. Serving as the chief officer in a special investigatory committee, she represented the key vote sparing Pitta (and their political godfather) from prolonged investigations. In the aftermath of the premature "archiving" of one proceeding held against the mayor, Athie had gained notoriety as an accomplice of the status quo. Alleging that there was not sufficient evidence against the mayor and the City Council, she had been colored by corruption in media coverage, even once admitting, "I … felt like a criminal stamped on all the newspapers."[9] Like many colleagues, Athie left Maluf's PPB in late 1999 for the right-of-center Party of the Brazilian Democratic Movement (PMDB). It was also Athie who sponsored the Lebanese independence day event in the São Paulo City Council chambers.

COMMEMORATING LEBANESE ETHICS
IN THE SÃO PAULO CITY COUNCIL

As Middle Easterners made headline news in a corruption scandal broadcast throughout Brazil, Athie had orchestrated a *sessão solene* (ceremonial session) in honor of November 22, Lebanon's independence day. First held in 1999, the Commemorative Day of Lebanese Independence was held again in 2000, soon after the incumbent city councilor had won municipal elections. Although many such celebrations are officially slated for more than forty ethnic groups in the São Paulo city government, this Lebanese celebration put a particular emphasis on ethics. What follows is an ethnography of the opulent ceremony held in the Salão Nobre (Noble Hall) of the São Paulo City Council chambers.

Handed a small pin in the shape of Lebanon and decorated with its flag, I signed my name with a gold pen in the leather-bound register on the eighth floor of the City Council chambers in downtown São Paulo. Offered a glass of champagne by the deferential wait staff, I grasped a slender chalice decorated with the national symbol of Lebanon, the cedar tree. Like the sparkling bubbles from the champagne and the shining colors from my lapel pin, the eighth floor glowed with men dressed in sleek suits sporting gold watches and women adorned in shiny dresses and jewelry. The chandeliers of the Salão Nobre glittered while a film showed tourist sites of Lebanon. Older members in the sizable crowd—who were not rubbing elbows in the adjacent hallway packed with people—watched it with many "Oohs" and "Aahs."

In attendance were several notables of the Lebanese and Syrian community, including religious figures, state congressmen, diplomats (from Middle Eastern and European countries), and mostly second- or third-generation subjects from about fifty social and political associations of the Arab community in São Paulo. Their names were announced and "registered" for the public record. This roll call of important individuals and entities lasted for fifteen minutes at the beginning of the ceremony. Even a handful of telegrams and letters from "illustrious figures" were read aloud and greeted with applause. Congratulating both the city councilor on her initiative and honored guests of the Lebanese community on their independence day, a federal deputy and governor not in attendance stressed that they "pride[d] themselves in being of Lebanese descent." As Lebanese names were outlined in media headlines of corruption, the ceremonial session's participants embraced their ethnic appellation with overt pride.

After the Lebanese and Brazilian national anthems were played, the master of ceremonies invited Councilwoman Athie to take the podium for the next ten minutes. First, she thanked the audience for participating in the commemoration of Lebanon's national day of independence, promulgated on November 22, 1943. She declared that "the tribute we carry out today is directed toward some Lebanese descendants who distinguished themselves in São Paulo and Brazil." Whether peddlers or physicians, businessmen or judges, artists or sportsmen, Athie continued, descendants "distinguished" themselves in all professions. "The presence of Lebanon," she concluded with a sound bite, "is a constant in this [Brazilian] nation that has so caringly received us." In this light, the celebration of Lebanese independence day in São Paulo concerned not only "Lebanon" but also Lebanese in the Brazilian nation.

Athie stressed the strong presence of "Lebanese descendants" in the Brazilian state. In fact, two influential federal statesmen of Lebanese descent were seated next to her at the head table. In deference to Michel Temer, then the president of the federal Chamber of Deputies, she smiled and noted that a *filho de libaneses* (a son of Lebanese [immigrants]) held the third most powerful post in Brazil. Temer, who also belongs to the PMDB, smiled as his ethnic persona was extolled. Athie next turned to admonish the senator from Rio Grande do Sul, Pedro Simon, a presidential hopeful in the 2002 elections. While press coverage pinpointed Arabs as corrupt politicians in São Paulo, their ethnicity was exalted via the presence of Brazilian federal congressmen in this ostensible celebration of Lebanon's independence.

Athie finally mentioned the Lebanese homeland. Alluding to Lebanon's bloody fifteen-year civil war, she explained that "Lebanese and their descendants can speak of the moral and physical wounds etched into the body of

Lebanon." Even today, she said, the country cannot celebrate its "true independence," which "exists only on paper." With close to half of the population
living in poverty, the economy faltering, and "security" imposed by a "third
party" (Syria), "the Country of the Cedars" was stated to have its "sovereignty"
threatened. Despite such challenges, countered the righteous Athie, Lebanon
was blessed with a "spiritual and human wealth" from the Phoenicians. Inher-
iting "faith, determination, boldness to conquer an ideal, love and patience,"
present-day "Lebanese and descendants," she insisted, will remain upright in
their quest for "justice" amid so many "adversities." In conclusion, she made
an appeal to Lebanese "ascendants" and "descendants": "It will be up to us ...
a grandiose mission ... of the formidable Phoenician adventure, who discov-
ered the world and the continents, struggling for the defense of our culture
and our dream of liberty." Lebanon's independence day was thus configured
by Athie as a struggle for justice and sovereignty.

After the consul of Lebanon in São Paulo hailed the Lebanese contribution to Brazil, fifteen Lebanese Brazilians (fourteen of them men, and one
woman) were individually called to the front of the Salão Nobre. Only two
were naturalized citizens, the majority being either *filhos* (sons) or *netos*
(grandsons) of immigrants. Proudly calling out each name, the master of ceremonies first read a short biography of the venerated guest, highlighting a long
list of economic positions or political posts once achieved or currently held
in Brazil (never Lebanon). Also enunciated was the *cidade originária* ("sending" or "originating" city) of the parents or grandparents. The honorees
seemed to have little contact with the homeland, but the acknowledgment lent
authenticity to the political event itself. Awarded a plaque in the shape of
Lebanon's national territory adorned with its flag (a cedar tree with one white
and two red stripes), honorees posed for pictures as the audience applauded.
Thanking parents, families, and the city councilwoman, each honored guest
expressed pride not only in Lebanese "roots," "origins," "blood," or "descent,"
but also in "being Brazilian" and "living in the Brazilian nation." Recurrent references made to Brazil were not "out of place" in what was a Lebanese independence day celebration. After all, ethnic elites were praised for their economic and political achievements not in the Lebanese homeland, but in Brazil.

The emphasis on the Lebanese presence in Brazil became more pronounced in the speeches of two federal congressmen at the end of the ceremony. For his part, Senator Pedro Simon took the podium abdicated by the
master of ceremonies. Using all of the eloquence and ardor for which he is
notorious, Simon addressed the audience for more than ten minutes. In one
of his lyrical flashes, Simon announced that "there are folks who think that the
Brazilian people ... it has even appeared in the headlines ... [are] a people

atavistically turned toward corruption." Referring to the São Paulo City Council corruption scandal, the senator gave a non sequitur response. "Brazil," he
stressed, is "a great people," because it *fez a mescla* (made the mix) of "white,
black, Indian, Caboclo ["mixed" Indian], Portuguese, Italian, German, Arab,
[and] Lebanese" peoples.[10] He continued, "We integrated ourselves into what
we can call the Brazilian race. It's within this Brazilian race ... that we look to
the Lebanese people as one of those who contributed the most." Simon thus
distanced Lebanese descendants from the spectacle of corruption and rein-
serted them in the nationalist narrative of race mixture (Skidmore 1974).[11] This
praise of Lebanese integration into Brazil was repeated in later press coverage.

Temer, who was then the president of the Chamber of Deputies (akin to
the U.S. House of Representatives), was the last honored guest to be invited to
the podium. Stemming from the same right-of-center political party as Senator Simon and Councilwoman Athie, Temer first engaged in statistical praise
of his ethnic political brethren. "In the Chamber of Deputies," he noted in passing, "10 percent of its membership are Lebanese descendants." Alluding to such
upward political mobility, Temer rhetorically asked the audience before him:

> What country would allow for Myryam Athie to be such an efficient City
> Councilwoman ...? For Pedro Simon, ex-governor of Rio Grande do Sul,
> Senator of the Republic, to be a candidate to the presidency of the Repub-
> lic? For a modest Tietense [an inhabitant of Tieté, São Paulo State, and a
> reference to himself] to get to Brasília to be the president of the Cham-
> ber of Deputies? What country would allow for this if it weren't Brazil?

Attributing the "efficient" and "modest" ascension of Lebanese political elites
to the "blessed country of Brazil," Temer situated himself and his two colleagues in an allegedly ethical state and nation. Concluding his speech, he
remarked that everyone should express "thanks to God" for "having Lebanese
parents and having been born in Brazil."

While that "Lebanon" in the Middle East was pushed to the background,
honorees and audience members glorified the Lebanese in Brazil. The material motivation of this sleight of hand became most evident when Temer
stepped off the podium to make room for Athie, who brought the event to its
official end. Ostensibly overcome with "emotion," she addressed the deputy,
senator, and other parliamentarians by saying, "Thank you for being able to
transform this chamber, which during some time was an object of criticism
by a press that would only show its bad side." Under media scrutiny, an array
of Lebanese politicians came together to project their ethnically righteous
place in the Brazilian state.

COLORING CORRUPTION IN THE IMAGINED
TRANSPARENT STATE

Striving to make Lebanese appear ethical, Athie was rivaled by non-Arab authorities who claimed transparency in press coverage. An appointee of the mayoral administration, for instance, announced steps to reduce omnipresent "kickbacks" and proclaimed: "I want transparency in the work [of inspection]."[12] A center-right city councilman also claimed "to show transparency and to facilitate any type of investigation. I can't be put in a common sack and [be] called a crime boss."[13] Likewise, Celso Pitta severed ties with Maluf and removed appointed administrators, which, in his words, would "better give transparency in the investigations."[14] Even his lawyer remarked that "Pitta was held hostage by *malufismo* for years, and now, having liberated himself, he's going to show transparency in his administration and help end this true canker of corruption that took over the city."[15] Such claims to transparency deflected suspicions of corruption in national headlines.

Ethics and transparency were likewise emphasized in the 2000 elections. On both the right and the left, political aspirants proclaimed their stance *pela ética* (for ethics) and *pela transparência* (for transparency). While the mayoral candidate Paulo Maluf claimed to be victimized by accusations of corruption, the Workers' Party (Partido dos Trabalhadores, or PT) attained far-reaching political victories due to an ethically righteous appeal. Satirized as the epitome of a *PT cor-de-rosa* (pink-colored PT), the victorious mayoral candidate, Marta Suplicy, was a political newcomer (though then married to a senator). As a one-time television talk-show host, Suplicy had gained fame as a psychiatrist in sexuality, popularly labeled a *sexóloga*. Above all, Suplicy was assured success because of her peripheral status to the establishment and her appeal to bourgeois and working-class disillusionment with its corruption. In her victory speech, the incoming mayor proclaimed, "One commitment I can have: absolute transparency."[16] Putting a radical spin on a similar keyword, the leftist icon Frei Betto spoke of the "ethical rebellion" of the São Paulo votership against a corrupt establishment whose ostensible apotheosis was the Lebanese Brazilian Paulo Maluf.[17]

Voting for Suplicy, however, was hardly a rebellion. In fulfilling her *compromisso ético* (ethical commitment) to "the people of São Paulo," the mayor negotiated a "partnership" with the World Bank within the first month of electoral victory.[18] Righteously dubbed the Program of Good Governance and Combat against Corruption, the partnership undertook an investigation of corruption in the São Paulo city government.[19] It was initiated when Suplicy and Jorge Mattoso, the head of the city government's new Secretariat of International Relations, met with World Bank authorities in Washington, D.C., in November 2000. Not incidentally, the $1 million program first focused on city administrative units, whence stemmed suspicions of corruption in the nearly two years leading up to elections.[20] Close to three thousand city officials were slated for interviews in the "mapping" of what the mayor herself dubbed "webs of corruption" in the São Paulo political establishment.[21] Far from being unique, the program's idealizers pointed out, the anticorruption program was similar to others implemented in countries throughout Latin America and Africa. In fortifying the "efficient" state around the world, the campaign against corruption was part of the World Bank's attempt to focus on the human and social aspects of globalization rather than solely on trade and industrial concerns, as shown in the Washington Consensus.[22] Stemming from the World Bank and covered in national media, this discourse of anticorruption reform helped remake the São Paulo city government. Although a similar claim to "sweep out corruption" had been made in midcentury times, it was magnified by the idea of transparency in the contemporary world economy.

As the language of transparency was used by city government, the ethnicity of politicians of Syrian–Lebanese descent became conflated with corruption in mainstream media. Figures in the mafia of kickbacks spectacle were depicted not only as dishonest politicians but also as corrupt Arabs in 1999 and 2000. Loaded with lingo and political satire, this representation of Arab corruption was realized via innuendoes about the popular Brazilian "Arab" fast-food chain Habib's, as well as "Arab food," such as tabouleh (a salad with parsley, tomato, and bulgur wheat), *kibe* (ground meat with bulgur wheat), baba ghanoush (eggplant pâté with garlic and sesame-seed paste), and even *esfihas* (meat pies).[23] One political pundit awarded "prizes" to the most unpopular figures in São Paulo, serving up the "Habib's prize" to Paulo Maluf. In early 1999, he wrote:

The Habib's Prize goes to doctor (doctor of what, eh?) Baulo Baluf [*sic*]. After one of those years in which the mayor's order turned into a *pita azeda* [bitter pita bread; a reference to Celso Pitta] and the fight that was to be tabouleh turned into raw *kibe*, all that's lacking the illustrious citizen is to open up a *cadeia* [double meaning of chain or prison] (no pun intended) of Arab food and give license to his charms to make all his opponents get cancer.[24]

As corruption was associated with Middle Eastern foods, including pita bread, tabouleh, and *kibe*, Paulo Maluf was mocked for his support of Celso Pitta's city government, which plunged São Paulo into one of its worst corruption scandals ever.

Within the next few months in 1999, another social commentator levied similar criticism of several figures involved in the mafia of kickbacks. Taking the form of a "Dear Gabby" column, a perhaps fictitious reader fretted:

> WELL DONE
>   My last votes went to Maluf, Pitta, Garib and Viscome. Will I eternally burn in the fires of hell, or will I be deserving of some divine clemency? Do I have some chance of being forgiven? How?
> —Fried *Kibe* in Boiling Oil

In "response," the political satirist wrote:

> DEAR SENHORA HABIB'S,
>   I fear that you will suffer the same punishment as other São Paulo city residents who committed the same sin: being condemned to live in an ugly, dirty, and wicked city.[25]

Although two non-Arab politicians implicated in the corruption scandal were mentioned (Celso Pitta, a self-identified black Brazilian,[26] and Vicente Viscome, of Italian descent), the discourse on Middle Eastern food ("fried *kibe*") and the reference to the Habib's fast-food chain colored corruption with the ethnicity of Paulo Maluf and Hanna Garib. Political corruption was conflated not with blackness or Italianness but with Arabness in São Paulo.

The media, however, was not the sole source of criticism. In June 2000, the Union of Bank Clerks organized a protest in which members distributed three thousand *esfihas* (Middle Eastern meat pies) in front of the City Council chambers. Angered by the failure to impeach Paulo Maluf's handpicked successor, Celso Pitta, protestors expressed indignation by modifying a colloquial expression, *Vai acabar em pizza*—literally, "It will end in pizza," meaning, "Nothing will come of it." In the words of one organizer, since the protest was *em homenagem aos árabes e libaneses* (in dedication to Arabs and Lebanese), the scandal would end not in "pizza" but in an *esfiha* (meat pie).[27] Covering the event, the journalist related:

> Instead of pizza, one group of fifty bank clerks, dressed as Arabs, gave *esfiha* meat pies to the people passing in front of City Hall in protest of the rejection of Mayor Celso Pitta's impeachment trial. The president of the Union of Bank Clerks ... said that the switch of pizza for *esfiha* was

motivated by the fact that "the godfather of Pitta, Paulo Maluf, is of Lebanese origin."[28]

Covering their heads with kaffiyehs (Arab scarves) and promising that a belly dancer would come on the scene, union members overlooked the backgrounds of other politicians implicated in the scandal and embodied Arabness as the canker of corruption in city government.

Curiously, the most cutting criticisms of Middle Eastern politicians stemmed from left-of-center media elites who identified themselves as "Lebanese descendants." José Simão, famous for writing a daily column in *Folha de S. Paulo*, was relentless in his witty and sometimes cryptic discourse on the corruption of fellow *turcos*. Satirizing the insignia of Paulo Maluf's PPB, Simão once wrote, "Since I am Lebanese, I can say that PPB means *Propinas Pros Brimos*. Hahaha!"[29] Roughly translated, "*Propinas Pros Primos*" means "Kickbacks for Cousins." Simão played on native Arabic speakers' difficulty in pronouncing the "p" in *primo* (cousin), enunciating it as a "b"—hence *brimo*. Simão also quipped in other articles that Paulo Maluf would take advantage of his time in the limelight to write and release an autobiography titled, *Minha Vida É uma Esfirra Aberta* (My Life Is an Open Meat Pie).[30] Satirizing Arabic language and food, this self-identified Lebanese journalist highlighted the corrupt character of Middle Eastern ethnicity in national presses.

Hanna Garib was mocked in equally creative ways. In the excerpt that follows, Simão commented on how Garib's forced departure from the political arena led to his replacement by another politician, Wadih Helou, who coincidentally also was Middle Eastern:

> Attention! It's the Turco-Circuit [*Turco-Circuito*] in Sampa [São Paulo]. 'Cash Garib' leaves and his replacement is Wadih Helou? One *turco* leaves and another enters? As a reader friend of mine says: "They switched a *kibe* for an *esfiha*? It's like an all-you-can-eat meal at Habib's! Ha ha ha! It [the corruption scandal] ended in *esfiha*, and not in pizza![31]

Using Middle Eastern food and the popular ethnonym of *turcos*, the Lebanese commentator outlined the corrupt contours of Hanna Garib and even his replacement, Wadih Helou (who had nothing to do with this corruption scandal itself).

Arnaldo Jabor, another well-known pundit who writes in the *Folha de S. Paulo* and makes brief appearances on the Globo television network,[32] accentuated the alleged Arabness of corruption and the servile role of blackness. He surmised that the mafia of kickbacks under the administration of Celso Pitta,

São Paulo's first black mayor, was orchestrated by Paulo Maluf and other *turcos*. Satirizing Middle Eastern politicians as a "mafia of baba ghanoush eaters with sesame dripping from their chins," he joked that the black mayor "will turn into *kibe* in the hands of the *turcos*." Celso Pitta was a *negro de ganho* (black servant) "put in his place" by Maluf and the Conexão Esfiha (meat-pie connection), who reaped lucrative profits from the kickback scheme.[33] The blackness of Celso Pitta was referenced insofar as it came to symbolize his subservient position in relation to shrewder *turcos*. While blacks were servants, Jabor insinuated, Arabs were the masters in the "Casa Grande" of corruption.[34] As the blackness of Pitta was depicted as fulfilling a subordinate role in nefarious governmental dealings, the Arabness of Garib, Maluf, and others was conflated with corruption itself. Briefly highlighting his own "*turco*" background in a later article, Jabor wrote:

> We have seen voracious Arabs commanding the money-laundering schemes [*maracutaias*]. .... the whole band of *turcos* (I am, too) eating *esfihas* and baba ghanoush and transforming São Paulo into a cavern of Ali Baba.[35]

Evoking Middle Eastern food and the mythic Ali Baba himself, Jabor accentuated the Arabness of corruption and, meanwhile, his own ethnic difference.

In 1999 and 2000, *turcos* gained visibility in a novel context. The allegedly inborn shrewdness of Brazilians of Middle Eastern descent shifted from economy to politics. Prepared and served up through the idiom of ethnic foods, the mass-mediated corruption of *turcos* was used to deflect criticism of the administrative structure of both outgoing and incoming São Paulo city governments. In press coverage, varied political leaders claimed transparency while corruption was conflated with Arab ethnicity. Legitimated by anticorruption discourse from the World Bank, the São Paulo city government's structure did not bear the weight of accountability but, rather, an ethnicized scapegoat. To be sure, some politicians of Middle Eastern descent were involved in nefarious political dealings. Ultimately, however, it was their ethnic difference that was charged with corruption in the public sphere.

This episode bears some similarities to the quagmires of other *turco* politicians in Latin America, such as Carlos Menem, former president of Argentina, as well as Abdalá Bucaram, former president of Ecuador. In parallel ways, each politician has been portrayed as an "embodiment of anti-reason and a threat to democracy and civility" (de la Torre 1999: 556; see also Jozami 1996; Roberts 2000). In particular, Bucaram's "Lebanese origins" were evoked by journalists "to explain his corruption" (de la Torre 1999: 566). Like Athie (as explored later), Bucaram honed a populist persona through a vast array of mass media, including a music CD (de la Torre 1999). But Menem and Bucaram have not intensified ethnicity in the ethical terms of their Lebanese counterparts in transparent Brazilian government reform.

These mass-mediated politics of *turcos* in Latin America, however, stand in contrast to the publicity surrounding Arab American politics in the United States. As I have already mentioned, any public acknowledgment of "Arabness" in the United States is constructed in relation to European Jewish colonialism (Massad 1993; Saliba 1999). In fact, Arab American public figures have shown that their activities—whether organizing the community or effecting public policy—have been closely monitored and often vilified by U.S. American pro-Israeli groups on Capitol Hill (Samhan 1987; Zogby 1986). Unlike their counterparts in Latin America, Arab Americans' involvement in U.S. American domestic politics remains encompassed (and marginalized) in ways that mirror the Arab world in U.S. American foreign policy.

ETHICAL STRUGGLE AND ETHNIC SHAME IN THE PUBLIC SPHERE

Of course, Myryam Athie made sure to publicize her own declarations of ethics from the Lebanese independence day event. The city councilor oversaw the publication of the celebration in two magazines of the Syrian–Lebanese community, *Chams* and *Carta do Líbano*, together distributed to more than fifteen thousand households throughout Brazil.[36] "With an impeccable ceremony," related the article in *Chams*, "the city councilwoman exalted the force of the Lebanese people." It further qualified that, "if the night was festive, there also did not lack moments of reflection about the peace process in the Middle East, a crucial question for the development of Arab countries." Providing excerpts about the homeland from Athie's speech, both articles portrayed the event as advancing the righteous struggles of Lebanon and the Arab world. Associated with corruption in mainstream media, Middle Easterners had been subsequently depicted with righteous esteem in ethnic press coverage.

In each publication, Athie prominently figured in dozens of photographs as well. The red headline on the cover of *Chams* read: "Myryam Athie Honors Lebanese Descendants."[37] Above it was a sizable photograph of the beaming city councilor in a light-green dress, positioned beside an image of the Lebanese flag in the country's geopolitical shape. Also captured in color within the centerfold pages of *Carta do Líbano* (normally published in black and white) were eighteen photographs of the individuals honored, and embracing each of them was the city councilor. Showing more photographs of Athie than actual words from her speech, the ethnic media coverage helped to cull her righteous persona.

Making use of the Brazilian press, Athie arranged for the publication of the Lebanese independence day commemoration in an Arab-owned but popularly circulated neighborhood newspaper, *Jornal do Brás*.[38] Read by those who shop and work in the Brás district, the biweekly publication covers news and events from the very place whence stemmed the most damning accusations of corruption against Hanna Garib and suspicions of the city councilwoman. Culling good relations with the editor-in-chief and sole owner of the paper, Athie had the event published in a full-page layout. Titled "Lebanon, Fifty-Seven Years of Independence," the article recounted, "As an initiative of the reelected city councilwoman, Myryam Athie, the Municipal Council Chambers of São Paulo sponsored a special night … in commemoration of Lebanon's day of independence." The concluding paragraph cited excerpts from Athie's righteous defense of the Lebanese homeland. "The Land of the Cedars and its children," it quoted, "clamor for justice, total sovereignty, and independence." Capturing the city councilwoman posing next to federal congressmen, the article's textual and visual construction lent an ethical aura to a politician and ethnic group tainted by corruption in national headlines.

Such endeavors to redeem the Arab name from shame, though, were not limited to ethnic and neighborhood newsprint. Also covering the Lebanese independence day event was the fourth-largest television network in Brazil, the Rede Bandeirantes. Not coincidentally, its second-generation Lebanese Brazilian founder was posthumously honored by the councilwoman for his "pioneering work" in national media development. Having invited his daughter to accept the honor and award, Athie was able to arrange for mainstream television coverage. During the ceremony, cameramen had taped sound bites and elegant poses that aired on November 23, 2000, in a four-minute segment on the Bandeirantes's midnight news show.

Opening with footage of religious, diplomatic, and national figures in posh poses, the narrator recounted that the "São Paulo City Council paid homage to Lebanese and descendants who distinguished themselves in Brazil." The male voice specified that the founder of the Bandeirantes radio and television network was one of the awardees. The program cut to a shot of the eldest daughter, who stated that her father, "being a person who dedicated his whole life to the integration between races in Brazil, [was] a man of [television and] radio. The prize is for this reason." Quickly proceeding to images of Pedro Simon and Michel Temer, the two federal statesmen in attendance, the narrator recounted that both had been honored at the event as well. Simon said, "Lebanese descendants [*pause*]. They have a very significant characteristic. They integrate themselves in Brazil. They identify themselves with Brazil. They adore Brazil." After Arabs were inserted and extolled within the Brazilian nationalist ideology of racial mixture and democracy, the narrator then concluded that "the author of the bill that honors the Lebanese is City Councilwoman Myryam Athie." Athie smiled and stated, "Lebanon contributed much to the formation of Brazil. ... Lebanon exported great personalities to this country." After being depicted as corrupt subjects in mainstream media, Arabs would represent themselves in ethnic glory in the "racially mixed" Brazilian nation.

Publicizing the Lebanese independence day event, however, did not offset the shame and frustration felt by the wider *colônia* in concurrent media coverage of the mafia of kickbacks. Several artistic, liberal, and business professionals emphasized how the corruption scandal *sujou* (dirtied) or *envergonhou* (shamed) the name of the *colônia*. Márcia, a sculptor, reflected on the difficulty of picking up the newspaper when the corruption scandal broke in the press because "there would appear the name, you would see all these Arab last names, all of them appearing as corrupt." Middle Eastern names, reflected Wlademir, an engineer, simply stood out more than other appellations. This media attention on Arabs involved in corruption "shamed the *colônia*" so much, said Ricardo, an architect, that an "internal ethics committee" should be formed within the community to prevent bad publicity. Even a socialite who had organized an event to honor Lebanese Brazilian professionals jestingly remarked, "Every profession will be represented but politics." Summarizing what many descendants felt, the 25 de Março merchant Beto declared:

> I'm annoyed in knowing that there are so many Arabs in politics ... making trouble. Stealing, appearing in the newspaper ... with names in the newspaper associated with the scandal, with stealing. So Arabs, sometimes they pick up the connotation of being clever ... meaning, there are so many Arabs in politics that they're making a curse. We are even at times afraid to elect one more Arab so that he doesn't do anything wrong, because he dirties the name of the *colônia*.

Overwhelmed by the seeming preponderance of their brethren in the corruption scandal, ordinary Middle Easterners were most disturbed at witnessing the name of the community dragged into the corruption scandal, notwithstanding the righteous expression of ethnic identity orchestrated by Myryam Athie in the Lebanese independence day celebration.

Politicians who supported the ethics investigation in the City Council employed similar language about Arabness and the kickback scheme. One right-of-center councilman stated that "the *colônia* was unjustly demoralized ... undergoing what it didn't deserve to undergo." He stressed that Lebanese, and Arabs in general, are not any more or less corrupt than other ethnic groups, though their name was associated with the scandal. A Workers' Party representative more directly noted that the scandal "really shook up the *colônia* ... because it associated them [Syrian–Lebanese] with those involved [corrupt politicians] who were from the community." The very clubs of the *colônia* frequented by the accused politicians, he added, were tainted by guilt due to the latter's corruption. Even a federal deputy who shares the last name of one of the convicted city councilors reflected that "some figures" in the mafia ring "marked as corrupt were of Lebanese or Syrian origin. ... They really dirtied our name." Bearing a distant relation to the guilty city councilor, the federal deputy lamented that both family and community names had become mired in the scandal.

Whether liberal, business, or political elites, these descendants did not necessarily consider the publicity *preconceitouso* (prejudiced) or *racista* (racist). In fact, the only two subjects who denounced the media coverage of corruption as "prejudiced" were right-of-center politicians who were initially embroiled in it. In contrast, for the majority of descendants, the scandal and its media coverage generated *constrangimento* (strained discomfort). Ricardo, the architect, commented, "We feel a certain *constrangimento*. Nowadays when you speak of Arabs, they're viewed with a certain mistrust [*desconfiança*]." Such wariness associated with Arabs, however, was understood by Wlademir as "not prejudice, but jealousy, envy, making fun of guys." This "jealousy" and "envy," he explained, was invoked especially when colleagues jested about his *patrícios* (countrymen) in corruption proceedings. Reminding them that Brazilians of various backgrounds were involved, Wlademir said that his response was: "Shit! What about yours [your countrymen]?" In high society, the image of Arab corruption was not only experienced as a strain on a comfortable lifestyle. As addressed in the next chapter, Middle Easterners' emphasis on the nondiscriminatory character of press coverage reflects the idea of racial democracy—that there is no, or very little, racism—in Brazil.

Instead of denouncing media reportage as racist, descendants reproached their political brethren for the ethical entanglement of the community in press coverage. Hassan, a medical doctor, proclaimed, "All of this [dirt on the Arab name] is Maluf's fault!" Employing the exact same words, Wlademir remarked, "*Tudo isso é culpa do Maluf.*" In parallel fashion, several observers placed blame on Hanna Garib and his well-known ego. Other citizens expressed sympathy and even pity for Myryam Athie, who was embroiled in the controversy as well. Such sentiments were reiterated by conservative and progressive-minded ethnics alike who were frustrated with or shamed by the seeming corruption of Arab political leadership. Tacitly accepting Arabness as the embodiment of corruption, these lay citizens not only upheld the belief in racial democracy. Middle Easterners themselves inflected the representation of Arab corruption while the city government lay claim to transparency.

Reflecting these intra-ethnic tensions, the lay leadership of the *colônia* took measures to ensure novel alliances with the rising left. During one of my meetings with a magazine editor, Ricardo, the director of an uptown Syrian club called on the telephone. Ricardo admonished his colleague to extend an official invitation to an upcoming club event to Vereador Nemer, a Workers' Party city councilor of Syrian descent who, until then, had steered clear of the *colônia*. The interloper expressed skepticism about allying with a "leftist." Downplaying the "estrangement" of the Workers' Party politician, Ricardo insisted that Vereador Nemer did not have anything against "the bourgeois." He simply had not been invited to participate in the community. "It's important to invite Nemer," advised Ricardo, "because he can be the bridge between the *colônia* and [Mayor] Marta Suplicy." The editor concluded that this intermediary role would not only "strengthen the position of the boy, but [would] also be good for the *colônia* … and [would] make his father very happy." Ricardo was successful. From late 2000 onward, I began seeing Nemer at community events (which Nemer had previously told me was "*a praia da direita* [the turf of the right]"). This personal exchange suggests that lay leaders took practical steps to align their "ethnic group" with dominant political powers.

INSTITUTIONALIZING ETHNICITY IN POLITICAL REPRESENTATION

Notwithstanding the failure to convince the lay Middle Eastern electorate, Athie's sound bites and visual shots point to the institutionalization of ethnicity in São Paulo city government. Before being convicted on racketeering charges, Hanna Garib proposed, and sometimes passed, legislation with explicitly ethnic ends.[39] Culling electoral and financial support of the *colônia*, he instituted the "Independence Day of Syria" as well as "the 'Day of Lebanon' in the ambit of the municipality of São Paulo" in 1995.[40] In fact, a 1997 *Chams* article that covered the independence day celebration at a country club referred to Garib as the "author of the bill that included the National Day of Lebanon in the municipal calendar."[41]

The convicted councilman's law thus predates Athie's own legislation that putatively created the Lebanese independence day event in September 1999.[42] Although Athie declined to speak with me, it seems that two concerns underlay her claim to authorship of the celebration. First, Garib was directly associated with corruption. Any reference to him as the "father of the law" would have compromised the event's ethical expression of Arab ethnicity. Second, Athie secured the post of *suplente* (substitute city councilor) only in the 1996 municipal elections. Garib's fall from grace in 1999 assured Athie a permanent seat on the City Council and enabled her to tap into those constituencies formerly culled by Garib himself, including the *colônia sírio-libanesa*. Any reference to Garib would have undermined her personal interests as being the alleged leader of an event that promised positive media coverage. By rewriting the law that instituted the Lebanese independence day event in her own name, Athie sought to cleanse the name of the Arab community shamed in the corruption scandal and, more important, claim its electoral and financial support.

Self-represented as the *mãe da lei* (mother of the law) who instituted the commemoration of Lebanese independence day, Athie's legislative record makes clear her political aims. Municipal bills proposed or passed into law by the councilwoman include changing the name of public thoroughfares in honor of local leaders (non-Arab and Arab),[43] declaring a "sister-city" accord between São Paulo and another (non-Arab) international metropolis,[44] and instituting official commemorative days in the municipality.[45] No fewer than thirteen of the twenty-eight bills proposed by the councilwoman up to 2001 served symbolic functions that target specific voting publics and potential campaign financers.[46] The Middle Eastern votership, for its part, served as one of her constituencies. Yet this institutionalization of ethnicity was not peculiar to Athie or others mired in corruption proceedings.

Common to the activities of the *colônia*'s City Council notables, second- and third-generation Middle Easterners have garnered similar legislative records. Through the 1990s, they have proposed or passed laws to change the names of public thoroughfares, donate public property to Syrian–Lebanese "philanthropic" groups, and establish sister-city accords with other international metropolises.[47] Several parks in the city of São Paulo, for instance, have been slated to be renamed either in honor of Syrian–Lebanese elites in Brazil or in homage to sending towns in the Arab world. Sister-city accords with Amman, Beirut, and Damascus have also been proposed or passed into law in the São Paulo City Council chambers. Invariably crowned with posh events or ribbon-cutting ceremonies, these legislative activities were crucial for politicians to gain positive publicity and curry both electoral and financial favor with the ethnic votership.

This institutionalization of Arab ethnicity in the City Council has reflected the neoliberal "government of reconstruction" in São Paulo. As mentioned earlier, Mayor Marta Suplicy founded the Secretariat of International Relations within the mayoral administration soon after she won the elections in 2000. In addition to maintaining partnerships with "multilateral organizations," such as the World Bank and IMF, and international NGOs, the Secretariat of International Relations has official ties with the "thirty ethnic communities in the city of São Paulo," as well as with the consulates, embassies, and other entities of their respective homelands. Its self-envisioned "strategic role" is summarized on the city government's website:

> With the advent of globalization and the acceleration of international flows of commerce, metropolises such as São Paulo come to have a strategic role in the articulation of decentralized cooperation at the local level. … The exclusionary character of globalization accentuated the role of cities as potential protagonists of another politics, that of social and citizen insertion … and the creation of another international institutionality, less competitive and more regulated, unified, and just [*e mais regulada, solidária e justa*].[48]

Using the language of justice and, if only implicitly, ethics, the Secretariat of International Relations is portrayed as an institutional intermediary that, one hopes, will ameliorate, if not correct, the negative impact of global forces on metropolitan cities such as São Paulo.

In particular, the Secretariat of International Relations provides special services for varied *colônias*. In March 2002, the secretariat launched an Internet portal, "São Paulo: A Cidade dos Mil Povos [São Paulo: The City of the Thousand Peoples]." It reflects the "priority" given to advertising in the Suplicy administration, which had already spent 82.1 percent of its annual publicity budget within the first three months of 2002.[49] Dedicated to thirty ethnic groups in São Paulo, the site stores a plethora of information that celebrates and exhibits the particular histories, neighborhoods, and characteristics of communities that trace their origins to Europe, Latin America, Asia, Africa, and the Middle East. In addition to documenting the numerous "sister-city" accords struck between São Paulo and other metropolises of the world,[50] the site provides a list of "official and commemorative dates" that pay tribute to ethnic and racial communities in São Paulo. Nearly twenty "peoples" have been honored with such days. After the days for Germany, Hungary, Austria, and the "Afro-Brazilian Community" in October and November comes the "Day of Lebanon" in late November. These "commemorative events" have served as a way for city councilors or the mayor to target and cull the support of ethnically or racially conscious voters.

Not coincidentally, Mayor Marta Suplicy and Jorge Mattoso, head of the Secretariat of International Relations, participated in the 2001 Lebanese independence day event. As metaphors of local government, they acknowledged, accentuated, and aimed to attract ethnic constituencies. In this light, the city government's celebration of Middle Eastern eth(n)ics has signified both recognition and its limits among dominant political alliances and rhetorics, pointing to the hierarchical reproduction and reorganization of ethnicity and national state powers today. Although scapegoated as corrupt elements in the public sphere, ethnics devised a project of ethical leadership that reflects and shapes the broader ethnicization and ethicalization of political power in neoliberal Brazil.

THIS CHAPTER HAS ARGUED that Arab ethnicity has intensified through the language of corruption and ethics in São Paulo. In 1999 and 2000, a corruption scandal challenged the conservative establishment and ushered in the left-of-center administration of Marta Suplicy. As outgoing and incoming city officials used the discourse of transparency—legitimated by the World Bank's anticorruption program—the ethnic difference of politicians of Middle Eastern heritage was conflated with corruption in media reportage. Represented as corrupt ethnics in national headlines, these politicians devised a project for the righteous acknowledgment of Lebaneseness and Arabness within the very chambers of the São Paulo City Council. Their declarations of ethical ideals, however, failed to convince media and lay co-ethnics who inflected the representation of an allegedly Arab corruption. Viewed in the context of such discordant views, the Lebanese independence day event shows not only the greater recognition of Arabness but also its limits in the eth(n)ically intensified São Paulo city government.

PART II

Remodeling the Nationalist Order

~

THREE

Turcos in the Market Model
of Racial Democracy

A S SHOWN IN THE PREVIOUS chapters, *turco* (Turk) has served as a general designation for "Middle Easterner" in Brazil. Originally, it was used by early twentieth-century Brazilian elites to denigrate immigrants as economic pariahs. Rejecting the lowly classification, however, Syrian–Lebanese merchants sought a higher status by sending their children to private and postsecondary institutions. This generational strategy for upward mobility has continued in similar courses undertaken *no exterior* (abroad; mostly to the United States). In this current context, white-collar Syrian–Lebanese continue to be labeled *turcos* but have now self-identified with the category, even considering it an "affectionate" or "joking" term of reference.

Intrigued by the transformation, this chapter asks how Syrian–Lebanese ethnicity has been projected through market imagery and racial ideology. In upward mobility, Middle Easterners' relation to the *turco* category has shifted through two paradigms of the Brazilian economy: urban industrialization through the 1970s and white-collar restructuring thereafter. While Middle Easterners viewed "*turco*" as a derogatory misnomer in mid-twentieth-century mercantilism, descendants have stressed its nondiscriminatory meaning in present-day liberal professions. Through market mobility, Syrian–Lebanese have now appropriated the *turco* label using the nationalist language of racial democracy. Expressing nostalgia for the ethnic past of peddling, Middle Easterners have been identified, by themselves and others, as *turcos* in this novel context of seemingly higher but increasingly competitive liberal professions.

Attentive to this ethnic acknowledgment of white-collar Middle Easterners in the current model of racial democracy, this chapter engages with scholarship on race, class, and ideology in Brazil. While early seminal pieces viewed
race as a result of economic structure (Fernandes 1969; Harris 1964), later
work has tended to view race as the determining force in economic mobility
(Andrews 1991; Hanchard 1994; Twine 1998). In a more balanced approach,
however, the anthropologist Peter Wade (1997: 112) has reflected that we must
see "economics, politics, race and ethnicity as mutually influencing each other,
rather than privileging one or two of these as determinative." Following Wade's
insights, I grasp the dynamics between ethnicity, market mobility, and racial
ideology "*through* the medium of culture" (Wade 1997: 112).

Liberal professions were assumed to ensure greater nobility and material
security at midcentury but have garnered increasingly lower prestige and
salaries today. In this context, upwardly and downwardly mobile professionals of Middle Eastern descent have romanticized the past of peddling, including the label *turco*. This novel admiration of what had been considered low
status has developed with the public representation of Syrian–Lebanese
descendants as Horatio Algers rising from peddlers to *doutores* (university
graduates). In contrast to midcentury ethnics who rejected *turco* as a derogatory misnomer, present-day liberal professionals have self-identified with the
term as "caring" and "nondiscriminatory."

Such adjectives point to the continued power of racial democracy, but in
a novel context. In lay, media, and state criticisms, this nationalist "myth" has
been challenged by statistical representations of economic inequalities between
so-called "whites" and "blacks."[1] Yet in this chapter, I assert that market
imagery has not just undermined, but has also confirmed, nationalist ideology. *Turcos* have been represented by themselves and others as *doutores* rising
above commercial origins, numerically and publicly. Stressing the slight existence, or nonexistence, of prejudice in liberal professions today, Middle Easterners have gained ethnic acknowledgment in what I consider to be the market remodeling of the nationalist ideology of racial democracy.

IMAGINING UPWARD MOBILITY IN THE
EARLY TWENTIETH CENTURY

In the 1940s, liberal professions and university educations grew in extraordinary importance with the expansion of urban and industrial classes, thanks
in part to Getúlio Vargas's state-led industrialization program. The novel category of white-collar professionals developed within government administration, business organizations, and related service sectors of burgeoning urban

spaces. As noted by the historian Brian Owensby (1999: 91), the liberal professional class in the first half of the twentieth century was principally composed of the sons and grandsons of immigrant shopkeepers and industrialists. Graduating from postsecondary institutions, medical doctors, lawyers, engineers, and others experienced an unprecedented opportunity for mobility in a social order that historically inhibited it.

Although Middle Easterners had amassed material wealth, the attainment of a higher status was thought possible only by ensuring education for children. For many immigrant parents, a college degree was fundamental to the economic well-being and cultural enhancement of sons and daughters. Take for example the seventy-plus-year-old Sami. Having supported the university studies of his six children in law, medicine, and sociology, Sami recounted that "the Arab father ... would take from his own mouth, from his own clothes. ... He would do everything for his children to be instructed. The [Arab] immigrant [wanted] his children to have strong roots, to have some kind of liberal profession, of nobility, of culture."

In this regard, Oswaldo Truzzi has found a striking educational pattern between immigrant and second generations in Syrian–Lebanese families. Over half of a select number of Middle Eastern graduates from medical, law, and technical institutions until 1950 were the children of immigrant parents who worked in commerce or industry (Truzzi 1997: 125–26, 244–47). "Seeing a son as a *doutor*," reflected Truzzi, would "'clean the blood' of the lineage," because second generations would "exercise professions of a more universal intrinsic value, of a more legitimate knowledge than that of commerce" (Truzzi 1997: 143). Other ethnic groups—like the Jews and Japanese (Lesser 1999)—likewise sought greater legitimacy through a liberal professional strategy. What distinguishes the Middle Eastern case, however, is the historical referent of commercialism.

Rising into liberal professional ranks, second-generation subjects have boasted of parents' sacrifices for their own educational advancement. "In the first place," began Rafael, a lawyer turned politician with a flare for metaphor, "the Lebanese was a peddler but he didn't want his son to be a peddler. If he carried a trunk with his hand, he wanted his son to have a pen in his hand, right? ... That was basic." Others reiterated the importance of a college degree. "Every father who couldn't study in [his] lifetime," noted Samir, a medical doctor, "one of the things [he] demanded from his children was a diploma. Really, a diploma was fundamental." Valéria, an older college graduate turned housewife used almost the same words: "All parents wanted their children to go to college." She concluded that pedigrees could provide younger generations with better lives. Financed by immigrant parents' commercial livelihoods, the educated professions of descendants were viewed as the symbolic departure from them.

In the mid-twentieth century, however, college degrees and liberal professions were basically limited to engineering, law, or medicine. The engineer Wlademir, a second-generation Lebanese, noted: "I got into college in '58—that is, forty-three years ago ... and the liberal professions that existed at the time were law, engineering, and medicine." Though he enjoys his profession, Wlademir qualified that his choice of engineering had more to do with his "lack of aptitude" in medicine or law. This random selection of a vocation was implied by the second generation Assad as well. Today a successful lawyer, Assad recounted that he first enrolled in medical school but, after coming face to face with a human cadaver, dropped out and entered a law program instead. Continuing to work in his father's clothes shop on 25 de Março, however, the youth still harbored doubts about the legal profession. But on the day of his graduation banquet, Assad, sharply dressed in a tuxedo, was inadvertently referred to as the *moço da lojinha* (the boy from the little store) by a female colleague who frequented his father's clothing store on 25 de Março. In his own words:

> That "boy from the little store" really moved me. And I said to myself, "I really don't pass for anything more than a boy from a little store. I don't have anything to do with this banquet." That really moved me. It was then that I resolved to do law. It was like this that I convinced myself that I really should do law.

Assad decided to work harder to become something more than a *moço* in a *lojinha*. Whether younger generations chose medicine, law, or engineering, it was the desire for distinction, and not only the profession, that fed their strategies of upward mobility.

Assad was not alone. Middle Eastern names dot the record books of the famous *Centro Acadêmico XI de Agosto* of the Law College of São Paulo (Machado 1998), today part of the University of São Paulo (USP). In contrast to the small fraction of Middle Easterners who graduated from the law school throughout the 1930s, 4.5 percent of the 1940 graduating class bore Middle Eastern surnames (9 of 206). Twenty years later, in 1960, the number had risen to 5.7 percent (16 of 280). As recently as 1985, the number of Middle Eastern names reached 7.5 percent of the sum total of graduates (28 of 374).[2] Syrian–Lebanese descendants have departed from the "little stores" on Rua 25 de Março in São Paulo.

Arabesques likewise cross the rosters of the renowned medical school in the University of São Paulo (Associação dos Antigos Alunos da Faculdade de

Medicina da Universidade de São Paulo 1995). Although only two or three Middle Eastern names appear in graduate records up to the early 1930s, around 7 percent of the 1940 graduating class appear to be from the *colônia sírio-libanesa* (6 of 80). By 1960, the proportion of medical-school graduates with Middle Eastern names remained relatively stable at 6.3 percent (5 of 80). Twenty years later, the average had decreased slightly to about 5.5 percent (10 of 180).[3] Nonetheless, they have composed 7 percent of the sum total of graduates living and practicing their degrees in the present-day city of São Paulo (roughly 130 of 1,900). This seems due to the fact that the majority of Middle Easterners settled in the region. In law and medicine, the children of immigrant merchants have joined the educated ranks of the city and nation.

But the pursuit, possession, and practice of a university degree were rife with gender inequalities. Though enrolling in professional and postsecondary courses, women were discouraged from exercising their degree. Lena, a second-generation Lebanese woman in her late forties, recounted that her father had motivated her language studies in high school and college. Yet he grew worried when she began to work as a French and Spanish interpreter in the São Paulo state tourism agency. In Lena's words, the father asked, "Daughter, what is missing here at home? What am I not giving you that would make you want to work?" This present-day homemaker surmised that her father "wanted his daughters to study and to graduate, but he didn't want them to work." In this vein, Truzzi found that the "objective of studying for women never was the exercise of a profession, but only to become educated" (Truzzi 1997: 130–31; see also Osman 1998: 19–20). As Thorstein Veblen (1899) noted at the end of the nineteenth century, women were educated to advance families in the competition and "invidious comparison" of the leisure class, including strategies to marry into and ally with higher-status families.[4]

As women were limited to the home or philanthropic groups (Truzzi 1997: 130–32), men were encouraged to exercise professional work. Fourteen out of eighteen white-collar interviewees, for instance, had established offices or firms in medicine, law, and engineering in post–World War II Brazil. In these cases, one or more siblings continued to operate family-run businesses, received income from renting vacated real-estate, or sold storefronts or properties to establish professional practices. Wlademir, now sixty, heeded the advice of his immigrant father (who worked on 25 de Março) and became a civil engineer in the late 1950s. Gaining experience in remodeling the residences of family friends, Wlademir and another *patrício* established an engineering firm together. Today, he makes an upper-middle-class living in civil construction. Meanwhile, his brother took over the family property holdings, shifting from wholesale to retail operations on Rua 25 de Março. Providing a degree of contrast, the second-generation Syrian physician Samir secured a steady clientele and livelihood in his practice by joining the ranks of the Hospital Sírio-Libanês. The property owned by his father (who worked in textile wholesaling) is now rented out. Its earnings supplement the income of his sister, who works as a teacher as well. In a different vein, two brothers in the Ghantous family were sent to law school in the 1960s by their father, who had attained success in the textile market. Closing and selling the family-owned property because "no one wanted to remain working on 25 de Março," the eldest sibling, Liam, explained that the three brothers used the earnings as start-up capital for their now successful law firm near Avenida Paulista.

The distinct trajectories of these three families indicate not only the manifold accumulation strategies available to second generations, but also the continued relevance of ethnicity. Particularly for those who departed from ethnically marked commercial occupations of immigrant parents, middle- to upper-class livelihoods were ensured by family, friends, and colleagues in the *colônia*. Common to many other immigrant groups in Brazil (Fausto 1999; O'Dougherty 2002; Owensby 1999), the white-collar mobility of Arab Brazilians was initiated by way of intra-ethnic relations in post–World War II times.

TURCOS AT THE MARGINS OF RACIAL DEMOCRACY IN THE MID-TWENTIETH CENTURY

Professional mobility for immigrants and descendants became a real possibility, if not a lived experience, in the Vargas era. At the same time, however, a powerful ideology of race would render more rigid and fixed the imagination of the changing social order. Narrating a mythic past on colonial plantations, Gilberto Freyre's *Casa grande e senzala* (1977 [1933]) depicts the country's seemingly harmonious race relations within a patronage system between masters and slaves. In this scenario, whites were cast in the role of benevolent, if occasionally sadistic, patrons, while brown and black subjects were positioned as intermediaries and subordinates. In Freyre's vision, these patron–client relations helped to preserve the slight existence or nonexistence of racism. Admittedly fraught with inequalities, the maintenance of the occupational placement of white, brown, and black subjects in a changing social order was thought to uphold the country's racial harmony. Conceived at a time when patronage in the plantation economy intersected with the meritocracy of the urban industrial market (Owensby 1999), the nationalist ideology of racial democracy reinforced the status quo of race in midcentury Brazil.

Middle Eastern immigrants were absent in this racial patronage system of the Freyrian mythic past. As described in Chapter 1, they were generally viewed as *turcos* by Brazilian elites in the first half of the twentieth century. Yet these so-called *turcos* responded in equivocal ways. As a proud second-generation Lebanese who wrote about Lebanon and the Lebanese in Brazil in 1945, Jorge Bastani understood *turco* as a mere misnomer:

> The Lebanese who emigrated were carriers of a passport issued by Turkish authorities. ... They were classified as "Turks" for Turkey having given them official permission to travel. ... Any mortal stemming from that Oriental region was also known as "Turk," whether he was Egyptian, Persian [*sic*], Syrian, Palestinian, or Lebanese. (Bastini 1945: 123)

At the same time, Taufik Duoun (1944: 56) surmised that Lebanese, Syrians, and Palestinians "were called '*turcos*'" because the region from which they immigrated was under the dominion of the Ottoman Empire. But he qualified that there was a "hidden intention that completely altered the meaning of the term applied, making it synonymous with degrading." Wadih Safady added that "the word TURCO was a natural synonym" for Middle Easterners due to their status as "Turkish [or Ottoman] subjects." But due to economic competition, he mused, the "name Turk ... began to be used as a deprecating adjective" (Safady 1966: 140–41). Summarizing the various designations for "Arabs" in Brazil, Jamil Safady (1972a: 117) noted that "turco is the vulgar term that is commonly given to the countryman who sells, in all parts of Brazil." Explaining the plausible history of *turco*, most Syrian–Lebanese intellectuals recognized its derogatory meaning through post–World War II times.

But in a quasi-justification, Taufik Duoun (1944: 57) reflected that "the first immigrants maybe deserved, in appearance, the deprecating term." His reference to the "little respectable appearance" of recently arrived Middle Easterners implied that the category connoted not only innate shrewdness, but also a lack of "distinction" (Bourdieu 1984). "*Turco*," as the second-generation Lebanese Valéria corrected me, "means not only *pão duro* [cheap-skate]"; it also implied that Middle Easterners were "*não refinado* [unrefined] and *grosso* [crass]" because of their manual work, poor dress, heavily accented Portuguese, and inadequate culinary habits (discussed in Chapter 5). Recognizing the term's negative valence, these Syrian–Lebanese elites have faulted their cohorts' own apparent lack of distinction in earlier times.

In response, Middle Easterners turned to liberal professionalism as a way to elevate themselves from the "low" status of *turco*. A *brincadeira* (joke) still told in the *colônia sírio-libanesa* suggests how immigrants and descendants associated the category with lower commercial origins. "When the guy first arrived," begins the joke as told by Samir, "he peddled, was really a pauper, and was a *turco*. He started to make a little bit of money and turned into a Syrian. When he became a millionaire of high society, he turned into a Lebanese."[5] Since the distinction between "remediated" Syrians and "wealthy" Lebanese is explored in Chapter 5, suffice it to say now that this "joke" equated *turco* with lower origins. Liberal professional status was viewed by Middle Eastern descendants as granting the material and symbolic power necessary to raise Arab ethnicity above its lowly place in Brazil.

As the first step to achieve greater distinction in the mid-twentieth century, immigrant parents enrolled their children in primary and secondary institutions frequented by traditional elites, such as Colégio Sion, Sacre Couer, and Des'oiseaux. But these second-generation Syrian–Lebanese found themselves categorized as *turcos* (Greiber et al. 1998).[6] "The classmates, when they wanted to fight," recalled one *senhora*, "they'd call me *turca, turquinha*" (cited in Greiber et al. 1998: 253). Another *senhor* in his seventies remembered that, "when we were children at school ..., the classmates would call me 'Oh, little Turk!' [*Ô turquinho!*]." Teachers also singled out so-called *turcos*. "At school," began another *senhora*, "there was discrimination against the 'turca' origin. The nuns themselves were really stupid [and] tormented us a lot. At that time, we were really disdained. The discrimination was more or less general" (cited in Greiber et al. 1998: 179). Its underlying cause, surmised the second-generation Inácio, lay in the commercial origins of immigrant parents. Even though his own sisters "frequented good schools," Inácio qualified, "we were viewed as inferior beings—first because of the humble origins of our parents, who came, peddled, and all that. Who came educated? ... In the group of my generation, I think that, medical doctors, there were one or two [who] graduated, only" (cited in Greiber et al. 1998: 153–54). Enrolled in elite schools, Middle Eastern youth were made aware of the alleged inferiority of their ethnic difference in the mid-twentieth century.

Even though they "moved up" from their immigrant parents' commercial origins, students were (re)categorized as *turcos* in primary school and continued as such in their educational and professional trajectories. Bastani (1945: 163–64) recounted one such occurrence involving an immigrant Lebanese father and his son from the state of Minas Gerais. He related that the Middle Eastern father sacrificed much to enroll his son in a military college in Rio de Janeiro. "Since he was very intelligent and always surpassed his classmates" at school, writes Bastani, "the son was the target of the most bitter attacks on the part of some colleagues who, to morally put him down ... constantly called him "son of Turks [*filho de turcos*]." Developing an "inferiority complex," the son grew disillusioned but concluded his studies. On the fateful day of his graduation banquet, the son made a speech in front of his colleagues and "radiant" father. In Bastani's words, however, the son

> did not touch on another subject except for his ascendance, and in the attacks suffered, in the humiliations, and in the disdain of his classmates, in order to finally declare that everything had been in consequence of being a "son of a Turk" (*filho de turco*) and that he "was ashamed of his race and in its ascendants." (Bastani 1945: 163–64)

Despite Bastani's emphasis on the gradual rise of "Lebanese descendants" into medicine, law, and engineering (Bastani 1945: 171), the story of the estranged son and his diligent father suggests that the "lowly" label *turco* still tormented Middle Easterners in upwardly mobile trajectories. In my own reading of the narrative, a military cadet was still a "*filho de turco.*"

Another case narrated by many Middle Easterners concerns the well-known judge and statesman Alfredo Buzaid. At the time of his oral examination to attain a professorial chair in the Law School of the University of São Paulo, *patrícios* recalled that Buzaid experienced "prejudice" at the hands of the examining committee, who said it "would prefer a *preto* [black] to a *turco*," as Samoel, a successful medical doctor, remembered. Samoel reflected that Buzaid's examination was a matter of contention because it broke the long tradition of Luso-Brazilian elites (*quatrocentões*) who attended and taught at the school. For Buzaid, "What was difficult was not entering into the College of Law as a student, but more so as a professor, and even more so as a full professor," which gave him a permanent seat on the faculty (Truzzi 1997: 140). Viewed as *turcos*, Syrian–Lebanese have remembered past white-collar prejudice.

Truzzi described similar barriers faced by Syrian–Lebanese professors at USP's College of Medicine (Truzzi 1997: 142). Dr. Bussamara Neme, for instance, reached the rank of associate professor in the 1950s but was forced to wait nearly twenty years before the competition was opened for the post of full professor.[7] Truzzi relates that Dr. Neme endured such comments as, "Don't open it for the *turco* to enter" and "This little Turk [*turquinho*] is wanting too much." Dr. Sami Arap, a successful medical doctor, likewise recounted that although *patrícios* began graduating from several medical schools in the mid-twentieth century, full professor posts were reserved for *quatrocentões*. Specifically, at USP, physicians of Middle Eastern descent were said to have "never arrived at a titled [position] here inside." Even Dr. Daher Elias Cutait, who was trained in the United States and Europe (see Cutait 2000), remained part of the faculty as an "associate professor, but never was a full [professor]." Though seeking to rise above commercial origins, Middle Easterners were kept in their place as *turcos* by Luso-Brazilian elites who remained atop the changing social order in mid-twentieth-century Brazil.

WHITE-COLLAR PRESENTS AND THE ETHNIC PAST IN NEOLIBERAL RESTRUCTURING

In remembering past prejudice in market mobility, white-collar ethnics, such as Dr. Arap, reflected that, "after the decade of the '80s, this barrier was broken." Yet it was at this time that the liberal professions of medicine, engineering, and law began to show signs of increasing competition, wage cutting, and de-skilling. With the opening of the economy and the privatization of the state sector, this tendency has become most pronounced in the field of medicine, especially due to the introduction of so-called *convênios*, or health-management organizations (HMOs), by European and U.S. American transnational groups.[8] Six middle-aged physicians explained that the main problem with HMOs is their standardized low wages for medical doctors, regardless of ability or effort. Recent graduates of medical school, they reflected, encounter great difficulty in making a good living today. Dr. Riad Younes, a very successful doctor, pointed out:

> It's getting worse year to year, meaning the saturated market, principally in large cities, and the options get less and less. … Unfortunately, the majority [of medical-school graduates] will have to do penance because [the market is] saturated and the HMOs are taking over that population that can really pay you something. So you are going to earn a lot less because HMOs pay little.

Medical-school graduates are now forced to work for *convênios* or the failing state health system (Sistema Único de Saúde, or SUS), explained well-established practitioners such as Dr. Younes. In this way, the material rewards thought to be easily obtained with liberal professional status have been undermined by the neoliberalizing economy in Brazil.

In these circumstances, well-to-do practitioners stressed the importance of distinction in making a good living. While the "large majority of doctors live in the *convênios* and live relatively bad," explained Dr. Arap, "only those of us with a lot of professional prominence and prestige" can open a private clinic and join the medical staff of respected hospitals. Dr. Younes likewise noted that a spot on the medical staff of a good hospital can be achieved only by being "a little distinguished." Securing a job in an institution with an upper-class clientele can enable physicians to earn higher salaries from HMOs and supplement them with co-payments and honorariums individually negotiated with patients. Distinction in the medical profession thus reflects the increasing struggle for middle-class status in Brazil (O'Dougherty 2002).

Not incidentally, both Dr. Arap and Dr. Younes have partaken in residency programs and conferences *no exterior* (abroad). Dr. Arap is a renowned specialist in urology, born in Brazil to immigrant Syrian parents who supported his early studies abroad. The father earned a middle-class livelihood as a shirt maker and came to own property in downtown São Paulo. Lacking personal connections to the medical establishment, his father and mother believed that an "international diploma" was the only way to ensure their son's success as a *doutor* in Brazil. It did just that. Having studied with famous urologists in France, Germany, England, and other European and North American countries, Dr. Arap became a full professor at USP and now heads the urology department at a local hospital. Similarly, Dr. Younes explained that after attaining his medical degree from the USP College of Medicine, he joined a specialized cancer treatment center in New York City as a resident physician for two years. In his youth, Dr. Younes fled Lebanon with his family during the civil war. As his father earned a middle-class income as a mathematics teacher, Dr. Younes excelled in postsecondary studies. Like Dr. Arap, Dr. Younes is a full professor at USP and treats patients at the Hospital SírioLibanês. Attending annual conferences around the world, both Dr. Arap and Dr. Younes recognized the institution where I was enrolled as a Ph.D. student, Syracuse University. In separate interviews, they each asked me if I had contact with their colleagues who practice medicine at the university's hospital. In the contemporary economy, training "abroad" has been crucial to ensuring professional success.

These effects of cosmopolitan capital were evident in the offices and biographies of other Middle Eastern liberal professionals as well. João, a naturalized Syrian Brazilian who practices dentistry, highlighted his own participation in international conferences. An entire wall in his office was covered with at least fifty certificates from meetings in which he had participated during the past fifteen years, including the American Dentistry Association and other professional association conferences from Puerto Rico to Japan. During one of our conversations, João stressed that, although his children and grandchildren will choose their own vocations, he wants them to travel the world because it "opens the mind." Said, a second-generation Lebanese specialist in intestinal disease who graduated from USP, also mentioned his annual participation in conferences across the United States and Europe. Even Rógerio, a third-generation Lebanese, earned his engineering master's degree from Stanford University and soon after returned to work in São Paulo. Liberal professionals have become increasingly worldly.

Parents and children are well aware of the necessity to work or travel *no exterior*. Jorge, a merchant, explained that "the *colônia* … is in a phase wherein Arabs have become engineers, medical doctors, and lawyers today," adding that his own daughter had enrolled in a master's program in business administration in New York. Countless other twenty-somethings mentioned similar intentions. In addition, parents looked into cultural-exchange programs for high-school youth. A mother whose husband operates an architectural firm commented on her intention to enroll their son in a youth exchange program before college. "It looks really good on the resume," she surmised, asking me for advice about study-abroad options. These worldly experiences, parents have stressed, enable youth to learn fluent English, a "*must*" (said in English) in any profession today. Whether earning a degree, or learning English, the need to journey abroad was not unique to Middle Easterners but demanded by the Brazilian market.

What distinguishes the case at hand is the fact that descendants have memorialized the peddling past of the immigrant generation. In 2001, for instance, the annual commemoration of the Day of Rua 25 de Março was held at an uptown São Paulo country club, Club Homs. Although the ceremony honored eight Syrian–Lebanese merchants from the 25 de Março environs, the speakers were a lawyer and medical doctor. The physician Samoel speaks ten languages and has attended medical courses and conferences throughout the world. His speech began with a rhetorical question: "Why was a medical doctor invited to be part of the main table and to give a speech?" Samoel, who was born and raised in São Paulo, first noted that he had worked as a youngster on "that university called 25 de Março." After providing an abridged version of Syrian–Lebanese immigration history, Samoel noted that "the people present in the ballroom are descendants of those who worked on 25 de Março." Overstating their present-day achievements, the lawyer later professed that "the struggle was not in vain. Now we are in colleges, law firms, medicine, and politics. Now, we've been here for only a century, and we already represent 22 percent of the Brazilian GNP."

Such praise was not lost on the more than one hundred persons in attendance, the majority being of Syrian–Lebanese descent. As hors d'oeuvres were served after the formal ceremony, colleagues in administration, architecture, law, psychology, and other professions recurrently commented on how the speeches regarding the Syrian–Lebanese economic role in Brazil provided an "interesting" opportunity for me to learn about the *colônia*. As we left the country club, a friend who had received his degree in law even noted that 25 de Março "is a tradition, a culture … that must be maintained." The past of commercialism has come to form an integral part of the liberal professional Arab ethnic project in contemporary Brazil.

But the turn toward "worldly" professions has not necessarily ensured greater material security. Miriam, a Syrian Italian psychologist in her late twenties, provides a telling case in point. Having excelled in her undergraduate studies in psychology at USP, she was awarded a Brazilian state-funded scholarship to enroll in a specialization course in England. At the time, Miriam explained, she and her parents thought it would provide a more stable means of income. After two years of advanced studies in England, she returned to the city of São Paulo in the mid-1990s. Miriam first worked as a salaried employee in the psychiatric office of a *patrícia* ([Lebanese] countrywoman). But the pay, she recalled, hardly covered her middle-class monthly expenses. Currently, her practice has official ties with HMOs whose subscribers frequent Miriam's office, run from her rented apartment in a middle-class neighborhood. Struggling to pay the bills each month despite a full-time schedule, Miriam's worldly education did not ensure economic contentment. Only those liberal professionals who have their own firms and offices with an upscale clientele have been able to obtain upward class mobility.

In a nostalgic tone, the competent but financially strapped psychologist noted that her brothers and first cousins "left the tradition of their parents." Her generation assumed that liberal professions would provide greater security than the commercial ventures of their forebears. But today, Miriam is convinced that "psychology does not give the salary that a business would." Her two cousins have even left their professions and returned to the retail sales occupations of their parents to make ends meet. If the family business were still open, she reflected, her brothers and sisters could maintain a more comfortable lifestyle. Although Miriam's generation received an education that went far beyond that of the immigrant generation, it did not guarantee an elevated lifestyle. In claiming an experience of downward mobility, she tacitly articulated nostalgia for the ethnic past of commerce in the present-day market. This suggests that even when descendants have not reached the upper middle classes, they have made sense of market mobility in terms of the Syrian–Lebanese memory of commerce. That is, Middle Eastern middle classes inflected the ethnicity of upper-class counterparts, despite their own experience of class struggle.

The children of upwardly mobile families were not alone in their perception of the greater material insecurity of university educations and liberal professions. Interviewed in 1985, a Lebanese parent expressed disenchantment with the value of a college diploma:

My dream, like the dream of every Lebanese ... is a dream I have that is today out of the question. ... But the Lebanese dream ... is to have all children with diplomas. ... I think today it isn't worth anything more, because ... a physician, a great psychiatrist, a great psychologist, a professor earns less than a tool maker or a good plumber. ... Meaning, that impression that was given thirty or forty years ago, that a diploma was absolute security, a security with which this person would be set in life. ... Today, it's not like that anymore. (Cited in Greiber et al. 1998: 302)

Noting that he earned more selling clothing items, this older man left no doubt that the dream of liberal professionalism once held by Lebanese parents for their children lost its meaning today. As O'Dougherty (2002: 22) observed, "The dream class is over" in late twentieth-century Brazil.

In a similar vein, Sarkis, a medical doctor, related a conversation he had with an elderly immigrant storeowner on Rua 25 de Março. Bewildered by a university-educated son who did not meet or surpass his own material achievements, the father asked his "more learned" colleague for advice. Sarkis explained:

I was speaking with a *patrício* in the region of 25 de Março. He said, "Doctor, you sir, who [are] more learned, explain me something. I arrived in this country in 1930. I had five dollars. And today I have that store, that store, and that store. I don't even now how much real estate I have rented out. My son, he was born with a golden spoon in his mouth. I put him in the best schools, and in the best colleges, and when he got married, I had to buy the apartment for him to live in. When he needed a car, I went to buy a car. ... Where did I go wrong?"

Concluding, the medical doctor generalized that "the son works, as a medical doctor, or as an engineer, or as a lawyer ... but he doesn't have the means to buy an apartment." Immigrant parents have expressed awe that a college education and liberal profession cannot provide more material security for their children today.

Such a dire perspective, however, contrasts with recent generational advances in three families (mentioned in the beginning of this chapter). In Wlademir's civil-construction firm, for instance, his niece—who studies architecture at a private university in São Paulo—began a paid internship and plans to continue working in her uncle's successful enterprise. Likewise, in the family of Samir, the eldest son entered his final year in medical school and has applied for residence experience in hospitals around São Paulo and Rio de Janeiro. In the Ghantous family, as well, sons of the two brothers began an internship or became junior partners in the family-run law firm. Some third-generation youth have thus been able to prosper today with the symbolic and material capital accumulated by the second-generation of Middle Eastern families who established engineering, medical, or law firms after World War II.

Whether flourishing or foundering in today's economy, Syrian–Lebanese descendants have understood their market placement through an ethnic narrative of peddling forebears. Experiencing both upward and downward mobility, *doutores'* common nostalgia for the past of commerce has bridged the fractured experience of class mobility. More tellingly, it has also served as an ironic counterpoint to earlier attempts to move up from the "lowly origins" of so-called *turcos* in the mid-twentieth century. Far from forgetting the past of peddling—a key marker of Arab ethnicity—liberal professionals have identified with it today.

LIBERAL PROFESSIONALS ETHNICIZED IN THE PUBLIC SPHERE

Romanticizing the peddling past, Syrian–Lebanese *doutores* have over-generalized Arabs as ethnic Horatio Algers. In matter-of-fact ways, they have quantified the number of *árabes* in highly esteemed professional circles. One instance can be seen in my discussion with a friend of a colleague, Pedro, in relation to the São Paulo state division of the Ordem dos Advogados do Brasil (analogous to the American Bar Association). At the time, I was interested in looking at the membership roster, and my original intention in speaking with Pedro was to inquire into the possibility of gaining access to it. Without pausing, Pedro explained that fourteen of the ninety lawyers in the division's directorship are of *descendência sírio-libanesa*, including its president. Pedro added, "That's more than 15 percent of the total number." Middle Easterners have counted their numbers among São Paulo's legal elites.

This enumerated professional mobility has been also manifest in the field of medicine. Around the time that Mário Covas, former governor of the state of São Paulo, underwent heart bypass surgery, several acquaintances made sure to point out, ad nauseum, that "three out of the five doctors" who operated on him were "Arab." More generally, many medical and nonmedical professionals joked about the *monte* (heap) and the *turcalhada* (bunch of Turks) now composing the highly renowned faculty of USP's College of Medicine. In response to my question regarding the context of Arabs' social ascension in Brazil, Dr. Younes entered into a numerical discussion:

In the College of Medicine of USP, it's packed with Arab full professors. Well, Jatene was full professor. ... Maksoud from Infantile Surgery. ...

Angelita Abergama. … Assad now. There's Gatas from Psychiatry. … Ah, there's a ton of them. If you were to get the entire faculty, I think that a third of the faculty—and we are not a third of the population—a third are descendants of Arabs, full professors. So it's a lot of people… It's an all-star team. … Really, there's a ton of them.

In fact, Middle Eastern descendants do represent roughly one-third of the total number of faculty members in the College of Medicine. More important, though, Dr. Younes had expressed a sharp awareness of it. Surpassing the glass ceiling of earlier times, physicians now proudly count Arab ethnicity in the highest echelons of this increasingly competitive field.

Aside from law and medicine, ethnics also recounted their rise in the field of visual and performing arts. Wlademir, the engineer, reflected:

Look, I think here in Brazil, the Arab has distinguished himself in all sectors, not only in quantity, but in quality. If you take the sector of popular music. … I'm speaking of Arabs in general. If you take João Bosco. He's a descendant of Arabs, who's … a great author of music, a composer, singer, and guitar player. If you take Fagner. He's a descendant of Arabs. Fagner says that he learned a lot about singing with Arab songs. … If you take the biggest duo of classical guitar music of the world, it's the Duo Assad. … If you take classical music, there's Jamil Maluf, who is a great maestro. … Now … in the field of arts, we have a lot of Arabs, in painting, music, and sculpture. If you take the spaces of theater, the best directors in Brazil are Arabs. There's Fauzi Arap, there's Antonio Abujamra, there's Samir Iasbek, you understand?

Liberal professionals imagined the presence of *patrícios* in such noble pursuits as music and theater. In spite of branching into many learned and professional fields, Middle Easterners have identified co-ethnics in the upper echelons of Brazilian society.

Of course, this sort of ethnic promotion is characteristic of other groups as well. What distinguishes the case at hand, however, is the fact that claims to upward Syrian–Lebanese mobility reference the ethnic past of peddling. Take, for example, the book *Médicos sírios e libaneses do passado* (Lacaz 1982), which contains biographies of world-renowned medical doctors of Syrian and Lebanese descent. It was written by the well-known Dr. Carlos da Silva Lacaz, who has published other volumes on Brazilian medicine (see Lacaz 1977). In the book's introduction, Lacaz first takes note of the Syrian–Lebanese commercial past in Brazil. He writes that Syrian–Lebanese peddlers "opened their stores, selling their merchandise—needles, pins, thread, lamb-skins, combs, buttons, staples, jewelry, cheap perfume, embroidery. ... Firmly consolidated in industry and commerce, few nationalities like the Syrians and Lebanese in Brazil, had such a sharp conscience of the social, economic, and political advantages of a good education." To this he adds, "To educate their children, they [Syrians and Lebanese] made enormous sacrifices and in this way deservedly elevated themselves in social scale." Mentioning a dozen Syrian–Lebanese colleagues with whom he studied at USP's College of Medicine, Lacaz represents Middle Easterners as Horatio Algers who have risen from commerce to medicine. In writing about successful physicians today, peddling is romanticized and celebrated as an ethnic origin myth.

Middle Eastern mobility was also represented in the October 4, 2000 edition of the newsweekly *Veja*. Titled, ""Patrícios, dinheiro, diploma e voto: A saga da imigração árabe [Countrymen, Money, Degrees, and Votes: The Saga of Arab Immigration]," the article's headline continues, "The first Lebanese and Syrian immigrants wanted to make a fortune and return. They stayed, worked hard, invested in the education of their children. They brought up generations of *doutores* (educated professionals) and a tradition of participation in politics." At the beginning of the text, the reporter, Flávia Varella, identifies Middle Eastern difference by name:

> Salim, Ibrahim, Fuad, Abrahão, Jamil, Nagib, Habib, Tufik, Salomão, Chafic. In the life of almost every "genuine" Brazilian [*brasileiro "de gema"*; lit., "from the yolk"], there is a Brazilian with a name like that—"*turco*," as one says even today, more out of habit than out of prejudice. There's the store owner, the factory owner, the politician, the medical doctor. ... In politics and medicine, the proliferation of Arab last names is so intense that it comes to be intriguing.

Middle Eastern names today are encountered in commerce and industry, as well as in politics and medicine. Despite the diverse occupational spaces now inhabited by ethnic citizens, their names "habitually" have been labeled *turco* by "genuine" Brazilians.

As suggested by its title, the article emphasizes the social ascension of Arabs in Brazil from commercial origins to liberal professional fields, especially politics and medicine. The names and photographs of twenty-six descendants who have distinguished themselves "on the stage and podium"—including actors, musicians, politicians, journalists, and doctors—are horizontally laid out over six glossy pages of the news article. A textual excerpt beside the visual roster of famous *patrícios* relates that "descendants of Syrian and Lebanese immigrants have [attained] distinction in various sectors of national life, from the arts to the universities, from politics to medicine. Some do not use the Arab last name, but no one denies his [or her] origins." Medical doctors such as Adibe Jatene and Raul Cutait and artists such as Fagner and João Bosco are among the famous individuals listed. One factor contributing to such upward mobility, Varella relates, are the networks among *patrícios* that have led to the commercial success of immigrants and the rise of second-generation descendants in "the market of liberal professions."[9] Masking the increasingly fractured experience of class among Syrian–Lebanese descendants, the article serves as an unequivocal celebration of Arab market mobility in today's Brazil.

As noted in *Veja*, upwardly mobile descendants have been identified by the *turco* label that marked the ethnic difference of their peddling predecessors. What the article does not mention, however, is how white-collar Arabs continue to be viewed as possessing innate business acumen, the essential marker of being *turco*. This representation manifested itself in the television appearance of Dr. Younes, who is a renowned cancer specialist in Brazil and the world. He was invited for an interview on the Globo TV network's *Programa do Jô*, a late-night show with the comedian Jô Soares that is similar to *Late Night with David Letterman* in the United States. Dr. Younes was dressed in an elegant suit, wearing a smile that is a mark of his well-known personable nature. His interview was dedicated to recent changes and advances in the field of medicine. At one point, Jô asked why certain percentages are established in medical diagnosis and treatment. Dr. Younes explained that there are percentile norms that oblige the medical practitioner to let a certain amount of liquid drain from the lungs after surgery. Such established understandings, qualified the doctor, can be found wanting. Based on his own experience, Dr. Younes reflected on his discovery that the patient recovers faster by allowing more liquid to drain from the lung following surgery, despite the smaller amount stipulated in medical texts.

Picking up on this metaphorical "exchange" of fluids, the indefatigable Jô Soares turned to Dr. Younes and raised the ethnic question, "*Ô Riad, 'cê é de origem árabe, né?* [Oh, Riad—you're of Arab origin, aren't you?]." Smiling, the doctor responded with a positive but firm tone, "Yes. Yes, I am." With a more sinister smile, Soares then asked, "So, could it be for this reason that you stay bargaining in the surgery room, 'Take a little less from the lung,' 'less from the heart,' and so on?"[10] Laughter and hand clapping grew from the audience, and both the interviewer and the interviewee appeared equally amused. Taking the *brincadeira* (joke) one step further, Dr. Younes corrected Soares: "No, actually, because of [my] origins, I should be taking more, more from the lung, more from the heart, more. ..."[11] Everyone in the audience laughed harder, and

Soares affectionately tapped Dr. Younes's arm. Even vis-à-vis a world-renowned cancer specialist, the image of the shrewd Arab who "bargains" was invoked on a highly rated late-night television program. Although Arab Brazilians have long since entered liberal professions with cosmopolitan backgrounds, the image of the commercially astute Turk remains quite popular in the Brazilian public sphere.

I had a similar experience while interviewing a (non-Arab) tax collector who oversees the Rua 25 de Março region in downtown São Paulo. At the beginning of the interview, I introduced myself as a Ph.D. student in anthropology from the United States, though the tax collector inquired into my Arab background. At the end of our encounter, he jokingly expressed doubt about my purpose in São Paulo. "Was I really an anthropologist?" he wondered out loud, or "was I interested in tax legislation to open a store in the region?" In response, I joked that I would lose money in business. Surprised, he asked, "But, how? You have the blood, the Arab blood! You're *turco*!" Such a close association between the label *turco* and the image of shrewd money handling—despite a university degree or status as a Ph.D. candidate—was echoed in a remark made by Fernando, a third-generation Arab Brazilian who recently graduated from a private university. He reflected that school friends would amicably joke about his background as a *turco* in the school snack bar or dance clubs. "Oh! Turk," Fernando mimicked his friends, "*Dá o dinheiro!* [Hand over the money!]." In this light, being called a *turco* still involves the idea of an Arab commercial essence, despite descendants' educational mobility.

MARKING MIDDLE EASTERN AS *TURCO* IN RACIAL DEMOCRACY

Such ethnic recognition in the context of professional mobility must be understood in relation to what I consider to be the market remodeling of the idea of racial democracy. In most cases of this reorganization of racial meaning, lay, media, political, and academic critics have employed statistical representations of the economic inequalities between "whites" and "blacks." Such quantitative imagery of the market-based reality of discrimination has been wielded to challenge the "myth" of racial democracy.

As a brief example, the newsweekly *Isto É* published criticisms of the so-called myth of racial democracy in its July 2001 coverage of the World Conference against Racism, Racial Discrimination, Xenophobia, and Intolerance in South Africa. Provocatively placed on its front cover was a photograph of a black hand with white paint dripping over it, accompanied by the inflammatory caption, "*Você é racista?* [Are You Racist?]." In the cover story, titled

"The Hidden Prejudice: Brazil Prefers the Myth of Racial Democracy and Closes Its Eyes to Intolerance," the history of slavery, as well as its current continuities in the market, were recounted in ways that would make Gilberto Freyre turn over in his grave. Most significant, statistical averages of the economic realities of race were cited from the Institute of Applied Economic Research (IPEA). The article, written by a noted public intellectual, stated that Brazil,

> where the myth of racial democracy has been hidden by statistics, *tem contas a prestar* [lit., "has accounts to confer," and fig., "has bills to pay"]. The labor market is proof of the size of the inequality. ... A white laborer earns, on average, 573 [reais, in Brazilian currency] a month. The black man, 262 [reais]. ... IPEA also concluded that, even if blacks had the same schooling as whites, their salaries would nonetheless be 30% less, around 407 [reais]. The difference is fruit of discrimination in the labor market, and in this field there have not been advances in the past century.

Statistical representations of the inequalities between whites and blacks in the labor market have served as *the* gauge with which to measure racial democracy—or, more precisely, its absence—in contemporary Brazil.

In contrast, the myth of racial democracy has been also confirmed in the representation of upward Arab market mobility. Uniformly depicted as "rising above" past commercial vocations, Arab *doutores* have stressed the gradual reduction of prejudice in their lives, most evidently marked by the label *turco*. When I asked about the term's meaning, several Arabs reflected that, although *turco* was employed in a pejorative or prejudiced way in the past, it is used in an innocuous or affectionate manner in the present. "There were a lot of people who used it as a pejorative term before," said Said, a physician, "but today, I don't see much of this." Likewise, a retired school teacher, Roberto, reflected that when "the Arab peoples came to Brazil, it was the Ottoman Turks who dominated the region. So immigrants had Turkish passports and were called *turcos*. It was pejorative, but now it's affectionate [*afetivo*]." A second-generation homemaker, Valéria, reflected that when one was called *turco* in the past, "It was pejorative. ... But today, it's not like that any more. No. No, not anymore. Today, I think that you call someone *turco* in a caring manner [*maneira carinhosa*]." This not only suggests that prejudice was shifted to the past and effaced in the present (Twine 1998). Such emphasis on the affectionate or caring character of a once marginalizing ethnonym also points to the continued power of racial democracy in a decidedly ethnic way.

In an interview conducted with Dr. Younes within a month of his television appearance, he pointed out that *turco* is not indicative of "prejudice" or "discrimination," which in his words are "very light and very tenuous" in Brazil. Rising from a medical student to a full professor at USP (with much experience abroad), this Lebanese Sunni Muslim medical doctor emphasized the absence of any ethnic- or religious-based discrimination in his biography of upward mobility. He also went on to mention that *turco* is the *apelido* (nickname) of one of his colleagues at USP's medical school. "It's become more of a joke today," he concluded. During the interview, we also laughed about the "joke" concerning Arabs' ostensible propensity to bargain in the operating room. Having taken their place among the liberal professional classes, Arab Brazilians such as Dr. Younes, have transformed the category of *turco* that indexed Arabs' marginal status in the past.

Indeed, Arab professionals have generally stressed the nondiscriminatory character of the *turco* category. In the words of another medical doctor, Sarkis, "the Brazilian has a caring way to call you '*turco*.' It's a form of caring, typically Brazilian ... that does not have a racist connotation or a discriminatory connotation. It is not prejudicial." After pointing out that *turco* is not discriminatory, Dr. Arap similarly stressed that "prejudice here in Brazil is a really light thing." Using even more suggestive language, the engineer Wlademir explained that "the majority of people now caringly call you *turco*, affectionately." In parallel fashion, a lawyer stressed that Brazilians "call us '*turquinho! turquinho!*' But it's not with the air of offense, of discrimination. It's an even caring way of joking." Valéria likewise explained that being called *turco* today "is caring. It is 100 percent caring. When you say, 'Ah, that *turco* there, my friend, that *turco*.' But you say it in a caring way, do you understand?" A successful business administrator, Jorge, stressed that *turco* should not be seen as "prejudicial" because "all the races are equal" in Brazil. Arab professionals' emphasis on the nondiscriminatory character of *turco* illustrates the ethnic contours of *democracia racial* in contemporary Brazil.

This ostensible nondiscriminatory meaning of *turco* has not been an easy matter for me. When I was first forced to analyze this marker academically with my U.S. American brand of identity politics, I wondered whether it derided Arabness, akin to "Ay-rab" (said with a hard "a," as in "say") in the United States. Given the U.S. American history of prejudice and racism, the many verbal ways of deriding Arabness had been my main point of reference. Indeed, almost all studies of Arab Americans make some mention of such discrimination in the United States (e.g., Abraham and Shryock 2000; Kayal and Benson 2002; Orfalea 1988; Shaheen 1984; Shakir 1997; Suleiman 1999). But all too aware of my U.S. Americanness, I have not been willing to dismiss Arab

Brazilian self-understandings as "false consciousness." This would be tanta-
mount to what Pierre Bourdieu (1991: 50–52) has called "symbolic domination." Arab Brazilian ways of expressing ethnicity must be understood on their
own terms.

In a more problematic fashion, though, colleagues explained that "*turco*"
is analogous to other labels of ethnic and racial difference. "The Brazilian,"
Sarkis reflected, "calls the Japanese descendant '*japonesinho*' [little Japanese],
right? He calls the *moreno* [brown], the *preto* [black], *negão* [big black]."[12]
Similarly, the 25 de Março association's president, Beto, explained that *turco*
"is a term that you give to people who came from the Middle East. ... It's like
you saying 'yellow' for Chinese, Japanese, and Korean. The *turcos* [*pause*] ...
It's become a popular kind of term." Likewise, Michel, a wealthy tycoon,
stressed that *turco* "is not an offense. It's the same thing if someone comes from
another state and they call him *bahiano*." After noting that the term *turco* "is
not about discrimination," Dr. Arap said that the ethnonym "is a vestige of the
time of the *quatrocentões*. *Turquinho, japonês, carcamano*. It's for all races."
Turco has served as another allegedly nondiscriminatory marker of ethnic or
racial difference within that unequal hierarchy imparted by the once dominant Luso-Brazilians and today remodeled by the representation of the
omnipresent market.

Some colleagues, however, stressed the importance of context in judging
the significance of the *turco* label. Take, for instance, Fuad, a well-to-do merchant whose children work in liberal professions. In response to my question
about the meaning of *turco*, Fuad responded:

> It depends on how you use it. ... It depends on my way of getting along,
> my way of speaking with you. And you can be rich and not get annoyed.
> Right? "Hi Turk. Everything good?" "Hi. It's good, kid. Been a long time."
> So it's a caring gesture. So, *turco* has two meanings—one that offends and
> one that privileges.

The label "*turco*" could thus undermine or confirm so-named subjects depending on the context and the relationship between the speakers.

But this situational meaning of the term was especially downplayed in
relation to liberal professionalism. Exchanges in four other interviews linked
the attainment of a "noble" profession and the positive valence of *turco* (as a
"caring gesture"). When I asked whether the meaning of *turco* was "pejorative," interviewees offered a seemingly non sequitur response. After noting
that the term was "affectionate" or "a joke," they explained the mobility of
Arabs in liberal professions. Succinctly, the seventy-plus-year-old Sami

captures this expression of ethnic difference through the idiom of market mobility in racial democracy:

> Now you call someone "*turco*" but as an affectionate term [*um termo afetivo*]. Because in the *colônia*, we have many liberal professionals, as many in the political world as in the medical world ... as in engineering, everything. Our children are brilliant and are our pride. So, now you don't speak of "turcos" as you did in the past. Even if you say "*turco*," "little Turk [*turquinho*]," it's a sign of affection [*é sinal de afeto*].

Sami lay stress on how *turco* has become an affectionate term through Arabs' attainment of an allegedly more lucrative liberal professional status. While market imagery has been often used to challenge the so-called myth of racial democracy, it has also been employed by *turcos* to privilege their place today in this remodeled nationalist hierarchy.

Tellingly, the *turco* ethnonym has been appropriated by Arabs themselves. Colleagues recurrently stressed that they call one another *turco* in a joking or "common-sense" way. An elderly merchant, Fathallah (whose children are well-established liberal professionals), jested, "When I go to have lunch with friends on 25 de Março, I tell my wife that I'm going to Turkey." Abdo, a second-generation Lebanese, likewise explained, "We ourselves between us, the children of Lebanese, we would say this to one another 'Oh, *turco*! Oh, *turquinho* [little Turk]! Oh, *turcão*! [big Turk]." Third-generation Fernando reflected, "Here between them [Syrian–Lebanese], they call each other *turcos*. My father calls his friends, "O *turcão*! Come here!'" Finally, Mário, a well-established second-generation Lebanese Brazilian lawyer whose son has followed in his professional footsteps, provided a detailed explanation of this ironic appropriation:

> The only pejorative term that had to do with us is *turco*. But we ourselves, descendants of Arabs, Syrians, and Lebanese, *esculhambamos* [messed with] the term. So when we refer to a *patrício*, we use the term. With this, the term was made banal. ... "What are you?" "I am a Turk." We made it ordinary. We made it a joke. So, "Oh, Turk? How are you? All right? *Turquinho?*" I call my friends like, "Oh, *turquinho!* All right, *querido?*" Did you understand? So it's done. There's no more of that pejorative sense. ... This is the spirit of the Brazilian. He...makes it banal. He transforms rancor into a joke. And he destroys any rancor. He destroys any animosity.

In using the *turco* category themselves, Arabs transformed a once marginalizing signifier into an explicit self-identification of Middle Eastern difference.

In this perspective, the "messing with" language suggests what it means to be Brazilian: the transformation of ethnic rancor through the long-standing nationalist ideology of "racial democracy."

In this light, Arab Brazilian professionals' understanding of *turco* as "nondiscriminatory" stems from neither false consciousness nor an objective reality per se. As was shown in Chapters 1 and 2, some Middle Eastern merchants and politicians have experienced discrimination. Whether used by street vendors in downtown environs or by journalists in the coverage of a corruption case, the *turco* category can carry a negative or positive meaning depending on the given context. For me, "*turco*" has remained an ambivalent label that can confirm or undermine so-named subjects depending on the context. Generally, however, liberal professionals who sought to legitimate the ethnonym on their own terms denied this situational variation. The fractured experience of the educated class in today's market has conditioned white-collar Arabs to disavow the pejorative meaning of *turco*. In a model of and for their upwardly mobile place in the nation (Geertz 1973), *turco* has been transformed from "rancor into a joke." As the nationalist ideology of racial democracy has failed to persuade a growing part of the public sphere, ethnic liberal professionals have used their symbolic power to claim an experience of nondiscrimination and acceptance. In this sense, the positive affirmation of a once negative label not only has reflected the dominance of those who rose above lower origins prone to prejudice. It has also helped to shield others from reliving the past.

CONSTRUED AS AN ETHNIC project, the recognition of Arab professional mobility has developed at the intersection of race and nation in Brazil. Having "risen above" the peddling origins of immigrant forebears, liberal professionals have been positioned in more privileged places than their predecessors' marginal circumstances. In this milieu, the label "*turco*" and its referent idea of inborn business acumen have been emphasized by ethnics themselves, whether in the university classroom or the doctor's office chambers. Jesting commentary about Arabs and their innate commercial propensity is no longer solely indicative of an externally imposed, marginal place in the nation. Rather than imply "prejudice" as it did in the mid-twentieth century, the *turco* category has been adopted by Middle Eastern professionals and others as a "caring" and "affectionate" reference via the market model of racial democracy in Brazil.

꙳

FOUR

Mixing Christians,
Cloning Muslims

R ELIGIOUS DIFFERENCE IS PART of ethnic recognition, especially in a historically Roman Catholic nation such as Brazil. Estimated to make up at least 80 percent of Middle Eastern immigrants in the early twentieth century, Christian Syrian–Lebanese were scrutinized by state immigration experts in terms of their tendency to wed in the homeland and their low rates of "miscegenation."[1] To be Brazilian, in such nationalist thinking, was to be "mixed." In the late twentieth century, however, this idea of mixture was removed from state immigration policy and, at the same time, adopted by Christian Syrian–Lebanese who now criticize their Muslim counterparts "who don't mix" in ways similar to their own past marginalization.

Often expressed in terms of marriage practices, this religious differentiation in Syrian–Lebanese ethnicity historically has taken shape through two national paradigms of immigration policy in Brazil: race mixture until the late 1970s and economic productivity from 1980 onward. In the earlier model, mostly Christian Syrian–Lebanese were devalued for their apparent endogamy (or in-group marriage). In contrast, the current policy has recognized and supported mostly Muslim Lebanese who engage in the same marriage practices. Attentive to how Muslim Arabs have been singled out as "marrying among themselves" by their Christian counterparts and in the soap opera *O Clone* (*The Clone*), this chapter suggests that there have been limits to the greater acknowledgment of Muslim Arabness in contemporary Brazil.

My wider aim is to situate this religious difference in ethnicity vis-à-vis national immigration policy. Until the 1970s, "race mixture" served as the main rationale of Brazilian state policy. Ideologues hoped that non-European immigrants, including Middle Easterners, would "mix" with natives and avoid the formation of "cysts" (Fausto 1993). In 1980–81, though, immigration policy was emptied of references to race mixture and given the primary task of regulating the flow of people for "economic productivity" (*Estatuto do Estrangeiro* 2000: 18).[2] As noted by Benedict Anderson (1994: 323), the regulation of immigration today is less about claims to national belonging than about rights to work in a labor market. The neoliberal policy change also brought about the reclassification of immigrant endogamy that worried earlier authorities. Characterizing marriage between a Brazilian-born citizen and a foreign national as "family reunification," the current policy has enabled predominantly Muslim Lebanese to marry in Lebanon and return with immigrant spouses to live in Brazil. Though criticized by Christian Arabs in the nationalist idiom of mixture, the neoliberal Brazilian state has tacitly approved of Muslim Arabs who, in the words of one official, "prefer to marry among themselves."

This chapter's focus on marriage politics engages with scholarship on Syrian–Lebanese immigration and Brazilian immigration policy. Historians have agreed that early twentieth-century Syrian–Lebanese immigrant families primarily avoided "miscegenation," while later generations increasingly married outside the community (Gattaz 2001; Nunes 1993; Truzzi 1997). Absent in this one-dimensional assertion is any reference to the Brazilian nationalist preoccupation with "racial mixture." Broader analyses of early twentieth-century Brazilian immigration policy have clearly shown that miscegenation was not a "natural" phenomenon but one of state policy based on nationalist notions of *brasilidade* (Brazilianness) and race (Fausto 1993; Seyferth 1996; Skidmore 1974). Whether alleged to be "mixed" or "pure," the practices and politics of marriage must be studied in shifting terms not only of family hierarchy, but also of nationalist ideology and state policy.

My sense is that the fundamental change that has taken place across Syrian–Lebanese generations in the twentieth century is not necessarily the ostensible increase of exogamy (out-group marriage) but, rather, the national context in which ethnic claims about marriage have been made, questioned, and validated. Although Christian and Muslim Arabs continue to practice endogamy to varied degrees, their mutually oppositional ways of marking marriage point to the intensification of the Arab ethnic project in Brazil.

DIASPORIC MARRIAGE CIRCUITS BETWEEN
THE LEVANT AND BRAZIL

In search of suitable wives, Syrian–Lebanese men in Brazil have traveled to *el-bilad* (the [home] country, in Arabic) since the early twentieth century. Marriage was not a matter to be taken lightly, as made evident in a tale told about my own migrant great-grandfather, Abidão (Abdo) Bichara, who resided in northern Brazil at that time. As he lay dying after a gallbladder operation in Belém do Pará, Abidão dictated three points of guidance for his Brazilian-born sons in the family trading business: "Never argue with a priest or taxicab driver"; "Never buy real estate in the middle of the block but on the corner where it's worth more"; and "Never marry Brazilian women. Always return to *el-bilad* to find your brides."

Abidão Bichara's three sons would travel to "find their brides" in Lebanon and return to northern Brazil. They were not alone. As an anthropologist in Lebanon in the 1940s, John Gulick noted that "quite a few [emigrants] came back temporarily to the old village for brides" (Gulick 1955: 62). The anthropologist Judith Williams also observed migrants from Brazil who sought wives from their mountainous Lebanese villages (Williams 1968: 98, 105). The historian Mintaha Alcuri Campos saw a similar pattern in her survey among elderly Syrian–Lebanese in the state of Espírito Santo. She found that fifty-seven of ninety-four male Lebanese immigrants had returned to wed in the homeland or arranged for Lebanese-born brides to move permanently to Brazil (Campos 1987: 125). Middle Eastern men sought their brides in *el-bilad* in the first half of the twentieth century.

Arab community intellectuals were well aware of this matrimonial migration (Duoun 1944; Kurban 1933; Jamil Safady 1972a; Wadih Safady 1966). But by the mid-1940s, they observed, immigrant men began to search for wives not in Syria or Lebanon but within the *colônia* in Brazil. Jamil Safady (cited in Jorge Safady 1972a: 50) reflected that "the custom of the male youth going to the homeland to marry relatives or neighbors is decreasing," but "Arab Brazilian families ... remain devoted to having their children marry only descendants of Arabs." Wadih Safady (1966: 223) likewise remarked that the flow of Arab men who sought brides in the homeland had turned into a "reverse wave [*onda revertida*]" by the 1960s. "Many young Lebanese men," he judged, "now look to find marriage in the bosom [*seio*] of the Arab Brazilian family." Such commentaries have been corroborated by Campos. She found that twenty-six of the ninety-four couples surveyed (27.7 percent) were made up of an Arab immigrant man and a (second-generation) Brazilian-born Arab woman (Campos 1987: 125). This diasporic arrangement of endogamy, specifically between immigrant men and second-generation women, would remain prevalent through the post–World War II period in Brazil.

Such marriages were not limited to intellectual musings. "All of us at that time," recalled a second-generation *senhora*, "married guys [*rapazes*] who came from Lebanon" (cited in Greiber et al. 1998: 179). Likewise, in my research, many second-generation middle-aged women explained that female cohorts in their age range differentiated between male suitors born in Brazil, called *nacional* (national), and in the Middle East, dubbed *importado* (imported). These playful labels, however, belie how little freedom Arab women exercised in marital choice. Researching in the Syrian–Lebanese community of São José do Rio Preto, São Paulo, the demographer Marileila Varella-Garcia noted that "mixed marriages involving non-Arabian women are nearly four times as frequent as those involving non-Arabian men (228 versus 55)." Arab men were far more likely to marry non-Arabs than Arab women (Varella-Garcia 1976: 164). Accounting for generational differences among Middle Eastern spouses, Varella-Garcia's contribution confirmed striking gender inequalities in marital patterns.

Such diasporic marriage arrangements reflected the gender ideologies of family regimes wherein daughters were persuaded to marry, or coerced into marrying, co-ethnic men, and if doing otherwise could be marginalized by patriarchal standards. An immigrant Lebanese man in Goiás put it simply: "The unease was not in relation to the marriage of the man of Arab descent with a Brazilian woman but ... with the marriage of the woman of Arab descent with [a] Brazilian man" (cited in Nunes 1993: 195). Heloisa, a divorced second-generation woman in her fifties, stressed the difficulty she faced when she wanted to marry her sweetheart of Italian descent. Her Lebanese father did not approve, and her Lebanese mother tried to indefinitely postpone the engagement party. Likewise, Raul, a second-generation Lebanese man, recounted that his mother had admonished his sisters to "be careful" with Brazilian men, who would take advantage of them. In embodying "cultural tradition," women and not men were pressured to marry within the *colônia*.[3]

Middle Eastern men explained their conjugal preference for immigrant or second-generation women in terms of cultural preservation.[4] My great-uncle, for instance, related to my cousin and me the rationale of his diasporic marriage. In response to my cousin's question as to whether his choice was due to an aversion to *misturar as raças* (mixing races), my uncle replied, "No, no. ... It was to maintain customs and habits." Antoine, a middle-aged Syrian immigrant, likewise spoke of women as central to maintaining the habits, customs, and traditions of Syrian–Lebanese families in Brazil. Because of the length of time and high costs of transportation in the first half of the twentieth century, another Syrian immigrant, Jorge, reflected that many *patrícios* ended up marrying Middle Eastern women born in Brazil. Such women, he added, unite the family and instill in children traditional mores "from the homeland." Men, in this light, spoke of diasporic endogamy in terms not of male dominance but of cultural maintenance.

Implicitly, religion was one of those "cultural traditions" to be preserved. Wlademir, a second-generation Lebanese, explained that he and others rarely differentiated between Syrians and Lebanese because of a common religious background. He stressed that many families from Syria and Lebanon were Orthodox Christians, frequenting the same social circles and courting one another. Sharing this religious background, Assad, a second-generation Syrian, also reflected that "it is difficult to encounter a family of Syrians ... who doesn't have a daughter married to Lebanese, and vice versa." A cohort, Edgar, added, "There's a lot of Syrians married with Lebanese, and many Lebanese married with Syrians." Marriages between Orthodox Christian Syrians and Lebanese reinforced the popular label *sírio-libanês* (Syrian–Lebanese). The designation was not only a creative marker of identity, as Jeffrey Lesser has noted (1999: 42); it also carried an implicit religious valence, consummated in marriage.

Yet this Middle Eastern preservation of Orthodox Christian religiosity enveloped and almost effaced Muslim religious difference. Estimated in small but significant numbers, Muslim immigrants represented roughly 15 to 20 percent of Middle Easterners in Brazil until the 1960s (Lesser 1999: 49; Osman 1998). But writers in the Christian-dominated *colônia* at the time reflected on the so-called assimilation of such early- and mid-twentieth-century Muslim immigrants. In the 1960s, Wadih Safady, an Orthodox Christian, commented that "Muslim Arabs are a minority in Brazil. In their majority, they were assimilated and now live like Christians, and married with Christians" (Safady 1966: 224).[5] Similarly, Nagib Assrauy, then the only Druze Lebanese intellectual in Brazil, reflected with obvious regret that his fellow Druze were marrying "women from another religious belief." In 1967, he wrote:

> Emigration ... has brought to the Druze man a serious problem ... in contracting nuptials with women from another religious belief with which he constitutes a family, had children, and, without wanting it, without desiring it, turned into an altering agent of the pureness of his race [*agente alterador da pureza de sua raça*] and in this way extinguishing the heritage that he received from his fathers and grandfathers. (Assrauy 1967: 39)

Assrauy sadly noted that Druze immigrant men were marrying non-Druze women. He did not mention, however, whether these women were Middle Eastern or native Brazilian. Perhaps for Assrauy the distinction did not matter much because it effectively produced the same result: the "altering" of the "Druze race."

The tendency of offspring from inter-religious families to deny their Muslim or non-Christian side further effaced Muslim difference in a predominantly Christian community. A middle-aged Lebanese woman, for instance, remarked that although her mother was a Christian Lebanese born in Brazil and her father was a Muslim Lebanese immigrant, she was brought up Christian and "could not even speak" about her Muslim roots. Similarly, Valéria, an elderly second-generation Christian, recounted that a Muslim Lebanese acquaintance had married a Brazilian-born Christian Lebanese woman. Their three children married not Muslim but Christian Lebanese and frequented not mosques but churches. At the time, Valéria concluded, the children could not speak about their Muslimness among Christian peers, who would gossip that "he [the father] is Muslim!" These vignettes suggest that Muslim difference was curtailed through the children of inter-religious families in the Christian-dominated *colônia*.

This is not difficult to grasp in view of dominant Brazilian images of Muslims and Middle Easterners in the first half of the twentieth century. Despite the xenophobia of Vargas-era immigration policy, Brazilian elites made positive references to the Christian difference of Middle Eastern immigrants (Araújo 1940; Junior 1935; Souza 1937). Manuel Diégues (1976 [1952]: 195) stated that "among us, Syrian and Lebanese are principally part of the Melquite Catholic Church and the Maronite Church."[6] Two decades earlier, Alfredo Ellis (1934: 197) not only remarked that the majority of *turcos* were Christian. He added that "the cruelties practiced against Christian populations [in the Middle East] made the latter search for salvation in emigration." Likewise, the journalist João do Rio (1928: 164–65) noted that "ferocious" persecutions by "Mahometans" and "Druze" led to the "slow exodus" of Maronite Christians. Aware of the Christian difference of Middle Eastern immigrants, early twentieth-century Brazilian observers wrongly depicted them as refugees from a putatively fanatical Muslim Arab world.

Lesser has shown how this Brazilian aversion to Muslim difference became manifest when a Christian group from Iraq, the Assyrians, tried to migrate in the early 1930s (Lesser 1994). A Brazilian proponent of Assyrian resettlement argued that this "Christian population" was persecuted by "a Muslim fanatic" (Lesser 1994: 26). A Brazilian statesman who opposed it likened the "Assyrians" to Muslims. Lesser writes that the statesman "tried hard to link the group to Iraqi Muslims, by referring to them as 'the Assyrians of Iraq' and to Muslims

as their 'brothers'" (Lesser 1994: 31). Although the Assyrian resettlement plan
ultimately failed, this exchange suggests that, while Christian Arabs may
have been welcomed, those perceived as Muslim had no place in the early twentieth-century Brazilian nation.

ARAB "CYSTS" IN IMMIGRATION POLICY
AND RACE MIXTURE

Immigration policy measures in early twentieth-century Brazil, though related
to the economy, were explicitly concerned with the racial composition of the
country. In hopes of improving and "whitening [*embranquecer*]" the nation
along eugenicist lines, Brazilian state and intellectual elites were forthright in
their desire for immigrants from Europe.[7] Indeed, an article of the Constitution of 1890 promulgated by the Republican government prohibited the
entrance of immigrants from Asia and Africa (Diégues 1964: 50–51; Neiva
1943: 23; Skidmore 1974: 137). By 1907, a new decree had altered the racist
policy, setting standards that made no direct reference to immigrants' "continent of origin" (Skidmore 1974: 137). With Getúlio Vargas's rise to power in
the 1930s, however, a quota system was put into place, greatly reducing the
number of non-European immigrants (Mita 1995: 439; Skidmore 1974).

   The preference for white immigrants was reiterated in an early 1940s publication of the Conselho de Imigração e Colonização, the Brazilian state agency
of immigration (Conselho de Imigração e Colonização 1943: 186–95). One
of its members, Artur Neiva, wrote, "I judge ... [that] it is indispensable to
place limits on or to preferably exclude black or yellow immigration, favor-
ing by all means waves of white immigrants" (Neiva 1945: 46). Similarly, revi-
sions in the statute law for foreigners in 1945 called for "the preservation and
development of the European descent in the ethnic composition of the population" (Cavarzere 1991: 250; Chavez 1950: 33). At least three other statute
laws were passed in the next five decades, but a racially based quota system
remained intact that favored European immigration (Cavarzere 1991). As late
as 1976, a juridical scholar wrote that "immigration policy should be planned
and executed in such a way to remain preserved the European descent of the
Brazilian population" (Carvalho 1976: 21). Even a present-day federal bureaucrat managing immigration records in São Paulo has admitted that the quota
system was "higher for Europeans, principally Portuguese and Spanish"
through the 1970s. In much of the twentieth century, immigration policy
served to whiten the Brazilian nation.

   As state immigration policy aimed to contain and homogenize racial difference, contemporaneous cultural production organized and venerated the

country's racially heterogeneous composition. Inaugurated with the publication of Gilberto Freyre's *Casa grande e senzala* in 1933, the idea of miscegenation between the Amerindian, African, and Portuguese became a bastion of Brazilian nationalist ideology. Constructing a mythic past shared by lighter male masters and darker female slaves on colonial plantations, Freyre claimed that interracial sexual relations created a unique Brazilian race that was "mixed" and free from rigid racial divisions.[8] Set on the plantation, this nationalist origin myth of *mestiçagem* had been conceived at a time when commerce and industry gained force in the Brazilian nation.

The idea of racial mixture and the racist policy of immigration influenced how Brazilian elites spoke about and scrutinized "foreign elements." Ostensibly gauged by marriage patterns, miscegenation rates informed how immigrants were assessed, questioned, or legitimized within the nation. Governmental studies of marriage practices among immigrant groups abounded in the first half of the twentieth century (Araújo 1940; Ellis 1934; Guimarães 1952; Neiva 1943; Souza 1937; Viana 1932; see also Lesser 1996, 1999). Without exception, researchers found that Portuguese, Italian, and Spanish immigrants were miscegenating well with "native" populations. The place of immigrants of European origin was thus confirmed in the workplace and the bedroom, laboring and whitening the Brazilian nation.

Yet, others perceived as non-white—such as Japanese, Jews, and Middle Easterners—remained an ongoing concern for state bureaucrats and intellectuals. Such immigrant groups were regarded as possessing "undesirable" traits for Brazil (Lesser 1994, 1995). Their ostensibly low rates of exogamy contributed to fears of the formation of ethnic *quistos* (cysts) in the nation's corpus and the determent of its whitening process (Fausto 1993; Skidmore 1974). The optimistic expectation was that these "foreign elements" would engage in miscegenation, intermarrying with native-born populations and thereby reducing possible negative effects. The nationalist ideology of racial mixture, in this light, served as the entry point for both European and non-European immigrants. The place of these "undesirables," however, was questioned rather than confirmed in Brazilian miscegenation.

Referenced by several designations (as mentioned in the introduction), Middle Easterners made up the fifth-largest immigrant group in Brazil until the 1940s, drawing the attention of early twentieth-century commentators (Araújo 1940: 230–36; Ellis 1934; Guimarães 1952: 87, 100, 106; Junior 1935; Souza 1937; Viana 1932). In their vision, the Middle Eastern immigration pattern was characterized as single male youth; this was confirmed by the sociologist Clark Knowlton decades later. Knowlton (1961:93) found that there were 214.2 Arab men for every 100 Arab women.[9] This preponderance of

Middle Eastern men should not have appeared so strange to Brazilian elites, especially in view of Portuguese immigrants, who made up the highest percentage of single men. Brazilian intellectual and state authorities, however, feared that Middle Eastern men were marrying in their countries of origin or with Brazilian-born Arab women.

In earlier works, statistics on Middle Eastern endogamy hovered around 50 percent (Ellis 1934: 197–211, Viana 1932: 120–22). Such "data" led to intense debates about whether the "fusability indexes" of Middle Easterners with Brazilians were "reasonable" or "low" (see Junior 1935). Lesser (1996) has observed that the same statistics were used to justify both sides of the polemical debate. The bone of contention, however, concerned not statistics per se but the categories underlying them. Well aware that generational data were unavailable, scholars noted that it was impossible to surmise whether Middle Eastern immigrants were marrying "Brazilians" or Brazilian-born Middle Easterners who were categorized as Brazilians. Amid inadequate statistical representations, Brazilian national elites voiced fears that a *quisto* could be forming in the national body (Fausto 1993).

Such quantitative imagery contributed to the debate on Middle Eastern miscegenation. Although earlier works found intermarriage rates "reasonable" (Ellis 1934: 197–211; Viana 1932: 120–22), later publications questioned such "optimistic" findings on methodological grounds. In one heated exchange, a non-Arab observer alleged that their "reasonable" rates of intermarriage were a "statistical effect [*efeito de estatística*]," because "Syrian immigrants" were marrying the "Brazilian children of Syrians" and thus were erroneously categorized as "mixed" (Levy, as cited in Junior 1935: 40). "Although in social circles they have become intimate with the rest of the population," another ethnologist qualified, "their [marital] ties almost always proceed within their own colony." He added that "*Syrios*" prefer São Paulo residents of the "ancestry of their own origin" (Souza 1937: 101–102). Citing and summarizing the contrary sides of the debate, a sociologist concluded that only future studies would discern whether "Syrians" tended toward endogamy, "with possible consequences, favorable or not, for the *Pátria*" (Araújo 1940: 236). Arab marriage practices constituted a matter of nationalist preoccupation.

Mid-twentieth-century elites' suspicions were later confirmed by Knowlton. He wrote that "many of them [Syrian and Lebanese men] wed women of Syrian or Lebanese origin who figure in the official statistics as *brasileiras*, because they are *nativas* to Brazil" (Knowlton 1961: 51, emphasis in the original Portuguese). He added that some Syrian–Lebanese men did search for spouses and lovers *fora da colônia* (outside the community). Whether Arab male suitors were successful in post–World War II Brazil, however, is questionable. As peddlers and store owners, they were not necessarily viewed as "good catches" by the traditional Brazilian elite, notwithstanding their relative freedom compared with women in Middle Eastern family regimes. In *Brasil: Terra de contrastes* (1964), Roger Bastide took brief note of how traditional Brazilian families disdained Syrian–Lebanese men who stemmed from humble origins:

> The traditional Brazilian family looks with a certain disdain at those *turcos*, as these immigrants are called still today. ... They became rich, it is certain; however Brazilians almost always see them as how they first arrived, carrying a sack on their backs, selling cheap goods from plantation to plantation. (Bastide 1964: 183)

Exercising mercantile professions, Arab men attained material capital, but their "origins" (which conflated class and ethnicity) limited the accumulation of symbolic capital or "distinction" fundamental to advancing marital pursuits among Brazilian elites (Bourdieu 1984).

In interviews and informal conversations, Christian Middle Eastern men frequently pointed to such *preconceito* (prejudice) and even *discriminação* (discrimination) faced by their forebears. After explaining the past preference for endogamy to safeguard family "customs" and "traditions," the second-generation Christian Lebanese engineer Wlademir emphasized that his father's generation had no choice but to look for eligible spouses among female co-ethnics. "In the past," he noted, "the Brazilian elite didn't want to [inter]marry, neither did the Arab, but also the Brazilian elite didn't want to marry with Arabs." Using similar language, Abdo explained that *quatrocentões* (Luzo-Brazilian elites) "never even mixed with those from here. ... So this difficulty made marriages really be within [our own] race." Another second-generation man reflected that in the past, "There really was prejudice" on the part of the *brasilii* (Brazilians, in Arabic) because of the "humble origins" of Middle Eastern immigrant families (cited in Greiber et al. 1998: 153). Brazilians, he explained, did not want to "mix" with *turcos*, who were viewed as "inferior beings." Older Middle Eastern men have thus remembered their own past derision by wealthy (non-Arab) Brazilians.

ETHNIC MASCULINITY, NATIONALIST IDEOLOGY, AND STATE IMMIGRATION POLICY

By the mid-twentieth century, Middle Eastern men were imagined quite differently in state and media spheres. In 1952, Caio de Freitas Guimarães, a researcher in the São Paulo State Statistical Bureau, reported that "Syrian men" showed an "elevated tendency" toward marriage with Brazilian women (65.03 percent) and, hence, evinced "miscegenation" (Guimarães 1952: 107).[10] Conspicuously absent was the skepticism of earlier scholarship that cast doubt on Middle Eastern men's high rate of exogamy and the undocumented descent of their supposedly Brazilian spouses.

Within the same decade, Middle Eastern men were depicted as "mixing" in Jorge Amado's *Gabriela, cravo e canela* (1998 [1958]). In the novel, one of the characters, seu Nacib (Mister Nacib), falls in love with the protagonist Gabriela, a metaphor for the Brazilian nationalist ideology of mixture. As the owner of a small tavern, Nacib first takes on Gabriela as a cook and later, as a lover. Nacib becomes so enamored of the cinnamon-skin-colored woman that he asks for her hand in marriage. The couple wed in a civil ceremony. "Only then," Amado writes, "one knew that Nacib was Mahometan." Although their inter-religious marriage cannot be sanctioned by the church, Nacib and the local Catholic priest agree that the couple's future offspring will be baptized (Amado 1998 [1958]: 321). This reflects the mid-twentieth-century erasure of the religious difference of Muslim men through the Christianization of their children. In courting and wedding the *mulata* Gabriela, Nacib epitomizes Middle Eastern men's entrance into the Brazilian nation.

Gabriela, cravo e canela takes place in a rural Bahian town "developing" with cacao monoculture in the 1920s. Inhabitants hail their town's "progress" but fret over the changing relations between men and women, especially in regard to sex and marriage. Stemming from a poor *mulata* family, Gabriela is not viewed as a suitable wife for the upwardly mobile Nacib. Not only do town elites look down on her; even Nacib's friends encourage him to keep Gabriela as a mistress and marry another woman for high-society circles. At the novel's end, Nacib and Gabriela annul their marriage and maintain their romance, not as husband and wife, but as proprietor and cook/mistress. In this light, Nacib confirms the place of Arab men in the Brazilian national narrative of mixture, but only by reproducing the hierarchies of race, gender, and class that repress poor women of color.

This Brazilian domestication of Arab masculinity contrasts with the U.S. American representation of the Middle Eastern man in Rodger and Hammerstein's musical film *Oklahoma!* (1955). As I mentioned in the introduction, one of the characters is the "Persian" peddler Ali Hakem. He is portrayed as comical and bawdy. Although he steers clear of marriage with U.S. American women, Hakem ceaselessly seeks to seduce them and is shunned by local townspeople for doing so. At the end of the film, Ali Hakem is forced to marry a U.S. American girl at the barrel of her father's shotgun. While Nacib is depicted as a "civilized man" who keeps a *mulata* as his mistress and sexually "mixes" into the Brazilian text, Hakem is represented as a sleazy hawker who must be forced to marry a white woman and thus assimilate into the U.S. American narrative. In this light, Nacib is sexualized in an ethnically dominant position and Hakem in an ethnically subordinate one within the nation.

In Brazil, *Gabriela, cravo e canela* was turned into a year-long soap opera on the Globo television network in 1975, and in 1983, it was made into a critically acclaimed film by Bruno Barreto.[11] Its theme about Arab men and interracial sexuality was further developed in Amado's *Tocaia grande* (1981). The novel focuses on a Maronite Catholic Arab peddler, Fadul Abdalla, known as *seu* Fadu or *Turco* Fadu. He is not only commercially adept but also sexually virile, called *Grão Turco* in rural bordellos. "Among experienced women," writes Amado, the Arab peddler "was bursting [*gozava*] with popularity." Fadul is said to "have a predilection for girls with plenty of flesh, with salient chests; voluminous breasts, good to squeeze with [his] enormous hand" (Amado 1981: 39). In compensation for services, Brazilian women working in cabarets receive boxes of rice powder, bottles of perfumed water, low-interest loans, and, in rare cases, metal rings with glass stones and other fake jewelry. In this macho cast, the Middle Eastern commercial essence is extolled in late twentieth-century Brazil.

Fadul's business prowess and sexual forays were recounted in a soap opera on the Manchete television network in 1995–96. The theme of Arab virility was not lost on Christian Middle Easterners. A middle-aged Lebanese man, Salim, who immigrated in the 1960s, commented to me that "Brazilian women like Arab men. There isn't a [Brazilian] woman who didn't try out an Arab man. Our race is hot, and the Brazilian women like it."[12] Similarly, Bassam qualified that Arab men are desired by Brazilian women and by their parents. Especially, parents wanted their daughters to "marry with Lebanese men," explained Zena, a second-generation Lebanese woman, because of their "fame" for being "good husbands, good fathers, with an open ... hand. ... That thing from our race." Her proud husband, Raul, agreed that Brazilians "wanted us to marry their daughters because we are good husbands [and] good parents." Arab masculinity was thus inserted into the Brazilian narrative of mixture.[13]

Ironically, around the same time that Arab men were represented as sexually mixing in the public sphere, the nationalist ideology of *mestiçagem*—as well as similar referents to the racial origins of potential immigrants—were removed from state immigration policy. Initiated in 1980, the Estatuto do Estrangeiro (Statute for the Foreigner) specified that the goal of temporary or permanent immigration was not to protect the nation's "ethnic composition" (as stated in previous times) but to advance its economic growth. Passed into law in 1980–81, the Statute for the Foreigner stated:

> Immigration will fundamentally aim to allocate specialized labor in various sectors of the national economy, in relation to the National Policy of Development in all of its aspects and especially to the growth of productivity, to the assimilation of technology, and to the attainment of resources for specific sectors (*Estatuto do Estrangeiro* 2000: 18).

The flows of people into Brazil have now been primarily justified and managed in terms of their potential to further "development." Although the necessity to help the national economy was stressed in previous statute laws, it became the stated primary rationale only in 1981, entailing the formal exclusion of racial criteria.

The statute's separation of nationalist ideology from state immigration policy was one current of a larger sea change. Felipe, who has headed the Federal Immigration Bureau in São Paulo for the past fifteen years, spoke about this and similar legislation in terms of the country's 1991 economic opening. He noted that new policies have been formulated to regulate the greater influx of "highly qualified executives" from multinational corporations in Europe and the United States and to protect the human rights of illegal immigrants who suffer as cheap, informal labor.[14] In the latter regard, a new resolution was passed to help immigrants' families. Specifically, "the concession of a temporary or permanent visa to entitle family reunification" was the normative resolution passed in 1999 (*Estatuto do Estrangeiro* 2000: 415). It finalized into law what had become common practice in the 1980s and '90s. Used to obtain residence and citizenship rights for immigrants' relatives and spouses, the "family reunification" clause represents the humanitarian face of a neoliberal Brazilian state that seeks to validate the influx of cheap labor.

"Family reunification," Felipe continued, serves as the legal mechanism with which current migrants attain residence and citizenship. Pointing to the residence request of a Lebanese migrant whose case folder was sitting on his desk, Felipe explained that the majority of Middle Eastern immigrants today come from southern Lebanon. Another major change, he explained, is their religion: Though mostly Christians came in the past, Muslim Lebanese overwhelmingly immigrate today. Working in family-run businesses, Lebanese were said to be honest workers fleeing from conflict and wanting to live in peace. With the "family reunification" resolution in immigration policy, Felipe explained, Lebanese immigrants have been able to obtain residence or citizenship through marriage ties with Brazilian-born Lebanese spouses.

Addressing the cultural logic of this marital arrangement, the state official then reflected on the idea of a "promised" marriage among peoples from
the "Orient." With an anthropological tone of voice, he stated that "promised
marriages" are prominent among Easterners—not only among Arabs but also
among Koreans and Chinese. "Orientals," he stated matter-of-factly, "do not
like mixing [*não gostam de se misturar*] with Brazilians, but prefer to marry
within their own race." In this light, not only has recent immigration policy
tacitly upheld Middle Eastern diasporic marriage, but state bureaucrats have
even spoken of it in a humanistic discourse. Dislodged from state structures,
the nationalist ideology of mixture has been replaced with a language that can
legitimate the influx of labor in the open economy.

Like the nationalist ideology of mixture, state immigration policy privi-
leges masculinity. The majority of Muslim Lebanese "family reunifications,"
explained Felipe, involve marriages between an immigrant Lebanese man and
a Brazilian-born Lebanese woman. But he qualified that he has never spoken
with a Lebanese Muslim woman. Although men have attained temporary residence status by wedding second-generation Lebanese women, the women's
fathers or brothers customarily have come to speak with him about the details
of a given visa application. This indicates that the state has had a direct hand
in the containment of Middle Eastern women by family regimes and that
masculinity has continued as the dominant basis for mixed and diasporic formations of Arab ethnicity. Upheld by both nationalist ideology and state policy, the ethnic project for Middle Eastern family reproduction has been forged
through male dominance. Whether in mixed or diasporic family ideals, men
have dominated the contours of Arab ethnicity in contemporary Brazil.

CHRISTIAN AND MUSLIM MARRIAGE IDEOLOGIES
IN THE PRIVATE SPHERE

Based on the conjugal histories of forty-four Syrian–Lebanese men in social and
religious associations in São Paulo, I discerned a subtle difference in marriage
practices among Christians and Muslims. In terms of endogamy, I found that
immigrant Christian men have been more likely to wed second-generation
Christian women, while immigrant Muslim men have tended to marry immigrant Muslim women. Seven of twelve immigrant Christian men wed second-
generation women, and four of seven immigrant Muslim men married
immigrant Muslim women. Similarly, second-generation Christian men
have been more likely to marry second-generation co-religionists, while
second-generation Muslim men have tended to wed immigrant co-religionists.
Ten of sixteen second-generation Christian men married second-generation

co-religionists, and five of nine second-generation Muslim men wed immigrant co-religionists. In exogamy, I found that among immigrants and in the second generation, Christian men have been more likely to marry non-Arab women (of European origins) than have Muslim men.[15] Nine of twenty-eight Christians married non-Arab women, while three of sixteen Muslims did likewise. My limited findings suggest that Christian Middle Eastern men have been more likely to marry second-generation and non-Arab Brazilian women while Muslim Middle Eastern men have tended to marry immigrant women.

Although Christian Arab men married second-generation women, they explained such endogamy in terms of *convivência* (conviviality or "coexistence"). "There still is a lot of marriage inside the *colônia*," related Dr. Charbel, a medical doctor, "only because they [Arabs] frequent the same clubs, they see each other a lot, and they end up going to the same parties and end up knowing and liking and marrying one another." Similarly, Ricardo, a second-generation man who married a second-generation Syrian woman, noted that "if you know ten people socially, and out of these ten, eight are from your *colônia*, the chance of your daughter or son dating someone from the *colônia* is greater." Likewise, the second-generation Syrian physician Dr. Arap explained that he and his two daughters married other Syrian–Lebanese descendants because they experienced a *convivência* in the clubs of the *colônia* where they each met their spouses. In this vein, the third-generation Fernando pointed out:

> You still are going to encounter a lot of marriage inside the *colônia*. ... But I think it is more because of being together, because of going to the same club. ... The social level of the *colônia* is upscale. It's not because of cultural isolation or isolation of roots. Frequenting the same club, the same bar ... you end up having a different relationship that will result in marriage.

Fernando, like many of his Christian counterparts, stressed that marriages between Syrian and Lebanese descendants have arisen out of frequenting the same social spaces. Although immigrant predecessors legitimated diasporic endogamy in terms of cultural preservation, their present-day descendants expressed it in a language of "conviviality."

Despite such endogamy, these Christians stressed that *o árabe se integra* (the Arab integrates himself) and *a colônia está aberta* (the community is open). Before noting his marriage to a "Lebanese daughter," Wadih, an immigrant Lebanese man, stated that "here [in Brazil], closed *colônias* do not exist. There is an inter-linkage between them." Likewise, the second-generation Lebanese Rafael—who did not mention his own marriage to a second-generation woman—explained, "You see that there doesn't exist a son of Lebanese or Syrians who isn't married to a daughter of an Italian, to a daughter of a Portuguese. ... The integration is total." Similarly, Lena, a second-generation woman who married a second-generation Lebanese man, explained that "mixed marriages are a good thing" because "we shouldn't remain closed. I think it's a good thing to join one with another." Even Mário, a second-generation Lebanese man whose daughter married a second-generation Lebanese, noted that "the Arab was the [immigrant] who most integrated himself, marrying into other *colônias*." Such contradictions between discourse and practice suggest that Christian Middle Easterners continue the marriage patterns of their co-religionist predecessors. But instead of speaking of Arab ethnicity in terms of "cultural maintenance," present-day descendants frame it in the idiom of integration and openness.

As a synonym for *mestiçagem* (mixture), this language of *integração* (integration) is based in reality. As mentioned earlier, a significant number of Christian Middle Eastern men married non-Arab Brazilian women.[16] In the nine interethnic marriages tallied, Middle Eastern men identified female spouses as second- or third-generation European "descendants," many (five of nine) referring to wives as *de origem italiana* (of Italian origins).[17] Although Middle Eastern men spoke of non-Middle Eastern wives in this "ethnic" language of *origens* (origins) and *descendência* (descent), their marital preference in terms of race was made implicit: They have wed white, not black or Asian, women.[18] This is mixture, but a kind that makes clear the still predominant, and thoroughly unequal, hierarchy of race in Brazil.

Ignoring the issue of race, several Christian interviewees articulated a culturalist identification when speaking of Arab and Italian intermarriage in Brazil. Wlademir, for instance, noted that "Arabs, ... in friendship and marriage, get along best with the *colônia italiana*, which is similar. They like music and dance." Likewise, Sandra, a third-generation Italian who married (and recently divorced) a second-generation Lebanese, explained that Arabs have "the same way, the same sense of family, that mania of everyone getting together to eat. ... They are two races that are well matched." Even Márcia, a second-generation Lebanese who wed a co-generational man, reflected, "I see more marriages with Italians. I think it's because they have a lot in common with Arabs. [Italians] are a talkative people. Arabs are talkative, as well. So I think it's a people to integrate more easily with." By way of this talk of culturalist integration, Christian Arabs have joined the national narrative of (whitening) mixture.

A mixed ethnicity seems to be developing in such marriages between Christian Middle Eastern men and women of European origins. One instance arose in the inauguration of a park named after the city of many Lebanese descendants in São Paulo, called Marjeyoun. Several mixed and diasporic families were present. Standing with her father and grandfather, a little girl seemed confused with the Arabic being spoken and asked whether "Brazilians" were in attendance. "Yes," the father responded. "Brazilians of Arab descent." Continuing, the father specified to his daughter, "Your granddad is a Lebanese descendant. You are a Lebanese descendant, too." The little girl then asked whether her other grandparents were also Lebanese. The father explained that the mother's family was Italian, not Lebanese. The little girl appeared even more curious, again asking, "And me?" The father concluded, "You are Italian and Lebanese. You're a mix [é uma mistura]." The inauguration of the Marjeyoun park thus provides a glimpse of a still emergent mixed ethnicity in Brazil. Forging a familial project in the model of mixture, Christian Arabs attempt to remain atop a shifting ethnic hierarchy in the nation.[19]

In contrast, Muslims have shown a greater tendency to practice diasporic endogamy (nine of sixteen). Although they did not adopt the language of mixture, interviewees lay stress on their nondiscriminatory motives. "Muslims marry in the colônia," stated Abdel, a second-generation Sunni Muslim Lebanese, "but not because of prejudice or discrimination. It is not a question of thinking that Brazilians are inferior. It is only a differentiation." Muslims do not discriminate, he added, because all races are welcome in Islam. A second-generation Druze Lebanese, Adnan, similarly explained that, although co-religionists are obliged to marry one another, they are not racist because Druze do not proselytize or convert outsiders into the religion. Likewise, Fuad, a Shia Muslim Lebanese, noted that, although he and his colleagues married co-religionists, "We have all races in the mosque." Although their Christian counterparts have tended to legitimate endogamy in the language of conviviality, Muslim Arabs have validated it in terms of racial equality, joining Islamic ideals with the Brazilian nationalist ideology of racial democracy.

Most important, Muslim Arabs, such as Hassan, have spoken of their endogamy in terms of cultural maintenance. Hassan, a second-generation Sunni Muslim, met his wife on vacation in Lebanon in the early 1980s. Sealing the union within the next few years, Hassan noted that non-Arab friends sometimes jested that he was "against Brazilians." In response to such criticism, Hassan stressed that it is "not about being against [Brazilians] ... but about us raising families." Brasilii, he continued, could not maintain his family's lifestyle, especially as regards the children. With some candor, Hassan stated, "What we look to pass onto the children is knowledge of this [Arab] culture, because this person tomorrow, he'll come to have two cultures [Arab and Brazilian]; he'll come to have the knowledge of two cultures. Is this wrong? No, it's important."

While present-day Christian Middle Easterners spoke of integration, the idiom of cultural maintenance used by co-religionists in the early twentieth century has been adopted by Muslim Middle Easterners. Fashioning an ethnicity through the ideal of a diasporic family unit, Muslims have reiterated the immigration policy of family reunification in contemporary Brazil.

Druze Middle Easterners have similarly formed a non-Christian Arab ethnicity in Brazil. The conjugal history of Adnan, a second-generation Druze Lebanese man in his thirties, is illustrative. Although his first marriage was to a Brazilian woman (of Italian descent), it came to an end several years ago. While visiting Lebanon in the 1990s, Adnan married a Druze woman. "All of the guys that I know," he noted, "went to marry there [in Lebanon]." Reflecting on this kind of conjugal union, Adnan remarked that women "influence a lot in this deal of the family"; the wife, he implied, is influential in instilling Druze Lebanese religious and cultural values in Brazilian-born children. Although the Druze intellectual Nagib Assrauy (1967) worried about the mixed marriages of co-religionists in the mid-twentieth century, Adnan and others have forged a Druze Arab ethnicity in the model of family reunification upheld by the neoliberal Brazilian state.[20]

Both Hassan and Adnan illustrate how Muslim difference in Arab ethnic hierarchy has been strengthened by the separation between nationalist ideology and state policy. But as I stated earlier, a small percentage of their co-religionists have wed non-Arab women (three of sixteen). In contrast to their Christian brethren in mixed marriages, though, Muslim Middle Eastern men have put emphasis on how their non-Arab wives (of European origins) learn Arab culture and language. For instance, Mohammed, a Sunni Muslim Lebanese immigrant, is married to Fabiana, a "Brazilian descendant of Italians and Portuguese." At the time of our conversation, Fabiana had traveled with the couple's young son to visit her in-laws in Lebanon. "She's so content there," commented Mohammed, "that she called last week to say that she's staying ten more days." After mentioning his wife's journey to Lebanon, Mohammed stressed Fabiana's fluency in Arabic. A colleague talking with us at the time reflected on his and others' contentment with the Arabic-speaking Brazilian woman. "It's a pleasure to see!" they exclaimed. Mohammed's contemporaries in the oldest Sunni mosque in São Paulo likewise pointed out that a number of non-Arab wives frequent religious services. Abdel, the second-generation Lebanese man mentioned earlier, reflected that the "Brazilian women who married Arab men are well integrated." Even in mixed marriage, Muslim men have affirmed Arabness through the ideal of diasporic family.

Of course, the world of non-Arab women who marry Muslim Middle Easterners is more complicated than such blanket statements suggest. Fabiana, for example, learned to speak Arabic because of her own interest in Arabness, and she is admired as a role model by male leaders of the community. Yet non-Arab women such as Fabiana experienced more difficulty relating to Arab women. Nayla, a second-generation woman "of Lebanese origin" (who does not speak Arabic well), once asked how this "woman outsider" could speak the language if she was not Lebanese. Fabiana responded, "Yes, I'm Brazilian but I speak Arabic. And you who are Lebanese, why don't you speak Arabic?" Although Arab men claim that Brazilian women are smoothly integrated, tensions surface between non-Arab and Arab women. It is the gendered politics of cultural preservation, however, that lies at the heart of such friction. Many non-Arab women who have Middle Eastern husbands and who converted to Islam were said to have been drawn to the lifestyle because of an affinity for Arabic dance and language. Respected as newfound guardians of Arab culture, non-Arab women can take over a role once relegated to and shouldered by Middle Eastern women. In this practice of exogamy, Arab ethnicity has gained greater emphasis in ways that potentially make irrelevant Arab women themselves.

INTENSIFIED IMAGES OF MUSLIM ARABNESS IN THE PUBLIC SPHERE

In 2001–2002, Muslim Arab conjugal lifestyles were featured in a popular Brazilian nighttime soap opera, *O Clone* (*The Clone*), on the Globo television network. Diverging from past emphases on Syrian–Lebanese men's commercial and sexual affairs in Brazil, *The Clone* focused on a *família árabe-muçulmana* (Muslim Arab family) living between Morocco and Brazil. The soap opera narrated the love story between a Brazilian boy, Lucas (Murilo Benício), and a Brazilian-born and -raised Moroccan girl, Jade (Giovanna Antonelli). In the first episodes, Lucas's twin brother, Diogo, is killed in Rio de Janeiro after cutting short a family excursion to Morocco. Having unknowingly slept with his father's new Brazilian girlfriend in Fez, Diogo dies before he has made peace with his estranged father. The father is heartbroken and holds himself responsible for his son's ill-fated destiny. No one, however, is more shook up than Albieri (Juca de Oliveira), a geneticist and the godfather of the twins. In a last-ditch effort to recover his preferred godson, Albieri miraculously clones Lucas's tissue cells and implants the embryo in an unsuspecting woman who gives birth to a boy who looks just like Diogo. As the title suggests, this boy is the "clone." But it is not the only one.

Central to the soap opera's main theme is Jade's unwavering pursuit to be with her true love, the Christian Lucas. In the wake of her mother's death in

Rio de Janeiro, Jade packs her bags for Fez to reside with a maternal uncle, 'Ali (Stênio Garcia). She falls instantly in love with Lucas during a chance meeting, and they become sexually involved in subsequent rendezvous throughout Fez. Jade nonetheless has been "promised" in marriage to a young Moroccan man, Said (Dalton Vigh). Swearing that she will marry only *por amor* (for love), Jade cannot convince her uncle 'Ali to approve her marriage to Lucas and is forced to wed Said. For the next several years, Jade frequently tries to flee from her husband in Morocco. Only in the last episode, however, is she reunited with Lucas in Brazil, nearly twenty years after their first encounter. By placing special emphasis on a Muslim Arab woman's struggle against male dominance and allegedly Islamic rules of marriage and sexuality, *The Clone*'s screenwriter Glória Perez sought to show that "Muslim women love, too. Muslims do not have anything against sexuality. … If you take the women of Islam, they transgress rules the entire time."[21] Subtextually, however, *The Clone* emphasized Muslim families' supposed adherence to patriarchal rules of marriage and sexuality. Justifying his control of women's marital choice in terms of Koranic principles, uncle 'Ali arranges the marriages of his daughter, Latiffa, and niece, Jade, to two Moroccan brothers, Mohammad and Said. Having immigrated with Latiffa to Rio de Janeiro, Mohammed would likewise plan the endogamous engagements of his two children nearly twenty years later.[22] Similarly invoking Islam to prevent Muslim women from marrying non-Muslim men, uncle 'Ali sought to arrange Jade's marriage to Said to prevent her permanently from marrying the Christian Lucas in Brazil. However, in response to Jade's unfailing refusal to submit to male authority in Morocco, Said initially condoned a failed public whipping of Jade in the penultimate episode. In focusing on the transgressions of one Muslim Arab woman, *The Clone* subtextually represented Muslim Arab family regimes (run by men) that defend allegedly Islamic rules of marriage and sexuality. Although it gave more visibility to Islam in a historically dominant Christian community, the soap opera presented Muslims as clones of the Orientalist imagination, as critiqued by Edward Said (1978).

Reproducing these dominant images, Christian Middle Easterners spoke about Muslim counterparts in terms of their allegedly religious aversion to mixing, despite little firsthand contact with non-Christians. Salim, an immigrant Christian Lebanese, remarked, "It's more difficult for Muslims to mix with Brazilians, because they're Christian." Especially in raising children, Salim noted, "Brazilians are really open and Muslims are really closed"—so much so that Muslim children "live in a military regime. They can't even go out with Brazilian children." Likewise, the second-generation Lebanese Christian Valéria reflected that Muslims do not "integrate themselves" not only because

Christianity is the major religion in Brazil, but also because parents do not let children socialize with non-Muslims. Another Christian Lebanese declared, "Here there are divisions in immigration—I think it's on the side of the Muslims, since they are conservative, they prefer to remain far from people, always remaining apart" (cited in Gattaz 2001: 208). Similarly, a second-generation Christian Lebanese youth reflected that

> Muslims from here [Brazil] are more closed in their community, only socializing with one another and avoiding contact with Brazilian society. The Muslim parents that I know ... do not motivate their children to study, be they men or women ... the men because they have the family business to keep going, and the girls because they are only prepared for marriage inside the community. (cited in Osman 1998: 299)

Christian Arabs have spoken of their Muslim counterparts as averse to martial and familial mixing. Both influencing and influenced by representations of 'Ali, Said, Mohammed, Latiffa, and others on *The Clone*, Christian Arabs have reproduced the stereotypical images of Muslims as religious zealots. Increased ethno-religious visibility thus does not necessarily mean the reduction of prejudice or discrimination.

Such assumptions of alleged Muslim isolationism arose during a family gathering of Bassam, an Orthodox Christian who left Lebanon in the 1960s. Now living in an upscale penthouse in a residential high-rise located in the posh Jardins neighborhood of São Paulo, Bassam first married the daughter of a Lebanese immigrant family in Brazil. After their divorce in the early 1980s, he was happily remarried to a third-generation Italian woman, whose several relatives were present at the soiree. Nibbling barbecue and sipping a whiskey on the rocks, I was introduced to Bassam's third-generation Italian brother-in-law, Marcos, and second-generation Lebanese nephew, Samir. After I mentioned my research interests, the conversation turned to the history of Lebanese and Italians in Brazil. After a few more barbecue skewers and whiskies, Marcos and Samir began to speak about the changing religious composition of the Lebanese community. Marcos noted that his brother-in-law's new neighbors in the building were a Muslim Lebanese family, adding, "Muslims don't mix." Samir nodded in agreement and repeated, "Yes, *o muçulmano não se mistura*." The two affinal relatives, who shared a Christian background, reflected that, although the new Muslim neighbors drank and ate with them, they never invited Christians to their parties in the same building complex.

In referring to the Muslim neighbors' alleged aversion to mixing, Marcos was alluding not only to their seeming social isolation, but also to their marriage practices. He and Samir gossiped about the Muslim neighbor's brother who was sent to Lebanon to marry a woman "promised" to him. The arranged engagement, however, had unfortunately ended in the brother's death in a car crash in Lebanon. What made matters worse was that the brother was found drunk with two girls in the car. "What a shame!" they bantered. Although it was not overtly expressed, the moral of the story seemed to be that Muslims who do not mix in Brazil lead lives that end in tragedy. Concluding, Marcos reflected that "the [Christian] Lebanese is better accepted [in Brazil] because he integrates himself." Standing beside his third-generation Italian in-law, Samir nodded in agreement and repeated: "*O libanês é melhor aceito porque se integra.*" By marginalizing their Muslim counterparts, Christian Middle Easterners have positioned their own ethnic and religious difference in the Brazilian nationalist ideology of mixture.

This intensified image of Muslim Arabness has developed alongside Christian Arabs' transformation of their own religious difference. Christian Arabs' religious roots lie in the Orthodox church (of the Patriarchate of Antioch) or in the Eastern Rites of the Roman Catholic church (the Maronite and Melkite). But many qualified that family members and relatives are now baptized in or irregularly frequent Roman Catholic churches. Curiously, while such Christian Arabs have been "Latinized"—to use the terminology of a Maronite priest—Brazilian Roman Catholics began to frequent Orthodox or Eastern churches. Claiming that São Paulo is home to the largest Orthodox Christian cathedral outside the Hagia Sophia in Istanbul, second-generation Valéria qualified that "very few *patrícios* go. It's mostly [non-Arab] Brazilians who go to mass now." In a related vein, Ricardo, a second-generation Orthodox Christian Syrian and churchgoer, noted that many "Brazilians from the Roman church" are not only marrying within the Orthodox church but formally joining the parish. "They find our mass beautiful," Ricardo said—"more beautiful than that of the Roman church." Flows of parishioners between Roman Catholicism and Eastern Christianities suggest that Christian Arabs' religious difference has been made innocuous in Brazil.

Muslim Middle Easterners, for their part, concur that Christian co-ethnics more fully "integrate" in Brazilian society. Abdel, Adnan, and Hassan assumed that Christian Middle Easterners have integrated with Brazilians socially and through marriage because of a shared religious background. However, they also reflected that such mixture has diminished Arabness. "Christians integrate themselves more," Abdel observed, "and for this [reason] lose their ties with the Arab world." Likewise, Adnan commented that "Christians marry more with Brazilians and lose a lot of their ties with being Arab." Qualifying that the Arabness of Christians becomes more "emotional,"

Adnan jested that Christians are *árabes de carteirinha* (card-carrying Arabs). Frequenting ethnic associations, Christians of Syrian–Lebanese descent were said to use Arab identity like an identification card, showing or hiding it in circumstantial ways. For Muslims, the "mixture" of Christian Arabs has implied cultural loss or inauthenticity.

In a similar vein, Nadia, a second-generation Muslim Lebanese, charged Christian co-ethnics as those "Brazilians who discriminate the most [against Muslims]." She commented that they had probably heard immigrant parents' or grandparents' stories about Muslims' alleged persecution of Christians in Mount Lebanon and Syria (supposedly precluding their emigration). Since descendants learn of the Arab world only through the sectarian lens of their Christian forebears, Nadia concluded, they end up discriminating the most against Muslims. Perhaps as a consequence, Abdel noted, Christians rarely frequent the gatherings organized by Muslim Arab-run associations: "We go to their events more than they go to ours."[23] Such perspectives, however, are silenced by the public representation of Muslims as alleged isolationists. Although Muslim Arabs have gained greater visibility today, they continue to be subordinated in relation to historically dominant Christian Arabs. But this hierarchy has shifted in a significant way since the early twentieth-century effacement of Muslim difference in Brazil. The current intensification of Muslimness seems likely to continue in neoliberal immigration policy and the nationalist ideology of mixture still relevant in the Brazilian public sphere.

IN MARRIAGE IDEOLOGIES, the Arab ethnic project has reflected the neoliberal separation between the nationalist precept of mixture and state immigration policy. In earlier times, Arab ethnicity was homogenized and questioned in Brazilian nation-making. In the late twentieth century, however, Christian Arabs situated themselves within the ideology of mixture and spoke of their endogamy in the nationalist language of integration. At the same time, Muslim subjects fashioned their own ethnic identity in the ideal of diasporic "family reunifications." Upheld today by Brazilian immigration policy, Muslim Arab family regimes have been cloned by a soap opera in their alleged Islamic adherence to patriarchal rules of marriage that forbid mixture. As Christian Arabs emphasized their own social, religious, and marital mixture, Muslim Arab ethnicity—and its fabricated isolationism—has intensified in the contemporary Brazilian public sphere.

This chapter's inquiry into the religio-political and racial overtones that inform Middle Eastern marital regimes pushes one to reconsider the relationship between alleged "national integration" and seeming "ethnic preservation" in ways that go beyond an either–or perspective, beyond thinking it must be one or the other. As Jeffrey Lesser has pointed out, the ideology of *mestiçagem* not only implies "the emergence of a new and uniform Brazilian 'race' out of the mixing of peoples," but also the "joining (rather than mixing) of different identities, as the creation of a multiplicity of hyphenated Brazilians rather than a single, uniform one" (Lesser 1999: 5). My exploration of the religious dimension of this multiplicity has revealed that Muslim ethnic difference— once "assimilated" into a Christian-dominated community—has now been acknowledged by the Brazilian state and ironically limited by greater media visibility.

PART III

Marketing
Ethnic Culture

〜

FIVE

Ethnic Reappropriation in the Country Club Circuit

S YRIAN, LEBANESE, OR ARAB nationalisms—in addition to Eastern Christian and Islamic traditions—inspired dozens of social, charity, and religious associations in early twentieth-century São Paulo. Today gaining renown in the *colônia* and the public sphere, these institutions have become luxurious spaces for the consumption of hummus and caviar, belly and ballroom dances, as well as lute-like *oud* and karaoke performances. In these hybrid leisure circles, though, socialites of Syrian–Lebanese origin have emphasized Middle Eastern culturalist styles of food, dance, and music that have been popularized in the increasingly diverse Brazilian market.

This chapter traces the consumptive formation and transformation of Syrian–Lebanese ethnicity in Brazil through the assimilationist paradigm that lasted until post–World War II times and the diversified service sector model in the late twentieth century. Middle Eastern cultural forms were marginalized in the earlier paradigm but have gained popularity in the current moment. Deemed to be unappetizing, raucous, or exotic by past Brazilian pundits, food, music, and dance with an Arab appeal have been now marketed to those with highbrow and lowbrow tastes. My contention is that Middle Eastern country club directors and members have gained symbolic power in this context and converted it into social capital among (non-Arab) Brazilian elites.[1]

Situating this development within a large body of scholarship on the politics of food, music, and dance in Brazil, I aim to challenge conventional ways of thinking about cultural appropriation. Whether focusing on *feijoada* (blackbean stew with meat), Carnival samba schools, or Candomblé, earlier works emphasized their usurpation by national elites and market forces (Fry 1982; Queiroz 1985). Later work on the same cultural staples has put stress on the ostensible authors, especially their resistance to or contestation of the meanings of the appropriated cultural forms (Browning 1995; Guillermoprieto 1990; Sheriff 1999). I suggest that these approaches employ a similar dichotomy in power relations between "appropriator" and "appropriated." Even in recent emphases on the agency of the appropriated, scholars depicted appropriators as the primary possessors of power. But what if the appropriated enjoy significant social power? This chapter shows that when a group whose culture is appropriated enjoys such power, it can retake the cultural appropriation in a way that further benefits itself.

In the late twentieth century, Middle Eastern culinary, music, and dance forms have been appropriated by the Brazilian national market. Whether it is the lowbrow Habib's fast-food chain, with more than 150 franchises in the country, or belly dancing in uptown studios and a prime-time soap opera, "Middle Eastern culture" is produced through national circuits (Luxner 2000; Vasconcellos 2000). Ethnic subjects have viewed this popularization of *coisas do árabe* (things Arab) not as obstructive or degrading, but as a creative integration of Syrian and Lebanese in Brazil. In this milieu, Brazilians of Middle Eastern descent have made claims to more authentic forms of cuisine and dance in their community-owned clubs, despite contracting restaurant staffs and professional dancers from the mainstream market. Inviting influential Arab and non-Arab Brazilians to memorial, culinary, and other events, socialites have converted the newfound symbolic power of ethnic commodities into social capital (Bourdieu 1977: 179–83). Retaking the appropriation of Arab culture, Syrian–Lebanese descendants have sought and gained greater recognition in a consumptively diversified Brazil.

"UNSAVORY" DIASPORIC LEISURE CIRCLES IN THE EARLY TWENTIETH CENTURY

Departing Mediterranean harbors to Brazilian ports in the late nineteenth and early twentieth centuries, immigrants traveled alongside emergent Lebanese, Syrian, and Arab nationalist ideas. Such flows resulted in the establishment of more than one hundred Middle Eastern associations in Brazil during the first half of the century. One of the first such entities in São Paulo was the Esporte Clube Sírio (Syrian Sport Club, or ECS), founded by a group of sports-minded *moços sírios* (Syrian male youth) in 1917. Fundraising in later years enabled the club to purchase a large piece of real estate in the now "noble" neighborhood of Moema. These leisure affairs were romanticized by an Arab Brazilian intellectual as a "spiritual revolution of the immigrant and ... a symbol of the idea of civic struggle" (Jamil Safady, as cited in Jorge Safady 1972a: 27).

But this "spiritual revolution" engendered another rebellion. At the same time that the Syrian club was praised, some Lebanese "withdrew" to establish the Clube Atlético Monte Líbano (Mount Lebanon Athletic Club, or CAML). Dubbed a "cessation" by a former Syrian club president, the "Lebanese" withdrawal arose out of a *briga de família* (family quarrel) involving the powerful Jafet family, who donated a sizable piece of land for the Lebanese club in the same neighborhood. A second-generation Syrian medical doctor, Dr. Samoel, reflected that, although many Jafet family members were sympathetic to Arab nationalism, an older brother, Basílio, and his wife, Adma, were ardent, even fanatical, "Lebanese nationalists."[2] The couple joined forces with other Lebanese nationalists in São Paulo, including the journalist Chukri al-Khuri, in clamoring for Lebanese distinction in the erstwhile *colônia "síria."*[3] Remembering that Lebanon was really part of the greater Syrian nation, Dr. Samoel went on to explain that the division between the Lebanese and Syrian social clubs derived from the French colonial separation of "Lebanon" from "Syria" in the 1920s.

In addition to the ECS and CAML, there were at least a dozen smaller *clubes* founded by brethren of the same city or region. Immigrant families from the city of Homs (in western Syria), for instance, formed Club Homs in 1924. Families from other areas in Syria or Lebanon likewise established Clube Aleppo, Sociedade Antioquina, Clube Hasbaya, Clube Marjeyoun, Club Rachaia, and Zahlé Club in early twentieth-century São Paulo. A middle-aged socialite explained that the Esporte Clube Sírio served as the "mother club" of smaller clubs named after cities in Syria (such as Aleppo and Homs), and Monte Líbano was the "mother club" of those entities named after cities in Lebanon (such as Marjeyoun and Zahlé). Although families frequented events in several associations, the majority possessed membership titles to a respective smaller city-based club and the corresponding "national" club, either the ECS or CAML. In the early twentieth century, nationalist ideologies in the Middle East shaped the boundaries of Middle Eastern leisure spaces in Brazil.[4]

Regional and nationalist rivalries in the Middle East were also transposed onto the *colônia*, frequently expressed through the idiom of sports competition between country clubs. Sami, a member of the Sociedade Antioquina, narrated a story about a *torneio de taulé* (backgammon tournament) sponsored by Club Homs in mid-twentieth-century São Paulo.[5] Since its members made up nearly half of the participants in the competition, the Club Homs board of directors had a one-meter-tall bronze cup made for the champion, assuming that one of its own members would win. But a member of the nearby Antioch Society won the contest, and a festive parade was planned by that club's members. In the words of Sami:

> Since the cup was [at Club Homs] on Avenida Paulista … and our club was on Rua Cubatão … the distance was two kilometers and a bit, I made the suggestion that on a Sunday afternoon we'd bring musicians there, *da própria raça* [from our own race], who play the violin, acoustic guitar, and *derbake* [Arab drum], and we went there and started to take turns carrying [the cup]; we came on foot, playing [music] and saying, "Long live the champion! Long live the champion!"

Thus, the club named after the former Syrian city of Antioch reveled in its upset victory over *homsienses* (natives of Homs).[6]

But these spaces did not fit into the dictatorial regime of Getúlio Vargas and the xenophobic Brazilian state during the World War II era. As was described in Chapter 4, while immigration quotas were passed to stem the entrance of undesirable non-Europeans, a related gamut of laws ensured the assimilation and mixture of resident immigrant communities (*colônias*). Their perceived "linguistic difference" drew special attention from state elites. In the Estado Novo regime, the Decreto de Exigência Patronímica (Decree of Fatherland Name Demands) "nationalized" the "foreign" names of immigrant associations.[7] Dozens of immigrant-run associations that bore "foreign names" were required by law to adopt so-called Brazilian appellations.[8] The Esporte Clube Sírio, for instance, temporarily changed its name to Club das Bandeiras (Club of Flags). The Liga das Damas Ortodoxas (League of Orthodox Ladies) permanently adopted the name Sociedade Mão Branca (White Hand Society). Enforced by the Vargas regime during World War II times, "naming" was an inherently nationalist undertaking.[9]

Luso-Brazilian elites, called *quatrocentões*, also disparaged Middle Eastern immigrants. As examined in Chapters 1 and 3, Syrian–Lebanese had solidified their rise from peddlers to store owners and industrialists by the 1920s. Although they commanded increasing amounts of material capital and property, however, they continued to be derided by *quatrocentões*. These decadent aristocrats still held on to the reins of power in elite country clubs, such as Clube Paulistano, Jockey Clube de São Paulo, and the Iate Clube de Guarujá. Middle Easterners amassed enough material capital to afford the latter's exclusive membership costs, but they did not garner the cultural capital still monopolized by those elites *de berço* (from the crib). Assad explained, "I recall that until the start of 1930, 1940, Syrians and Lebanese were even seen with a certain disdain by the so-called Brazilian *quatrocentões*." Such disdain, remembered Sami, was the reason that "so many Arab clubs existed" in pre–World War II times—namely, "because Arabs were badly viewed in Brazil." In the words of Sandra, a second-generation Italian woman who married into a Lebanese family and frequented Monte Líbano, "There was a lot of friction between the Paulistano and the Monte Líbano [clubs], a lot of friction." Its source, she noted, stemmed from the fact that the *quatrocentões* were "really closed and quite snobby" and barred Arab and Italian nouveaux riches from their social circles. Fomenting such resentment was the greater purchasing power of immigrant families, which allowed them to afford cars, real estate, and, most of all, leisure spaces that rivaled the clubs of the traditional aristocracy.

In this context, food was used by Brazilian elites to mark Middle Easterners' unsavory difference. Journalists who reported on Rua 25 de Março in the 1950s and '60s, for instance, reveled in the "foreignness" of the smells and sights arising from taverns of "Oriental foods." In the *O Estado de S. Paulo* article "A velha rua do quibe cru," the reporter Gabriel Marques was pleased with the "commercial puissance" of 25 de Março, though he did not digest its culinary elements.[10] Entering a *barzinho* (small tavern), he related, a *sírio* asked him, "Now, what would you prefer? '*Humus b'tahine*' or simply '*kafta*'?" Perplexed with such strange-sounding dishes, Marques replied, "What?" His Syrian friend, Salim, then translated, "Do you want chickpea paste or a ground-meat patty?" Like all "hospitable Arabs," according to Marques, Salim continued to offer dishes: "And wouldn't you prefer an *esfiha*? Or would you prefer *kibe*? Or would you want a bit of raw *kibe*? Or would you like *kibe* with *labne*? The stuffed grape leaves are excellent! Choose, man! Choose!" "Frankly," Marques concluded, "none of it looked appetizing." Food marked Arabs' outsider or peripheral status in the nation.

Popular lore also serves up mouthfuls of the seemingly foreign culinary practices of *turcos*. Numerous middle-aged to elderly Middle Eastern professionals recounted that *turcos* who peddled across the hinterlands were often viewed by Brazilian landowners and peasants as cannibals whose favorite dish was children. The unflattering rumor was said to have started when a *patrício* was viewed eating a delicacy called *kibe nyi* (raw ground lamb meat mixed with bulgur wheat, served with raw onions and olive oil). Since the consumption of raw meat was unknown by most in the country at that time (though it is less so today), Brazilians mistakenly assumed that the meat was human, not lamb or beef. This suspicion of cannibalism is often attached to liminal figures who accumulate "fast wealth" (Smith 2001: 804).

In related ways, the exotic character of Middle Eastern music and dance also attracted journalistic scrutiny. In the early 1930s, Guilherme de Almeida wrote, "I am walking down [the street] under the screams of an ... unexpected gramophone. It's a swaying music, really murmuring like the noise from water shaking in cans. I see a belly and a bellybutton dancing in this music. There are swaying bellies and bellybuttons in all the doorways in step with the gramophones."[11] Having ventured into a tavern with this "swaying music," Almeida again expresses his Orientalist imagination: "On the counter, the eternal gramophone so easily murmurs a belly dance. From the monotonous melody, there at times jumps a woman's ululation."[12] Like culinary markers, Middle Eastern music and dance forms reinforced the foreignness of Middle Eastern difference in the nation. As we shall see later, however, these once alien cultural expressions have been transformed into familiar cultural staples in contemporary Brazil.

POPULARIZING ARAB CULTURE IN
THE NATIONAL MARKET

Linked to Middle Eastern nationalisms in mid-twentieth-century Brazil, Syrian–Lebanese country clubs have gained renown as extravagant spaces nearly fifty years later, with indoor or outdoor squash and tennis courts, Olympic-size pools, up-to-date gym facilities, and ballrooms large enough for two thousand guests. On Avenida Paulista, Club Homs, in the words of one director, is "worth its weight in gold." A membership title (*titular de sócio*) costs ten thousand Brazilian reais, in addition to the one hundred reais monthly charge. In the upper-class neighborhood of Moema, the Esporte Clube Sírio spans 55,000 square meters. A membership title there costs about twelve thousand reais, plus monthly fees in the range of two hundred reais. Within five minutes by car is the Clube Atlético Monte Líbano, occupying 45,000 square meters. The *titular de sócio* is sixty thousand reais, plus four hundred reais in monthly fees. Because these clubs serve upper-middle-class families, membership titles are granted only if they are accompanied by letters of reference from at least two members. Middle Eastern clubs, in these financial and social terms, have now become as exclusive as the clubs of traditional Luso-Brazilian elites.

Embraced by state authorities as well, the Clube Monte Líbano and Esporte Clube Sírio have recently joined the Association of Sport Clubs and Socio-Cultural Club Members of São Paulo (ACESC). The association was founded in 1995 by a dozen or so elite country clubs, as well as the São Paulo state government. The association is not limited to traditional elites; the select "in" crowd also includes so-called *clubes das colônias*, or "clubs of [immigrant] communities," such as Jews and Arabs. In addition to providing a wider network to all members, the ACESC brings together elite country clubs in "cultural marathons," where officials from the state Ministry of Culture evaluate the art, music, and theater productions of socialites from a dozen or so entities.[13] Whereas the Brazilian state sought to efface the ethnic difference of Middle Eastern "civic associations" during the Vargas era, it has added to their symbolic status and institutional basis today.

These class- and government-based alliances have been accompanied by Middle Eastern clubs' greater exclusivity in terms of race. Non-whites rarely frequent such spaces. In the few instances when I did see blacks or Asians in the three largest clubs of the *colônia*, their presence was met with racist or snide remarks. Once when two well-dressed black men attended an Arab gala, a club director noted, "They're probably bodyguards." When I asked how he could be sure, he answered: "They look it." Even Asians provoked surprise. As "*japoneses*" walked through the main entrance of another club, a forty-year-old woman joked, "They're in the wrong club! This is an Arab club!" Though exclusionary toward blacks and Asians, Arab clubs accepted Jews. Especially in the ACESC-sponsored competitions mentioned earlier, only kind words have been exchanged between Arab and Jewish bourgeoisie. Although subtle tensions have occasionally surfaced, both *árabes* and *judeus* have claimed to "get along well," reflecting Brazilian nationalist ideology itself (explored in the next chapter).[14]

In addition to the three largest sports/social clubs of the *colônia*, there are several others that garner smaller membership rosters and real-estate properties, such as Aleppo, Antioquina, Hasbaya, Marjeyoun, Rachaya, and Zahlé. In contrast to the ECS and CAML, city-based associations have been known for only "social" or "cultural" affairs—namely, because of their lack of athletic facilities. Most tellingly, these country clubs have been generally frequented by families of more modest middle-class backgrounds. Since relatively fewer descendants attend such clubs today, however, the executive directors of several of them have tried to institute a social calendar that appeals to younger generations and a wider audience. In one attempt, country club directors institutionalized weekly or monthly *jantares árabes* (Arab dinners), complete with Middle Eastern cuisine and entertainment. This undertaking by middle-class clubs, described more fully later, has emulated leisure projects in other, wealthier clubs, such as the Esporte Clube Sírio and Monte Líbano.

Alongside these transformations, "Arab food" has been popularized in late twentieth-century Brazil. As early as the 1970s, the anthropologist Arturo Ramos was cited as saying that Syrian–Lebanese Brazilians' "dishes and alimentary habits ... influence large cities: meat skewers (*láhme mixue*), *kibe*, the principal plate; *minjádra*, the popular plate of lentils; *fatuxi, tabúl-i*" and other sweets (cited in Diégues 1976 [1952]: 146). As colleagues pointed out, one can purchase a *kibe*, a cooked meat patty with bulgur wheat, or *esfiha* in any tavern or restaurant today. Sandra, the Italian descendant who married a second-generation Lebanese man, noted that "Arab food" has become popularized only in the past ten years. "In the past," she recalled, "it wasn't like this. You had to go to 25 de Março or be invited to dine in the house of an Arab family." But nowadays, "*esfiha* is like *pão de queijo* (cheese bread)," eaten "by everyone." Likewise, a Lebanese woman remarked that "Brazilians eat *esfiha* like rice and beans." As noted in Chapter 2, *esfiha* has even entered the political lexicon. In the context of formal state investigations of "irregular" political dealings in São Paulo, lay and media onlookers modified the popular expression "*Vai acabar em pizza* [It will end in pizza]," meaning, "Nothing will come of it," as "*Vai acabar em esfiha* [It will end in meat pies]."

Middle Eastern meat pies have gained prominence due to *Habib's, A cadeia de fast-food árabe* (Habib's Arab fast-food chain). Since its founding in 1988, Habib's arabesque marketing has been copied by a half-dozen smaller chains and hundreds of independently owned *esfiharias* (meat-pie joints). The chain's trademark is a genie named Habib, with a fez, thick moustache, and sleeveless vest.[15] Second only to McDonald's in profit, Habib's serves *esfihas*, tabouleh, baklava, and other fast food in its nearly 150 establishments, which are concentrated in Rio de Janeiro and São Paulo (see Luxner 2000). For Rení, a public-relations director, Habib's is "a chain that popularized Arab food because today, from north to south in the country, everyone knows something about Arab cuisine [*culinária árabe*]. They know that the *esfiha* is Arab, and eat it, and value it, and like it." As mentioned at the beginning of this book, journalists estimate that "in the capital [city of São Paulo] alone, 1.2 million *esfirras* are [served] each day; 55 percent come from the large chains Esfiha Chic and Habib's."[16] Ostensibly, Middle Eastern culinary forms have become familiar objects of consumption today in the Brazilian market.

But this arabesque extends beyond Brazil. In fact, Habib's Arab fast-food chain has recently expanded into the Americas. Since 2000, the company has opened dozens of restaurants in Mexico City and set its sights on the U.S. American market. Using the same "Arab" marketing strategy across the hemisphere, Habib's founder and chief executive, Dr. Alberto Saraiva, intended to open restaurants in Florida and California in 2001. But after September 11, 2001, the company's plans were indefinitely shelved in view of anti-Arab violence in the United States. The explicitly Arab advertising that Habib's has used in Brazil and Mexico, the company thought, would be shunned by the U.S. American public. It is perhaps for this reason that labels such as "Mediterranean" and "Middle Eastern" are often adopted by restaurants that feature Lebanese or Arab cuisine throughout the United States.[17] While eating establishments explicitly identified as "Arab" are lucrative across Latin America, they are usually called "Mediterranean" or "Middle Eastern" to attract clientele in the United States.

The contemporary Brazilian market offers not only Arab fast-food chains but also numerous middle- and highbrow restaurants. They are so familiar, in fact, that hip characters refer to *restaurantes árabes* on television sitcoms.[18] During my research, I located sixty-one such establishments in the greater São Paulo region alone. Concentrated in "noble neighborhoods," such as Jardins, Itaim-Bibi, and Moema, nearly half of these restaurants were founded in the 1990s, while the other half were established in the 1980s. Only three or four have operated for more than twenty years. Samir, who runs the elegant restaurant Folha de Uva near Avenida Paulista, was well aware of this growing concentration.[19] He recounted:

> We founded the restaurant in '89. ... From then until now it's changed a lot because the country's economy has changed a lot. ... Many firms had to lay off workers, and the job market shrank. ... Many big firms in Brazil also started to give incentives to high-salaried workers to step away from the firm. ... So if you worked for ten ... years in a firm, they'd offer you what you had the right to and one more [monthly] salary for each year you worked ..., and a severance package. ... So you'd always leave with a good bit of cash. The majority of people who left with this capital, the first thing that they thought they should do in life is set up a restaurant. So from then until now, there has been a very large increase in the number of restaurants.

As a more than ten-year veteran, Samir made sense of the recent increase in the number of restaurants vis-à-vis the overall decline of Brazilian industry in the 1990s.

Such reflections resonate with quantitative analyses of the sectoral distribution of labor in the Brazilian economy (Baer 1995). In 1950, 62 percent of the country's labor was allotted to agriculture; industry was 13 percent; and services were 25 percent. Forty years later, in 1990, however, labor distributed in agriculture plummeted to 23 percent; industry reached 23 percent; and the service sector overtook them both, at 54 percent. Equally telling has been the sectoral distribution of the gross domestic product (GDP). From 1980 to 1990, agriculture fell from 11 percent to 9 percent of the GDP; industry also declined, from 41 percent to 34 percent. But the service sector increased from 49 percent to 57 percent of GDP. In this postindustrial model of development (Parker 1999: 153), the diversification of culinary businesses forms part of the late twentieth-century expansion of Brazil's service sector.[20]

Favorable cultural representations have reinforced these structural forces. A close (non-Arab) family friend once remarked that a few *restaurantes árabes* can be very beneficial when one wants to "give a good impression for a client" and "seal a deal." Samir himself noted that the majority of his weekday clientele are business and liberal professionals. This newfound currency of Arab cuisine has been made especially apparent in the food columns of mainstream newspapers. The well-known food critic Josimar Melo has frequently reviewed middle- to high-brow Arab restaurants—Baalbeck, Halim's, Miski, Arábia, Khayyam, and Folha de Uva—in his weekly column in *Folha de S. Paulo.*[21] His reviews, however, stand in contrast to the "unsavory" opinions of Gabriel Marques and others of the 1960s. Take, for example, Melo's appraisal of the recently inaugurated Arguile, which was opened by the son of a well-known restaurateur from one of the first Middle Eastern eateries, Jacob's, in the 1970s. After taking note of this genealogy, Melo reveled in the restaurant's "elegant" surroundings, including tapestries, *narguiles* (water pipes, in Lebanese Arabic, or hookas), and antiques imported from Lebanon:

> The elaborate ... family touch is present in the menu. The patés are well balanced (of chickpeas, of eggplant, of yogurt cheese); the meat of the raw *kibe* is consistent; the *esfiha* is delicate ...; they're dishes that create a good impression. The stuffed cabbage has a good filling, in spite of the fact that the cabbage leaf almost dissolved from being so cooked (much better is the ... stuffed eggplant, nicely firm and savory). All this is part of a laudable rotisserie with a fixed price, with dishes carried to tables by the waiters. *Kibe* with yogurt, stuffed lamb viscera, *michui* [grilled ground meat, in Arabic; *sic*] of Argentine steak are other specialties that can be savored before taking a few drags on the aromatic tobaccos from the *narguilés* [water pipes, in Lebanese Arabic; *sic*].

Middle Eastern cuisine, represented as exotic and "unappetizing" in the past, has now made the newspaper columns of fine food critics, constituted by an elegant discourse of its "well-balanced," "impressive," "laudable," and "savory" flavor and display.

Middle Eastern music and dance forms have also become very popular in Brazil, especially since the soap opera *The Clone* aired in 2001–2002. Its televised images of Arab women and men helped touch off a consumption frenzy involving belly dancing classes, supplies, and music. Weeks after *The Clone*'s debut on the Globo television network, a newspaper article related that enrollments in São Paulo's belly dancing academies had "increased by as much as 80 percent."[22] Of the thirty-five dance schools that I non-randomly contacted, sixteen offered classes in *dança do ventre*. Praised as "benefiting" and "furthering" women's sexuality, belly dancing has not been ridiculed as a foreign custom but represented as a gender-specific and physiologically advantageous exercise.[23]

Capitalizing on this transformation, Globo television tycoons prepared several lines of merchandise to be released within weeks of the soap opera's first airing. Items included attached wrist and finger bracelets, "Moroccan" leather sandals, and Middle Eastern music CDs.[24] Concurrently, a third-generation Syrian Brazilian established a national franchising enterprise modeled after his twenty-year old Egyptian Tea House, Khan el-Khalili, which specializes in similar "Eastern" goods and belly dancing accessories.[25] A female proprietor in the same market niche captured the logic of this sudden surge in the popularity of Arab dance forms in Brazil: "What is on the eight o'clock soap opera becomes fashionable." Once viewed as exotica limited to the Arab-run business district in downtown São Paulo, belly dancing has become a mass-mediated and mass-marketed phenomenon today.

Likewise, there has been a recent boom in *festas árabes* (Arab fests or parties). In one niche, informal financiers have held bimonthly events in bars around the city with live Arab music bands and belly dancers. At these events, the partygoers—Arab men, some Arab women, and many non-Arab women—come together in the Lebanese folk dance, *dabke*. During interludes, Middle Eastern pop music and European techno rhythms are blasted. In another niche of this sector, established "theme-party" businesses provide a list of themes for clients, including romantic subjects such as "love" and ethnic ones, such as "Italian" or "Arab." Key culturalist elements of a *festa árabe* include serving *kibe*, *esfihas*, tabouleh, and other "Arab foods"; playing live or taped Arab music; and belly dancing. An executive in this market niche explained that popular interest in the Arab party theme was "influenced by the media ... [which] awakens curiosity about 'Oriental mystery.'" She concluded that "the world is more globalized, and we have more access to all cultures in a general way. Because of this, Brazilians are giving more respect to these cultures that are so different, like that of the Arabs." Today, Middle Eastern culturalisms have become popular commodities in the Brazilian public sphere.

SOCIAL COMMENTARY AND CONNECTIONS THROUGH ARAB CULTURE

Roughly eighty Middle Eastern entities have come to form part of an exclusive, "who's who" social circuit in contemporary São Paulo. The events held include thematic Arab dinners, independence day celebrations (of Lebanon, Syria, and Brazil), club anniversary galas, arts concerts, and even

simpler get-togethers. Such affairs almost always feature a formal announcement of the names and titles of figures from country clubs, charity leagues,
or political circles who attend, who send regards by mail, or who receive a *homenagem* (tribute). Lasting from five to twenty minutes, this protocol has
ensured amicable relations among cohorts, as well as appeased those who *que-
riam aparecer* (want to appear or make a show). This invidious comparison
seems to be a taken-for-granted dimension of *colônia* events. Among the
dozens of executives, politicians, medical doctors, and lawyers at gatherings,
I have met upwardly mobile professionals ready to make introductions and,
perhaps, exchange business cards.

This bourgeois ambience has led many Middle Easterners—especially
immigrants—to criticize cultural associations of the *colônia* in terms of class
disparities. "I don't like the clubs," stated Salim, a naturalized Syrian immigrant,
"because of those rich people who frequent them." "Birds of a feather," he
noted, "flock together." Since Salim does not consider himself one of "those rich
people," he has found it stressful to visit the clubs of the *colônia*. Likewise, an
immigrant medical doctor, Sarkis, noted that the "pioneers who founded the
clubs ... had the idea to leave the clubs open, but unfortunately, the second,
third generation do not know how to do this." In earlier times, membership
was contingent not on "the condition to pay a fortune" but, rather, on the ability to "collaborate with the work, not in money." Today, Sarkis concluded, the
clubs have "changed, and they're really closed." Only wealthy descendants and
their influential guests seem welcome in various associations of the *colônia*.

Other Middle Easterners have expressed annoyance with the invidious
comparison in the club circuit. "These clubs are all *papo furado* [hot air],"
related Iskander, a naturalized Lebanese immigrant who runs a travel agency.
"They don't help any Arabs. ... They [club members] only like to hear their
names announced at events." At these gatherings, Iskander purposefully reg-
isters using a title from a non-Arab organization to upset representatives of
other ethnic entities. An artist who is an avid club member likewise noted that
she spends more time in the gym than at social or cultural affairs, because
"people go really *chique,* I mean, really *alinhado* [well aligned or put together].
But I think that in Brazil, it's like this, but the Arab is also really like this with
clothes. Arabs seem to like to show off, so they're really *alinhado.*" Likewise,
Samir, the Syrian doctor, reflected:

> I am not an assiduous frequenter, and not ... how do you say? ... a club
> rat that passes all his time inside the club: "My life is the club. I dine at
> the club. I eat lunch at the club." On the contrary, I find so many clubs a
> pain! Still, the club that I go to is of the *colônia árabe.* If I could sell all of

my club membership titles from the *colônia*, I would buy a membership title from a neutral club that wasn't of any *colônia*, only to feel at home and to play sports with ease, because in the *clubes da colônia* everyone knows about everyone's life.

In spite of the ethnic "refinement" or "authenticity" pursued by club administrations, several Middle Easterners have expressed frustration and even annoyance with the upscale pretensions and prying intrusions of socialites in the varied clubs of the *colônia*.

Ethnics are not alone in differentiating and debating the exclusive character imputed to their community-owned entities. Rení, the (non-Arab) executive from Habib's mentioned earlier, reflected, "I know that in the *colônias árabes* ... the Sírio, Monte Líbano, all of those clubs ... they're *clubes elitizados* [elitist clubs]. They're not popular clubs, normal clubs. They're *clubes elitizados* ... *redutos de ricos* [havens for the rich]." Not specifying whether she entered such spaces, Rení emphasized that the ECS parking lot is frequently filled with Mercedes-Benzes and other "imported" and "expensive" cars. A non-Arab Brazilian who runs one of the thematic-party companies mentioned earlier likewise declared:

In spite of the fact that the *colônia árabe* is considered rich, it is also tacky. Women are dressed with too much jewelry, and the general public is not well received by Arabs who, in a certain way, discriminate against Brazilians. The first question[s] that an Arab asks you [are] always: "What is your last name? What family are you from?" They want to know your lineage to know your purchasing power.

While this businesswoman organized "Arab" theme parties for paying clients, she rejected socialites who were the ostensible genitors of such Arab culture. Countering the claims of authenticity staked by ethnics themselves, these reproaches of Middle Eastern leisure circles have been cast in terms of the consumptive markers of class.

Ironically, I found that those ethnics (and, I suspect, nationals, too) who voiced such criticisms of the *colônia* were frequently present at events. While Iskander, Sarkis, Samir, and others expressed disillusionment with lofty community standards, they made sure not to miss ethnic events that attracted famous individuals from the Arab community and Brazilian high society. Their motives could perhaps be discerned in an incident at the plush reinauguration of the Lebanese Brazilian Chamber of Commerce at Monte Líbano. As I partook of wine, *kibes*, cheese balls, and pleasantries in a small circle of Arabs and

Brazilians, a middle-aged man excused himself, remarking, "Let's go pick some pretty flowers." Just before the comment was made, a young man had approached us, shaken everyone's hands, passed out the business card of a state deputy of Syrian–Lebanese descent, and disappeared into the crowd. Other flowery exchanges have transpired at the most varied events. Despite frequent criticisms, ethnic leisure affairs have provided the opportunity for liberal and business professionals to make connections with both ethnic and national elites.

Social capital that is potentially generated in business-card exchanges has been secured with more ease during dinner engagements, especially those with Middle Eastern cuisine. Invited to the weekly *jantar árabe* at Monte Líbano on a cool evening, I made my way into one of the foyers for an art exhibition that showcased members' paintings and sculptures. Certain works would be chosen for a competition held between clubs that belonged to the ACESC. I was promptly provided with a glass of white wine by the *garçom* and conversed with one of the club's directors, Alberto, and two (non-Arab) guests, Sérgio and Daniela, who had also been invited for the evening.[26] After a half-hour, the room filled with elegantly dressed men and women who balanced small talk with brief glances at the artworks exhibited under fine light. As elbow room tightened, Alberto suggested that we ascend to the third floor for the weekly *jantar árabe* (which, in fact, was open to members of all clubs that belonged to the ACESC). Making our way into the spacious salon, we took our place at an elegantly arranged table with João and Estella, another country club director and his wife. Alberto explained that the ethnic dinner was buffet-style, and we could begin whenever we wished.

Introductions came first, however. Daniela mentioned her agroindustrial enterprise in a town just outside the capital, adding that the *alcachofras* (artichokes) on which we would be dining were supplied by her business. After her husband warned that we should praise the artichokes, Daniela volunteered that she and João, the club director, had a business partnership to develop a "farmer's market" (said in English) that would help small-scale agriculturists sell their products. Offering details about the land purchased and the building permits obtained, guest and club director expressed excitement about the potential success of their economic undertaking. Even Alberto chimed in that he would be interested in investing in the cooperative because it looked like *um bom negócio* (a good deal). Alberto also nonchalantly mentioned that, although he never expected or asked for political favors, his first cousin had recently been reelected mayor of the town in which the farmer's market was to be located. At the time, I was preoccupied with the exquisite meal about to be consumed, so I initially understood this exchange as mere coincidence or small talk. In retrospect, however, it seemed that interests in a political and economic alliance underlay the small gathering of bourgeois subjects who would dine on fine Middle Eastern cuisine at Monte Líbano.

Such material plans, however, were not the major topic of conversation that night. In contrast, the dinner conversation involved experiences of consumption that ranged from vacation trips to Tahiti and the United States to the "excellent quality" of "ethnic foods," particularly Middle Eastern cuisine. Only exalting language was heard about *comida árabe*. As we readied ourselves for the buffet line, one club director explained that the night's special dish was *mukhiie* (an "originally Egyptian" dish of green foliage eaten with rice, toasted pita, and either lamb or chicken). However, he suggested that we start with *meza* (appetizers, in Lebanese Arabic) before moving on to the main dish. Making our way through the buffet, we all filled our plates with salads and appetizers, including hummus, baba ghanoush, and *kibe nyi*. As we found our way back to the table, Sérgio told everyone that his "favorite food" is "Arab." Alberto then quipped that Monte Líbano was known for having the best Arab food in São Paulo, even though the club's master chef, nicknamed Salim, was really a *nordestino* (northeastern migrant). Smiling, Alberto later added that the artichoke hearts from Daniela's company were the most delicious he had ever tasted. Through the consumption of kind words and delectable cuisine at the *jantar árabe*, social connections were laid out for potential future intercourse. Claiming the most authentic Arabisms in a national market full of them, socialites converted the symbolic power of ethnic cuisine into social capital among the ranks of high society. Such incidents turn the tables on past ethnic and national hierarchies and point to the ethnic project of Arabness in a consumer-diversified Brazil.

COMMODIFIED ARABISMS IN ETHNIC
LEISURE SPACES

Historically, the consumption of Middle Eastern cuisine, music, and dance was imagined and realized in several clubs in the *colônia sírio-libanesa*. Men would come together, munch on Syrian–Lebanese foods, play a folk drum called the *derbake*, sing old tunes, and dance the *dabke*. Yet such "get-togethers" (*sahras*, in Arabic) were informal and improvised events. Today, the consumption of Middle Eastern cuisine has a more institutional character, complete with pricey tickets (twenty to fifty reais per person), arranged dates (from weekly to bimonthly), and novel material ties to upscale Syrian–Lebanese restaurants in the national market.

High-end restaurants such as Folha de Uva are contracted to cater "Arab dinners" and general events at small clubs and religious associations. After the religious condecoration of two members, for instance, the Syrian Orthodox cathedral held a reception catered by Folha de Uva, whose owners (not coincidentally, Orthodox Christians), were present. In a similar way, the executive directors of the larger and wealthier Clube Atlético Monte Líbano, which has it own food service, have made sure that the club's "culinary director" is the (Lebanese) proprietor of the poshest Lebanese restaurant in São Paulo, Khayyam. At the same time, however, the master chef in the club's kitchen—the aforementioned "Salim"—is from the state of Pernambuco in the underdeveloped northeastern region of Brazil. Like many of his counterparts, Salim migrated to work in São Paulo. Joking about the labor arrangement, one cultural director wrote in the club magazine, *Shuf*:

> When I bring a guest to eat lunch or dinner, after the laudable meal, the customary question always comes: "Who's the cook?" I answer with a serious and convincing air, "It's Salim." [And they respond:] "Ah, good! It had to be one of the race to prepare these delicacies." I keep to myself until after dessert, when the eulogies increase, then I say to my guest: "Salim is a *pernambucano* [native of the northeastern state of Pernambuco] whose name is Adelito Ferreira Cavalcanti, who has [worked at] the club for twenty-two years ... and made his career in the kitchen, where today he is chef."[27]

As is captured in this tongue-and-cheek reflection, the cultural directors at Monte Líbano are well aware of the linkages between their club and the wider market. Monte Líbano, in fact, has gained status among Arabs and Brazilians alike as one of the most authentic establishments offering Middle Eastern cuisine, notwithstanding the fact that entrees are overseen by a highbrow restaurateur and prepared by a chef who migrated from the northeast.[28]

In parallel fashion, the belly dancers that these clubs regularly contract have been non-Arab women from the Middle Eastern dance market in Brazil. Informal agreements have been customarily made between female dance professionals and Arab male club directors. A non-Arab belly dancer, Priscilla, explained that dance performers are contracted by a particular country club to perform a certain number of shows over a specified period of time. In her informal contract with a small Lebanese club, for instance, Priscilla was guaranteed employment at weekly *jantares árabes* (Arab dinners), as well as at any other event that featured belly dancing during the club's 2001 fiscal year. Another non-Arab belly dancer, whose stage name is Fairuza, had sealed a contract with a different Lebanese social club that holds bimonthly *festas árabes* and more sporadic family reunions and get-togethers. Both Priscilla and Fairuza have taken note of the "turf boundaries" between dance professionals in competing for these desirable contracts in the dozen or so clubs that feature belly dancing in the *colônia*.

Ethnic and national interlinkages have informed other activities in the clubs as well. Belly dancing and Arabic language classes, for instance, have been instituted at the ECS, Monte Líbano, and Homs, the three largest clubs in the *colônia*. Whether making stomach undulations or guttural sounds, teachers in these settings have also used their skills in administering courses for paying students in the outside market. In addition to teaching belly dancing at Club Homs, for example, Gabriela has administered classes at the large Academia de Danças Étnicas (Academy of Ethnic Dance), where gypsy, flamenco, and other "ethnic" dances are taught, and has given lessons in her home. Georges, a naturalized Brazilian citizen from Syria, has had a similar experience as the Arabic-language teacher at Club Homs and the ECS.[29] While teaching three times a week in two clubs of the *colônia*, he has worked as an official translator for the São Paulo state judicial system and administered a host of private classes for higher-paying students. Ethnic commodities of dance and language in Middle Eastern country clubs have been interlinked with the "relations of production" of Arabness in the wider Brazilian economy.

Such ethnic and national market imbrications are best illustrated in the following description of a *festa árabe* at one of the smaller clubs of the *colônia*. Having been invited to Clube Marjeyoun, named after a small village in southern Lebanon, I found myself enveloped by a family and festive environment. The partygoers ranged in age from their twenties to about seventy, although most were forty-something. Samer, a colleague who is a cultural director at the club, later commented that 90 percent of those who had attended the *festa árabe* were connected to the village of Marjeyoun, either as immigrants or descendants. Everyone was dressed in casual attire: The men sported blazers and slacks with fine watches and polished shoes, while the women wore dark-colored dresses with equally fine jewelry. One enthusiastic man in his early thirties even wore a *kaffiyeh* (head scarf, in Arabic), along with a caftan fit for a sheikh in Orientalist grandeur. As everyone sat down at the more than twenty elegantly decorated tables, there was a solemn moment to pay tribute and award a plaque to a long-time club member.

Appetizing aromas soon enveloped the audience, as waitresses dressed in black shirts and hats bearing the name "Jacob's" brought out entrees for the buffet. Catered by the Jacob's restaurant, the "Arab dinner" consisted of such culinary staples as stuffed squash, *charutinhos* (stuffed cabbage and grape leaves), raw *kibe*, hummus, baba ghanoush, tabouleh, and *fatush* salad. Table by table, people served themselves in a buffet line and returned to their seats. Samer's aunt, who sat at our table, frowned when asked how the stuffed cabbage leaves tasted, though the other entrees were savory. Soon after, the desserts served (also buffet-style) included fruit and many *doces árabes* (Arab sweets) such as baklava, "bird nests," and *helis delous*. The Arab foods consumed in this venue had been produced by a well-known and "traditional" restaurant from the Brazilian market.

As everyone finished dessert, the band began to play, and Sonia Athie, an immigrant female singer known in Arab leisure circles, was introduced and wailed in harmony. Within the next ten minutes, four non-Arab belly dancers swayed into the salon. Later I learned that one of them, Fairuza, had a "contract" to give such performances at the club. When Athie announced the performers' arrival, friends frantically moved dishes to the sides of our table to make room for a belly dancer to climb it and shake for everyone's delight. Several other tables did the same and invited the performers to dance on table tops, as mostly men slipped five reais and ten reais bills into their low-cut belts. This seemed to be welcomed mostly by men, but also by some women.[30] It was a clear demonstration of male predominance in such leisure spaces. When I expressed my surprise, a female colleague at the table reassured me: "*É coisa do árabe mesmo!* [It's really an Arab thing!]." This gendered dimension of "Arab culture" has received considerable criticism from some Arab women.

After a round of the *dabke* dance circle, another well-known, older male singer with an extravagant moustache appeared. He employed the "traditional" style of improvising lyrics as the band continued playing. Like many other second- and third-generation members in the audience, I did not catch the full message enunciated in formal, not popular, Arabic. The singer had praised the "liberation" of "South Lebanon," its rolling hills with winds of "freedom" (especially after the Israeli pullout in April 2000). This was met by applause and shouts from the audience. Sitting next to me, the father of my friend—an elderly immigrant from Marjeyoun—tried to wipe the tears from his eyes with his wrinkled hands before anyone noticed. His daughter and son saw and soon embraced him. It was *saudade* (longing) for the homeland, for its mountains and newfound liberty. Yet this was a *saudade* expressed in the context of a commodified Arabness made in Brazil.

DISTINGUISHING ETHNIC IDENTITY IN PUBLIC AND PRIVATE SPHERES

Such market manifestations of "Arab culture" reflect and shape descendants' particular sense of ethnicity in the nation. Whether restaurateurs or liberal professionals, they have looked down on fast-food chains such as Habib's and even middle-brow food establishments. Samir of Folha de Uva, for instance, remarked that the *esfihas* from Habib's are made with cheap ingredients, changed to suit "Brazilian taste buds," and marketed to the masses. Likewise, Lillian, an administrator in the São Paulo state government's Secretariat of Culture, noted that on the day that we met for an informal conversation, the main course offered in the cafeteria was *comida árabe* (Arab food). "Today," Silvia explained, "was an Arab lunch with *kibes*, *esfihas*, that dish with lentils and rice [*mjudra*] … but it wasn't as good as that of my aunt Yvette." Engaged in an "invidious comparison" of the ethnic variety, descendants have now taken a self-conscious pride in their own authentic culinary forms.

The commodification of Arabness has especially informed ethnics' sense of distinction on the country club circuit. Take, for instance, Mário, the Monte Líbano member who praised the club's *comida árabe* in the article from *Shuf*:

> The fame of our Arab food has already left the confines of the club and reached the city, neighboring municipalities, and even the hinterlands of the state [of São Paulo]. … We are always approached by our friends, principally the "Brasiliie" [non-Arab Brazilians, written in the popular Arabic pronunciation], so that we will invite them to dinner on Thursday or to lunch on Sunday.

After boasting about the fame earned by Monte Líbano's cuisine, Mário pointed out that its ethnic dishes have attained such distinction because of the directors who have "revolutionized the kitchen" and because of the members who have "very refined palates." The members, he continued, have made suggestions to improve the cuisine, including a petition with three hundred signatures "asking for more bulgur wheat in the *kibe*." Invoking the now elite status of "Arab food," Mário concluded that club directors and members "are responsible for this food [that is] delicious, savory, [and] worthy of presidents, sheiks, kings, and rulers." Once marginalized in the national market, Middle Eastern social clubs have been praised here as spaces of authentic Arabness in Brazil.

With the proprietor of the upscale Lebanese restaurant Khayyam heading food services at Monte Líbano, the club members claim culinary authenticity through the "buzz" about its kitchen in the public sphere. "The *comida árabe* of Monte Líbano is really famous" in São Paulo and throughout Brazil, began Sandra, who went on to recount a brief story about her neighbor, César Tralli, a famous reporter for the Globo television network:

> I said to him, "Ah, one day, let's have dinner at Monte Líbano on a Thursday. There's an Arab dinner." … I invited him and his wife, right? And he

[answered]: "They've told me that it's the best Arab food in São Paulo!"
... It's really famous, really savory, really put together.

Even a reporter on the Globo television network, implied Sandra, has heard of the exquisite cuisine at Monte Líbano. She added in passing that Tralli still asks, "When is it that you'll take me to eat dinner at Monte Líbano?"

Directors and rank-and-file members of another country club, Club Homs, have been equally outspoken about their own authentic Arabness in the Brazilian public sphere. In the words of one director, Ricardo, Club Homs sees itself as the "club of the *colônia*, the Arab community," which "has the obligation to manage [*gerenciar*] and preserve its cultural values." Amid the club's diverse program of classes and events, the board of directors has recently put a special emphasis on courses and spectacles that contribute to the *resgate cultural* (cultural renewal) of the club. "Events seek to bring to the club," related a Club Homs magazine article from 1998, "the knowledge and the tradition of Arab culture through presentations of diverse artistic–cultural manifestations."[31] With "Kibe Arak" theme nights, belly dancing and *dabke* performances, as well as poetry and *oud* recitals, Club Homs's administrators have advanced this ethnic project of Arab culture out of a more hybrid reality.

As part of this project, Club Homs remodeled one of its rooms in the late 1980s to serve as the *sala árabe* (Arab salon), with mother-of-pearl furniture, Orientalist paintings, and fine collectibles from the Arab world. Yet during my weekly visits, the room was always kept locked. One director, in fact, commented that it is opened "only on very special occasions when there are authorities and diplomats, because not even the club members know how to take care of it. They don't appreciate the value." As I sat in front of its closed doors one afternoon, a group of teenagers who customarily met to go to the gym downstairs reflected on the "Arab salon." One youth remarked that he had been a club member for three years and never once had seen the *sala árabe* open and lit up. Arabness, in this case, has been marked for public recognition and as extraneous for private consumption.

To better cater to its own membership, however, Club Homs has embarked on an extensive "revitalization program" which has included the expansion of Arabic-language classes, the inauguration of belly dancing instruction, and the planning for traditional Arab wood-carving and *oud* music classes in the future. Language and dance classes have been opened to the public at large to attract non-members and non-Arabs who want to learn about Arab culture. In the words of the club director Ricardo, "We want to bring the people to know *cultura árabe* so that they will really know it." In response to my remark that Middle Eastern dances and languages are taught in São Paulo's various academies or schools, Ricardo interrupted, "But to learn Arab dance or language ... there is nothing better than learning it within a club, an Arab club." Thus, the claims of ethnic authenticity made by Middle Eastern descendants today draw their symbolic power vis-à-vis Arab cultural commodities in the national market.

This consumption of culinary, music, and dance forms in Middle Eastern country clubs has intensified a hierarchy of authenticity among "Middle Easterners" themselves. In contrast to André Gattaz's remark that there is almost no way to discern differences between "Arab," "Syrian," and "Lebanese" identities in Brazil (Gattaz 2001: 239), I found that Middle Easterners, and even non-Arab Brazilians, have made particular distinctions between them. As I noted in Chapter 3, a popular expression, or *brincadeira* (joke), recounted by several Arab (and non-Arab) Brazilians refers to the Turk as a poor peddler, the Syrian as a "remediated" or middle-class store owner, and the Lebanese as a wealthy industrialist or educated professional. When I asked about the significance of this colloquial saying, Samir, the second-generation Syrian doctor, reflected on the high status of Lebanese in Brazil and the world:

> The Lebanese ... had a very large European influence. It was a country much more modern in terms of Westernized beauty [*belezas ocidentalizadas*]. ... The Syrian is more conservative. The Syrian maintains more of that closed posture. Internally in Brazil, this differentiation between the Syrian and the Lebanese really exists.

Rather than conclude that the Lebanese are materially wealthier than Syrians in Brazil, Samir, among other Arab Brazilians, have emphasized that the Lebanese are more modern and possess a greater degree of Western civilization than Syrians, who are more "traditional" Arabs.

Because Samir distinguished between Syrians and Lebanese in terms of consumption, I asked whether the distinction was related to the club scene in São Paulo. He immediately responded, "Without a doubt. ... [Monte Líbano] is extremely sophisticated ... refined and boastful, [while] Club Homs is extremely conservative." Club Homs, others noted, has gained fame as the Casa do Árabe no Brasil (the House of Arabs in Brazil), whose members made it "a point to play Arab music at parties," as well as to offer instruction in Middle Eastern dance and language. Sami, another second-generation Syrian doctor, frequents Monte Líbano and affirmed the alleged refinement of the Lebanese. "Monte Líbano ...*is* more refined," he said, and the Lebanese are "more Westernized, more cultured than Syrians." Similarly, the second-generation Italian widow of a second-generation Syrian man asked me (a

Lebanese descendant): "The Lebanese are really refined, aren't they?" Already sensitized to the matter, I responded, "Lebanese like to think they are more refined." Especially in view of the popularity of Monte Líbano's "Arab dinner" among elites in São Paulo, this order of Middle Easternness reveals the ironic limits to ethnic recognition: The seemingly higher status of Lebanese identity is partly due not to "authentic tradition" but to "Western refinement."

This distinction between Lebaneseness and Syrianness in country clubs has been expressed in such terms today. When I told a Lebanese family friend who is a naturalized Brazilian citizen that I had enrolled in Arabic-language classes, he responded that I must exercise caution when choosing the teacher and course. I was told to enroll not at a Syrian club but at Monte Líbano or another Lebanese club, because Lebanese Arabic is more beautiful (*mais bonito*) than Syrian Arabic. In fact, both Monte Líbano and Club Homs now sponsor Arabic-language classes. However, while Monte Líbano's classes have few students, Club Homs's courses boast several dozen. When I asked him about the lack of interest in learning Arabic at Monte Líbano, the club's cultural director reflected that Lebanese in general are "Westernized" and do not *valorizam* (value) their Arab roots as much as the "more traditional" Syrians do. Club Homs's directors agreed, repeatedly emphasizing that Syrians have upheld "Arab tradition" through public classes in the Arabic language (as well as instruction in other cultural forms). In Middle Eastern social circles, language-class consumption, or its absence, has informed both Lebanese "Westernization" or "refinement" and Syrian "authenticity" or "tradition."

Belly dancing instruction and performance has also reflected this hierarchy of Middle Easternness. Although belly dancing shows are prevalent during *festas* or *jantares árabes* at several clubs, the actual institutionalization of belly dancing instruction has been eschewed by the Lebanese Monte Líbano and outwardly espoused by the Syrian Esporte Clube Sírio and Club Homs. Priscilla, a non-Arab former belly dancing instructor at Monte Líbano, explained that fathers at the Lebanese club opposed their daughters' studying belly dancing. In fact, a few students were able to take classes only because their fathers thought they were involved in other activities. Priscilla emphasized that men at Monte Líbano "want a belly dancer, but a mother, an aunt, a sister cannot be dancers. But there has to be a dancer." Hence, a *brasileira* (Brazilian woman) is contracted for club events. Although male socialites never raised this issue with me, it seems that Monte Líbano's "ethnic refinement" has showcased belly dancing but has prevented its instruction to female club members.

In contrast, belly dancing performances and instructional courses have been institutionalized at Esporte Clube Sírio and Club Homs. But the Arab dance instructor at Club Homs, whom I will call Gabriela, was equivocal when asked about the club's sponsorship of belly dancing shows and classes, especially vis-à-vis the almost entirely male board of directors. In one private talk, she praised Arab women's essential proclivity toward belly dancing, reflecting on how students who are "descendants" learn the dance form more rapidly than others. At the 2000 Belly Dance Show at Club Homs, Gabriela thanked the administration for allowing her to "reclaim [Arab] culture, reclaim the belly dance." Moreover, Gabriela dedicated the show to her parents, thanking them for "the Arab blood that they gave me." However, in another private conversation, she noted that the performers contracted for club events that feature belly dancing have been almost without exception non-Arab Brazilian women (and non-members). Although the club's directors never commented to me about such gender disparities, Gabriela indicated that Club Homs's "Arab authenticity" has permitted belly dancing classes for women so long as they do not perform individually at club events. Whether ethnic refinement or tradition, the hierarchy of Middle Easternness has been based on patriarchy.

P ROCEEDING FROM THE EARLY marginalization to the contemporary commodification of Middle Eastern cultural forms and spaces, this chapter has focused on the greater recognition of Arabness in the diversified Brazilian national market. Once indicative of the peripheral place of Arabs in the Brazilian nation, Middle Eastern food and dance have become popular among elites and masses. This national appropriation, however, has been felt as having had a positive impact on Arab ethnicity in Brazil. Attentive to the growing distinction of Arabisms in the public sphere, directors and members of Syrian–Lebanese country clubs have expended considerable time, energy, and resources in developing *jantares árabes* and belly dancing spectacles. Claiming an authentic Arab culture in the national market, socialites have converted the symbolic power of ethnic commodities into social capital within the upper echelons of the Brazilian nation. While consuming Middle Eastern staples, ethnic and national connoisseurs have made potentially lucrative social connections. This creative outcome suggests that, when the group whose culture is appropriated enjoys significant social power, it can retake the appropriation in a way that further benefits itself.

SIX

~

Air Turbulence in
Homeland Tourism

JET-SETTING TO DISNEY WORLD or Tahiti, Brazilians of Syrian–Lebanese descent are avid consumers of international travel.[1] Although their preferred destination, like that of many well-to-do Brazilians, is the United States, their itineraries began to diversify in the late 1990s, as suggested by weekly tourism ads and reviews in the mainstream press. In fact, Middle Eastern tourist packages have been familiar features in Brazilian newspaper travel columns since 1996.[2] In this context, Syrian–Lebanese descendants have expressed considerable interest in, and have been urged to visit, homelands in the Middle East. During such trips, though, they have toured sites of past bloodshed perpetrated by the Israeli military in Syria and Lebanon. This air turbulence has informed what it means to be *árabe* in contemporary Brazil.

Targeted by airlines and travel agencies, as well as by the Syrian and Lebanese states, Brazilians of Syrian–Lebanese descent have gained greater acknowledgment as a market niche for homeland tourism. Addressing their unexpected tours of anti-Zionist sites that commemorate past Israeli attacks in Syria and Lebanon, this chapter demonstrates that, while some tourists have reproduced the anti-Zionist tenets of Syrian and Lebanese nationalist ideologies, others have criticized them as encouraging "prejudice" among Arabs who relate well with Jews in a "racially tolerant" Brazil.[3] Using the exclusionary language of Brazilian nationalism, some tourists have subverted anti-Zionist ideology in homeland tourism, showing that nationalist ideas can counter the very logics of exclusion that derive from them.

Mindful of novel unfoldings in the diversified travel market, this chapter interrogates the intersecting agendas of Brazilians of Syrian–Lebanese descent, travel enterprises, and Syrian and Lebanese state powers. Second- and third-generation Arab Brazilians have partaken of homeland tourism because of a deeply felt familial connection with Syria and Lebanon. Such personal motives, however, belie the increasingly precise marketing savoir faire of airline companies that targets *comunidades étnicas* (ethnic communities) presumably interested in flying to diverse homelands. Consonantly, Arab state powers have counted on the travel practices of second- and third-generation descendants to reinvigorate national tourist industries. Despite recognizing the multiple nationalist allegiances of these emigrants, Syrian and Lebanese state officials have sought to impart anti-Zionism to them in homeland tourism.

Among such desires and interests, I focus on a still emergent progressive form of identification. The sites of Israeli violence profoundly affected Syrian–Lebanese descendants, only some of whom internalized anti-Zionism. Notably, others expressed ambivalence or repulsion toward what was considered the "racism" of the Lebanese or Syrian states. Their "brainwashing" tactics, stressed Arab Brazilian tourists, were futile because such tensions did not exist in an allegedly racially democratic and mixed Brazil. Using the core language of Brazilian nationalist ideology, ethnic tourists have "enacted an unnamed cosmopolitanism in the space of a very specific institutional site" of Arab state-sponsored tourism (Schein 1998: 190). My work holds out the possibility that nationalist precepts can serve as the first step toward this existing yet unacknowledged cosmopolitanism between Brazil and the Middle East.

EMOTIVE CONTOURS AND CHARACTERISTICS OF ARAB BRAZILIAN TOURISM

Narrating antecedent intentions in homeland tourism, second- and third-generation Syrian–Lebanese have spoken of wanting to know one's origin (*conhecer a origem*). A second-generation woman, Márcia, traveled with her uncle to Lebanon in the late 1980s. "Your emotional side speaks a lot, because … there [in Lebanon] you see where your family is from, you know where your origin is really from," she explained. "I loved having gone there and seeing where my father was born." Similarly, a second-generation Syrian–Lebanese man reflected, "I went to know my origin. I went to know where my parents came from. … I went to know the land of mother, the land of my father. [Syria] and Homs … Lebanon and Zahlé."

In a similar vein, Arab Brazilians specified the desire to know the very village of parents or grandparents. Abdo, a tourism-industry executive, explained,

"I wanted to know the land of my parents, my grandparents." He stressed that his mother had "transmitted" to him and his siblings "a love for Lebanon" and especially "a love" for their small village in southern Lebanon, called Mimes. In a shaky voice, he recounted:

> Mimes peopled our infancy ... because she [Abdo's mother] would speak about Mimes, Mimes, and we would stay imagining what would Mimes be like, right? She would speak about how it was located on the top of a mountain, really beautiful ... and she didn't get it wrong. The first time that I went there, I saw Mimes on top of the mountain, those clear houses surrounded by olive groves. I mean, beyond beauty, it was really moving.

With his childhood "peopled" with the ancestral village of his parents—its mountain contours, winding roads, and olive groves—Abdo experienced a real-life homecoming.

Likewise, Mário, a middle-aged second-generation Lebanese, noted that his father's constant references to Baieth, in northern Lebanon, fired his desire to know that very village. "When I arrived in the land of my father," recounted Mário, "we were received there with a banquet that never have I seen the same in my life. Never have I seen the same in my life. And I got really overcome with emotion." With similar passion, second-generation Hassan recalled that, when he stepped foot on Lebanese soil, "It was mine! ... [T]his belonged to me." He then continued to Akiara, "the city of my father, where he was born":

> I felt even more still that this was mine, that this belonged to me. ... That village belonged to me. ... I felt that this [was] inside of me, that all those people who were there ... were connected to me.

Traveling to an ancestral village in Lebanon inspired a unique sense of belonging. Even Hassan's children, the family's third generation, have visited the village.

Such personal motives, however, have been coupled with the desire to know a "different" or "alternative" place. Ahmed, a second-generation Lebanese, noted, "We travel first to better know our relatives ... and to know various cities, historical and new." He enjoyed sites such as Baalbeek, Beitedine, and others that "have much history." Said, a medical doctor who was born in Lebanon but raised since an early age in Brazil, explained, "First, I liked seeing the relatives again ... and also coming to know Lebanon. I visited more places. ... I liked Baalbeek, I liked Jouneih, and I liked south[ern] Lebanon." Beto, whose father is an immigrant Lebanese and mother is a Brazilian-born

Arab, noted that during a one-week trip to Lebanon in 1999, he visited paternal relatives, as well as ruins in Baalbeek and the Jeita Grotta. Even Márcia, the second-generation woman mentioned earlier, related that, in addition to meeting relatives, it was "cool" to see new, non-Western things. The experience of ancestral villages, distant relatives, and tourist sites thus overlapped in heritage tourism.

This dual agenda to discover origins and see new places has been linked into homeland tourist programs. Lebanese state authorities and tourist agencies offer excursions not only to archaeological sites but also to villages of emigrant ancestors. During the 2001 youth camp sponsored by the Lebanese Ministry of Emigrants, for instance, two third-generation participants were temporarily detoured at the end of an afternoon visit to the city of Zahlé, famous for ice-cream parlors and souvenir boutiques. After buying ice cream and gifts, the two youths set out for the nearby village of their emigrant grandparents, Marjeyoun. Accompanied by a ministerial employee, one Lebanese Brazilian, Carlos, was taken to the house of the only living brother of his migrant grandfather. After embraces were exchanged between emigrant nephew and paternal great-uncle, stories were shared between two family sides that had lost contact for nearly forty years.[4] Back in Brazil, Carlos fondly recalled the encounter as the high point of his one-month trip. Scheduled amid museum and archeological excursions, the "family reunion" had been central to the tourist experience itself.

But this project "to know" or "to see" relatives, sites, and villages did not include the objective to live among them one day. In stressing how he was overcome with a sense of belonging in his father's village, Hassan slipped in that he had traveled to the country *não pra viver, pra ver* (not to live, but to see). Having participated in a group excursion to the Syrian "home country," João, a dentist, reflected, "A friend of mine asked me if I would move there [to Syria or Lebanon]. I said no. Here in Brazil, I am a king. I can buy a car and go out to the cinema." Said noted that "things there [in Lebanon] are complicated now," and his growing medical practice in São Paulo would not permit him to make a permanent move. With their livelihoods and lifestyles tied to the Brazilian market, Arab Brazilians have chosen only temporarily to travel to the Middle East.

Class and family composition are thus important factors. Tourists stem from middle and upper classes. In some cases, wives and children spend winter vacation (July) in Lebanon while husbands remain working in Brazil. In other cases, college students travel without parents in guided tours. In a few instances, an entire family travels together. Yet, in characterizing themselves, Arab Brazilians lay stress on religious difference. Muslims and Christians alike have pointed out that Muslims are more likely than Christians to visit the homeland regularly. Four travel agents who sell tickets to the Middle East, in fact, stressed that most of their clients are Muslim. Although some colleagues explained that this is due to the fact that Muslims have a deeper connection to Arabness, others viewed this religious distinction in historical terms. Since most Christians immigrated in the early twentieth century, reflected the second-generation Sunni Lebanese Abdel, they did not develop the "habit" of visiting the homeland. In contrast, Muslims who immigrated in the second half of the twentieth century have had an easier time visiting Lebanon annually or biennially because of cheaper and faster transportation.

Despite these class, familial, and religio-historical variations, I have found an increasing specification of tour packages for members of a given country club or religious association, as well as for circles of close friends or colleagues. Such collectively organized tours have been age-specific, involving middle-aged couples, youth (chaperoned by adults), or a mix of family friends and accordingly have been tailored with activities and events for each group. Not surprisingly, these group-specific packages to the Middle East are similar to other tours organized by travel agents to the United States and Europe. This detailed, but "modular," precision is a common phenomenon in neoliberal times.

In narrating antecedent intentions, however, travelers never specified a desire to visit the sites of past Israeli attacks or the recently liberated southern Lebanon. Generally, the Arab–Israeli conflicts in the Middle East have been contrasted with the so-called convivial relations between Arabs and Jews in Brazil. Historical business ties between Arabs in textile wholesales on Rua 25 de Março and Jews in clothing retail sales on the nearby Rua José Paulino are well known in each *colônia*. "We bought our store," recalled one Arab merchant, "from a guy of Arab Jewish origins." The daughter of a European Jewish merchant likewise remembered that her father would buy most of his retail material from a well-known Arab-owned textile factory named Paramount. She concluded, "The relationship between Arabs and Jews is really good here [in Brazil]." Notwithstanding such admittedly romanticized language, Arabs and Jews historically collaborated with one another in the wholesale and retail segments of the textile market, especially in downtown São Paulo

These complementary socioeconomic relations between Arabs and Jews, which were prevalent before 1948 (Klich 1998), were due partly to their shared Middle Eastern origins. So-named Arab and Jewish conviviality also had to do with the similar ways that Arabs and Jews were constructed as ethnics by the Brazilian nation. Jeffrey Lesser has shown that the "highly visible" urban commercialism of both Arabs and Jews led Brazilian elites to link and marginalize them in overlapping ways during the first half of the twentieth century (Lesser 1998: 40). Having undergone common experiences of marginalization, Arabs and Jews developed interrelationships in the liminal space of the early twentieth-century Brazilian economy.

Even today, Arab Brazilian liberal professionals recurrently acknowledge friendships with Jewish counterparts. The civil engineer Wlademir related, "I've already had Jewish clients, and they became friends." Five medical doctors also remarked that their colleagues and patients included many Jews. Even the dentist João pointed out, "I was the *padrinho* [akin to the best man] in a Jewish marriage." He concluded: "We are what they [Arabs and Jews in Syria] were before the Europeans arrived." Such "conviviality," however, did not necessarily carry over into this private sphere. "Who is living there [in the Middle East]," explained a community magazine director, "doesn't believe in what is happening here. But this doesn't mean that the Jew who goes to the store of the Arab will invite the Arab to his home. ... It depends." Yet this ambivalence was often overlooked when subjects spoke of Arab–Jewish "conviviality" in Brazil. As the second-generation Mário said idealistically, "Arabs and Jews integrated themselves a lot here. ... Brazil can break the structures of all sectarianisms. ... Brazilians, and Brazil, is able to transform all rancor." Validated by professional circles, this celebration of Arab–Jewish relations in Brazil reflects the ideology of racial democracy. It is this nationalist idea that came to challenge the anti-Zionism emitted in homeland tourism.

TOWARD TARGET MARKETING IN THE NEOLIBERAL TRAVEL INDUSTRY

Airline companies, tourism operators, and small privately owned travel agencies have shaped international travel consumption in Brazil. Major airlines have traditionally pushed ticket sales through tourism operators such as Stella Barros, Soletur, and Agaxtour. In turn, tourism operators have regularly combined airline tickets with "land-based packages," including hotel fares and day tours, purchased at reduced prices from parallel companies in the city or country of destination. Providing airfare, hotel accommodations, and tour options, such "packages" have warranted a good deal of attention from the Brazilian leisure classes.

Airline companies and tourism operators have also culled personalistic ties with small privately owned travel agencies. Wilson, the market-relations manager for Alitalia in São Paulo, pointed out that "there exists a great interest ... in having a good relationship with the agencies." The better the relationship, he noted, the more tickets the private agents push to customers. Similarly, Oswaldo, an employee of KLM Royal Dutch Airlines, explained that KLM uses incentives that target booking agents who specialize in different destinations.[5] Keeping handy the business cards of private Arab-owned travel agencies, airline branch managers frequently referred me to a handful of booking agents who specialize in the Middle East. While visiting one of them, Iskander, I stepped aside while a SoleTur representative made a pitch about his company's competitive prices. "Moreover," the representative added, "we can offer free trips for you and your family." With much grace, my colleague declined and, after the salesman's departure, remarked that airline and tourism agents often stop by with similar pitches.

Such flows of business contacts are not fortuitous. Iskander's agency is one of several dozen privately owned and operated *agências de turismo* whose forte is the Middle East. Airline enterprises, explained the Alitalia manager, seek to develop relations with these and other kinds of agencies. He recounted that airlines commonly make distinctions between "religious," "ethnic," and other sorts of privately owned travel agencies. He and other airline managers explained that tourism agencies specializing in the Middle East are referred to as *agências étnicas médio oriente* (ethnically Middle Eastern agencies), just as those specializing in Italy are called "ethnically Italian agencies." When I asked whether these agencies know that they are spoken of in such terms, one manager replied that "everyone knows. It's the breadwinner of each one of them." Ethnicity, in this light, has been built into wider personalistic relationships between distinct travel industrial segments in São Paulo and Brazil.

Such person-to-person relationships have changed since the early 1990s. Especially today, market managers at Alitalia, Air France, and KLM enjoy access to databases located at their company headquarters in Europe. At São Paulo airline branches, I was impressed with the ease with which managers logged onto computer networks and downloaded statistics on Brazil–Middle East flights. Printing out passenger totals for this route on several airlines,[6] one manager emphasized the confidential nature of the information. In 1999, the printout tallied nearly 19,000 passengers flying between Brazil and the Middle East, more than half of whom were destined for Beirut. On another list provided by Alitalia clerks, the financial total for all airline tickets from Brazil to the Middle East increased from $21 million in 1999 to $31 million in 2000. At the same time, the financial total for airline tickets sold in the world was roughly $1 billion and $350 million. The Brazil–Middle East segment thus totaled from 1.6 percent to 2 percent of the total market value in 1999 and 2000. Viewing the paltry number, I asked a manager why airline companies were interested in a segment with such a small percentage of the total market. "It interests us because it's sales," he replied bluntly. These flows of database statistics capture the increasingly detailed sophistication of the Brazilian travel industry.

In this regard, Air France recently began to use "target-marketing strategies." In 2000, the airline's Paris headquarters informed the Brazilian branch office to allocate a certain amount of its budget to "ethnic advertising." Air France directors in Rio de Janeiro then "elected" three *colônias* as "target populations:" Arabs, Germans, and Jews. They entered into contact with an affiliate of the airline's transnational advertising consultant, Carrillo Pastore Euro RSCG. Based in São Paulo, Carrillo Pastore was founded in 1995 and was partially bought out by Euro RSCG two years later in the liberalized economy. It spearheaded Air France's "ethnic advertising" campaign in São Paulo. Transnational business imperatives strategized in Paris thus linked into the ethnic politics of the national travel industry in neoliberal Brazil.

Carrillo Pastore marketers first contacted the recently formed Associação de Mídias Étnicas (Association of Ethnic Media, or AMET) in São Paulo. Made up of Arab, German, Jewish, Korean, and Japanese newspapers and magazines, AMET was founded with the aim to "compete with bigger sized [advertising] vehicles" such as *Veja* and *Isto É*. Ethnic readerships were represented as "1 million consumers active and ready to acquire your products."[7] AMET's ethnic diversity, however, was too much for Air France. Contracts were then individually negotiated between Carrillo Pastore and three magazines in each *colônia*. The so-called ethnic advertising campaign held a "contest" for the best essay on "Your Dream Trip." While contestants' vied for two airline tickets worth up to 3,500 Brazilian reais, the advertising agency built a database of their profiles. The campaign ran from November 2000 to March 2001 in nine media outlets from the Arab, German, and Jewish *colônias*.

Carrillo Pastore came up with a modular and detailed advertisement that could fit into all three ethnic publications, notwithstanding the different destinations of the intended audiences. The full-page ad featured a green highway sign with white trim and lettering against the background of a blue sky and fluffy clouds. On the highway sign was a downward arrow pointing to "São Paulo" and "Rio de Janeiro" and a skyward arrow indicating the cities abroad to which the given readership would be destined. In Arab community magazines, the ten cities in large white script included Beirut, Amman, Cairo, and Damascus.[8] In German magazines, three of the twelve cities were Berlin, Frankfurt, and Hamburg. Only Tel Aviv and Paris were listed in Jewish magazines.[9] Flying high above the highway sign in the blue sky was an Air France plane with the message, "Air France: Never have the continents been so close."

The contest rules appeared at the bottom of the ad. The reader was asked to write a twenty-line essay on "the trip of your dreams," to print name and address, and to check a box for information about Air France promotions. A Carrillo Pastore consultant, Eduardo, explained that "Air France wanted to know if it would work, if the stimulated reader would respond." To gauge the campaign's success in different *colônias*, the agency's media department created a procedure to identify entry forms by placing an inconspicuous flag and number on them. German magazines were labeled 1–3, with a German flag; Arab magazines were labeled 4–6, with a Saudi Arabian flag; and Jewish magazines were labeled 7–9, with an Israeli flag. In this manner, advertisers measured the rate of interest among readerships by counting the number of entry forms filled out from each magazine and ethnic group. "Was there a good return?" I asked the Carrillo Pastore employee. "Yes, there was," he stated. "Not as much as we hoped, but it was a good return." Target marketing has thus acknowledged and reorganized the place of ethnicity in the Brazilian nation.[10]

This ethnic campaign attracted a good deal of surprise among Alitalia and KLM sales representatives. Wilson, the Alitalia manager, called Air France's "target-marketing" approach a "novelty." It chose "to attack now," he added, because of improvements in the time schedules for connecting flights in Europe (for passengers departing from South America to the Middle East). In an anxious voice, he repeated, "Air France is attacking the market now because it has good connections." Concluding, Wilson stated that this "direct approach" to customers contrasts with that of Alitalia, which "has done 'marketing' through [tourist] agencies and … is not investing in magazines and never used direct advertising."[11] In contrast to "traditional" market strategies that involve personal relations between airline companies and tourist agencies, this "ethnic target marketing" suggests that ethnicity has gained recognition as a market segment for national and transnational interests in Brazil.

The Air France campaign coincided with other small-scale advertising strategies. Travel agencies specializing in the Middle East also began to advertise in four major Arab Brazilian community magazines: *Chams, Orient Express, Carta do Líbano,* and *al-Urubat.* More aesthetically modest, such ads provided the name and address of the agency, as well as special packages or ticket prices (not only for the Middle East, but also for Brazil and other destinations abroad). The Libantur agency, for instance, took out a full-page ad in early 2001 issues of *Chams* magazine. Announcing "unmissable tour packages" to Lebanon, Syria, or Jordan, the ad read, "Libantur has prepared travel packages ideal for you and your family to visit the best of the Middle East and to take advantage of its marvels." Referring to such advertising, *Chams*'s editor-in-chief mused, "I am certain that it gives a good return for a travel agency." In an earlier interview, the same editor had noted that "airline companies are satisfied" with the number of Syrian–Lebanese who "fill their flights."

Aided by ethnic community magazines, airline companies and tourist agencies have strengthened the emotional connection between Arab Brazilians and Middle Eastern homelands.

TARGET MARKETING AND THE DIASPORAN DESIRES OF ARAB STATE AND BUSINESS POWERS

Airlines and travel agencies are not alone in targeting Arab Brazilians. Syrian and Lebanese states and financial groups have embarked on similar initiatives. The Syrian state has co-sponsored seven excursions called the Encontro com as Raízes (Roots Encounter) since the early 1990s. Bringing together three dozen youth or adults of Middle Eastern descent, the tourist program has become a familiar, if intermittently offered, leisure opportunity for Brazilians during winter vacation months. The excursions' other co-sponsors are two Syrian Brazilian associations, Fearab and Club Homs, and government ministries are said to have ensured low rates for hotel fares and tour packages in Syria.[12] "In Damascus," reported an article in *Homs*, the Club Homs magazine, "Brazilians were received by the Minister of Immigration, Abdallah al-Ahmar, in a special meeting and two other dinners in Damascus and Saidnaya."[13] This focus on tourists of Syrian descent has been part of the Syrian state's concern with promoting "cultural tourism." The Minister of Tourism has explicitly expressed his desire to draw "expatriate" visitors from the United States and Brazil "who feel comfortable traveling to Syria."[14]

The Lebanese state has sponsored more systematic excursions for second-, third-, and fourth-generation youth, dubbed "emigrant youth camps." Begun in 1996, the annual program brings together "emigrant" Lebanese youth from Africa, Asia, and the Americas, including "Brazilians" (the largest delegation in 2001). For three weeks every July, the Lebanese ministerial department of emigrant affairs escorts youth to tourist sites and semiofficial encounters with political leaders. In sponsoring the camp, state authorities hoped to plant the seed for "emigrant youth" to vacation recurrently in Lebanon. Soon after the 2001 camp came to an end, for instance, one ministerial employee reflected, "We want them to come back to Lebanon," qualifying that participants will not return permanently but will, it is hoped, feel compelled to make periodic visits. Reflecting Hassan's remark noted earlier, Lebanese Brazilians would travel to Lebanon "not to live, but to see."

In addition, the Lebanese state has endeavored to recruit emigrant tourists to improve Lebanon's image in the world. In showing the ancient "marvels" and natural "beauties" of Lebanon to young progeny abroad, government officials have sought their collaboration in publicizing the "good side" of Lebanon.

In the opening ceremony of the 2001 camp, for example, state authorities beckoned: "We are faithful to you and we count on you to be an ambassador of Lebanon in your host country." An official tour guide later explained to campers that "the Lebanese government wants you to publicize [*divulgar*] Lebanese culture and tourism … in your countries of emigration." Young tourists were encouraged to give presentations about Lebanon in their respective nations of upbringing. In capitalizing on the flow of emigrant tourists, advertising has become useful not only to airlines, but to states as well.

The yearly emigrant youth camp also befits the stated goals of the Lebanese ministerial department of emigration affairs.[15] In the view of its public-relations director, Ahmed Assi, it seeks to strengthen the ties between emigrants and the Lebanese homeland, as well as the relations between emigrants and their countries of settlement, promoting "the best relationships between emigrants abroad and their countries of emigration." In sponsoring tourist excursions, the Lebanese state has sought to make participants into "diplomats" who take pride in being "hyphenated" Lebanese, identifying with both the "homeland" and their "countries of emigration." The transnational Lebanese state agenda does not demand or require the sole allegiance of emigrants. While strengthening their identification in being Lebanese, it has likewise reinforced their identification with their countries of upbringing. As Akhil Gupta once reflected, "Nationalism may need transnationalism to protect itself" (Gupta 1997: 182).

Lebanon-based tourism enterprises have implemented similar programs. Jacques, an employee of a major travel agency in Beirut, explained that if Lebanese descendants know the name of the village of their emigrant parents, grandparents, or great-grandparents, his agency can prepare an excursion to that same locale. Lebanese descendants "come to visit the villages of their ancestors, and they want to make family trees," added Jacques. A multilingual tour guide likewise specified that "Lebanese descendants" who contract him often request one- or two-day trips to their emigrant ancestors' villages. Qualifying that the majority of tourists from Latin America are Lebanese descendants, the guide concluded that "tourists of Lebanese descent" provide his material livelihood and a unique opportunity to show the homeland for children far afield. Such emigrant interest in the homeland did not escape the attention of the public-relations director at the Lebanese Ministry of Tourism, Madame Boushra Haffar, who reflected:

> I think that Lebanon should work on its descendants. There are big communities spread throughout the world. They know what Lebanon is from their grandparents, great-grandparents, that they're from Lebanon. These

Lebanese can be attracted much easier because they already know something about Lebanon.

This awareness of Lebanese descendants' potential significance for the homeland's tourist industry has been accompanied by an explicit recognition of Lebanese descendants in Brazil (as well as in Argentina). Madame Boushra continued:

> I told the Minister [of Tourism] that we need to make a campaign for Lebanese descendants in Brazil and Argentina. Brazil is home to the first-largest Lebanese community, and Argentina to the second. I'm sure that they'd be happy to come to Lebanon … because they've heard about the homeland from their parents and grandparents who keep beautiful images of Lebanon, who always speak about their villages and homeland. And so their children and grandchildren have these beautiful images, this myth of Lebanon in their heads. And when they come here, they will see the Lebanon that they have always heard about.

State and business authorities are eager to tap into the emigrant desire to know ancestral villages. They have good reason to do so. As described earlier, Lebanese Brazilians' own articulation of their personal motives confirm such expectations of homeland tourism.

In the late 1990s, Lebanese state and business groups joined forces to make this idea into reality. Investors interested in emigrant Lebanese tourist programs were brought together by an executive at the Emigrado Co. (Emigrant Co.), whom I will call Amir. "The idea," he began, "is that there are second and third generations of Lebanese throughout the world whose last connection with Lebanon is through their parents and grandparents." Three different "groups" would be targeted: "youth," "gamblers," and "high-class Brazilians." Amir explained that the idea for "youth tours" was developed from questionnaires filled out by participants in the Lebanese state's "emigrant youth camp." Amir's privately financed program intended to pair emigrant youth with Lebanese-born college students in tourist and nightlife activities. In developing relationships with fellow students in Lebanon, reflected the executive, descendants would feel more compelled to return:

> The idea was to bring them over to meet people, not just for tourism. We were arranging for them [emigrant youth] to meet three hundred Lebanese university students. This is the way that people become attached to a country: not to stones and ruins, but to people.

The idea of this "youth tour" was to link emigrant teenage travelers to Lebanese national residents themselves and, in the meantime, strengthen tourism in the country.

Brazil was one of the primary countries targeted. Brazil "has the biggest reserve of Lebanese descendants," Amir explained. "There is no other country in the world that has so many." But the Lebanese in Brazil are "neglected," he continued, because of the "different language" and "distance. ... So it's a virgin market." His Emigrado Co. thus set out on an ambitious advertising campaign. First, it printed colorful booklets in Portuguese that carried the official stamp of the Lebanese Ministry of Tourism. "This was to gain legitimacy," Amir noted. The twenty-page brochures were then distributed to Lebanese associations and diplomatic offices in Brazil. Titled "Lebanon 2000: Youth Tours," the booklet relates Lebanon's cultural and natural marvels in prose and image: the majestic ruins of Baalbeck; the water-sculptured Grotta of Jeita; and crusader castles in Sidon, Tyre, and Byblos, as well as reconstructed Beirut's "hot" nightlife. It concludes, "We believe ... that ... this visit to Lebanon will form the basis of a long-lasting tie that will flourish and transform the country ... from a vague dream into a reality full of life." In (re)presenting Lebanese tourism, Lebanese state and business powers marketed the homeland to Brazilians of Lebanese descent.

In addition, Emigrado Co. contacted two well-known Lebanese Brazilian newspaper columnists, Vera Simão and Alice Carta, who agreed to publish columns on the "youth tour" program. This, said Amir, would be accompanied by an official letter from the Lebanese Ministry of Tourism, which would give the program "more legitimacy." Meanwhile, Emigrado Co. contacted the Brazilian tour operator Agaxtour to collaborate in obtaining airline tickets. An Agaxtour representative was invited on an all-expense-paid trip to experience what the program would be like in Lebanon, according to Amir. "The idea is fantastic," he kept repeating. Indeed, a transnational panoply of state and business interests—including Lebanese state officials, financial groups, and Brazilian tour operators and columnists—had combined forces to tap into the "virgin market" of Lebanese Brazilian tourists.

As this campaign took shape in early 1999, however, Israeli planes bombed an electric generator near Beirut (allegedly in retaliation for Hezbollah attacks in northern Israel). Within days, Amir recalled, the Agaxtour representative canceled her free trip. With such effects from Lebanon's "war-torn image," the executive soberly noted that the program was put on hold. But Israeli bombings of Lebanon at least once a year since 1999 have forced him to shelve the "youth tour" program indefinitely. "These circumstances make it difficult to do," concluded Amir. Another tourist-agency employee likewise reflected,

"Every summer something happens during tourist time. Israel bombs Lebanon, and bad publicity is generated in Western media, especially American." She added, "We cannot have real tourism in Lebanon until we have peace in the Middle East." Of course, this turbulence from Israeli aggression has undermined the tourist industry in Lebanon. As we shall see, though, the sites of past Israeli attacks themselves have been transformed into tourist exhibitions.

A TOURISM OF TURBULENCE IN
THE MIDDLE EAST

Arab Brazilians have regularly spoken of sites or experiences of violence during tourist trips to Syria and Lebanon.[16] In the Syrian-state sponsored "Roots Encounter," Brazilians were taken to the "ghost town" of Quneitra, which was destroyed during the Israeli pullout after the 1973 war and has since been "preserved" as a testament to Zionist aggression. Official guides showed tourists the remains of bombed houses whose rooftops lay on the ground, a hospital that was "like a skeleton" after being used for bomb drills by the Israeli army, and other structures razed by Israeli forces. As part of the tour, visitors were also taken into a small house wherein stood a small replica of the hundreds of houses and streets of the town before Israel leveled them.[17] Attentive to the tour's strong political agenda, one participant, João, sardonically noted: "They [Syrian state officials] wanted to show us what the Jews did."

Most who toured Quneitra spoke at length about the horrors of the destruction. At a dinner organized in São Paulo for "Roots Encounter" participants over the previous five years, a speaker paused to denounce such a "violent act of hate." Those sitting at my table nodded their heads in agreement. Even a wealthy businessman commented to me that he "didn't see anything standing" in the once well-populated village, ending with an analogy: "It's as if one day to the next, all the buildings on Avenida Paulista would be destroyed." Another participant, Ismail, later noted to me, "We went there ... to this place, out of this world. It shows how the war was, that war that they had. I even have a book [about it] that I brought from there. I have the book from there." Even around this site of bloodshed, there was a chance to purchase history books and other keepsakes. This was tourism: a tourism of turbulence.

Tourists also have been taken to the southern Lebanese village of Qana. When Israel launched a sixteen-day artillery attack on southern Lebanon in 1996, Qana found itself caught in the crossfire. In an operation called "Grapes of Wrath," Israeli military forces allegedly aimed to stomp out Hezbollah bases but "mistakenly" dropped bombs on a United Nations shelter in the village of Qana, killing more than one hundred innocent civilians and some

U.N. peacekeepers. To "remember" this brutal attack, the Lebanese government made the bombed United Nations compound into a memorial shrine. The Qana Memorial is now a tourist attraction for individuals and groups alike and is identified as an interesting spot to visit in the newly "Liberated South" by local tourist agencies and even the *Lonely Planet* guide (Jousiffe 2001). The memorial was also one of the sites visited by the 2001 emigrant youth camp.

Our tour buses ground to a halt. From my window, I made out a bombed building whose unsteady tower had "UN" written on it. Like other parts of the United Nations station, it had been left intact as a testament to Israeli violence. Two dark-green tanks were parked next to it. As sixty members of the Brazilian delegation in the emigrant youth camp made their way off the buses, several boys climbed onto the tanks and asked friends to take pictures. The festive nature of the entourage continued into the actual memorial, despite signs that read, "The New Holocaust: 18 April 1996 United Nations Hospital." No one took note of the six or seven eight-meter-long marble tombs in which rested the remains of 106 people killed in the Israeli attack. Losing patience with the youngsters, one tour guide screamed for everyone to show respect. "This is the place of the holocaust of the twentieth century," he bellowed. Continuing in an angry but controlled voice, he stated: "This is where the Israelis massacred 106 Lebanese. ... [T]he number-one criminal for the Lebanese is the Israelis who killed 106 unarmed civilians here in 1996." Indeed, this was tourism of an Israeli bombing attack where Lebanese blood was spilled.

Everyone was made somber by the soliloquy. The youth began to walk up and down the aisles between the tombs. We were soon escorted into other spaces of the memorial still undergoing construction. Inside an adjacent room were two walls full of photographs taken in the aftermath of the bombing raid. Images of strewn body parts and women grasping the spilled entrails of their children shocked us into silence. One of my Brazilian friends pointed to a picture where a baby's head was blown off. Moving with the flow of numbed tourists, everyone shuffled toward the back of the destroyed complex, where the remains of a church lay enclosed within glass windows. We gazed at it. The official tour guide spoke out, "This is our resistance." The Qana Memorial— its white tombs, bloody photographs, and broken cement remains—had brought emigrant youth face to face with a war that they neither did nor could experience firsthand. Like other tour groups that visited the destroyed United Nations compound, however, our entourage was quickly escorted back onto buses and taken to the next tourist site: nearby Christian rock carvings that may suggest that present-day Qana is the biblical Cana. In this fragmented sense, the destroyed United Nations compound had been just one of many tourist sites visited during that day in southern Lebanon.

The emigrant youth camp, including sixty members of the Brazilian delegation, visited another tourist site of turbulence, al-Khiam prison near the border with Israel. Historically, it was here that Israel and its proxy army, the South Lebanese Army (SLA), tortured Lebanese resistance fighters and suspected accomplices. After Israeli forces withdrew from southern Lebanon in April 2000, however, the prison was turned into an "impromptu museum and memorial for its victims" (Jousiffe 2001: 240). Today run by the Hezbollah political party, the prison-turned-museum receives busloads of tourists eager to consume the misdeeds of Israel in southern Lebanon. As the *Lonely Planet* guide for Lebanon reads, al-Khiam prison's "appalling conditions make for a sobering visit" (Jousiffe 2001: 240). Like other tour groups, the 2001 emigrant youth campers were escorted to this "sobering" space of violence.

We approached a large yellow and red banner that read "Al-Khiam Camp." It was the first of many signs in English and Arabic. As we entered the prison complex, a sign on our right said, "Men's Bathroom," and a sign on our left, "Room for Investigation and Torture by Electricity." Passing by detainees' cells, some emigrant youth knelt down into the caged cubicles. They "played prisoner" for the day. Camera flashes lit the dark, festive air. This tourist glee, however, soon turned into silence as bearded men, former prisoners, spoke about their experience in the camp. Standing in an open-air space within the camp, Brazilian youth struggled to listen while a tour guide translated the ex-prisoners' stories from Arabic to Portuguese. "They [Israelis] passed electrical shocks on our face, on our body," began one man. "We suffered a lot. They would beat us until we couldn't walk. They'd throw water on us and then whip us." Another ex-prisoner reassured the campers, "This prison is known in the entire world, and now you will know it." If emigrant tourists traveled to Lebanon "to know their origins," they would surely leave knowing the misdeeds of Zionism as well.[18]

At the end of the tour, we returned to the buses. On the way, though, many of us stopped to stare and take pictures of a large mural on one of the camp's walls. On the left side was a dove flying out of a cell whose bars were broken apart. On the right side was a Star of David with visible breaks. The explicative sign in Arabic might have been lost on emigrant youth who only spoke Portuguese, English, and Spanish, but its visual message was clear: the Lebanese resisted and broke free from Zionism. We stood in both awe and ambivalence.

A few weeks after the youth camp ended, I met with the officials who had overseen the program in the Lebanese Ministry of Emigrants. The public-relations director and assistant were very aware of these intense experiences in the tourist sites of past Israeli aggression. In the emigrant youth camp, both director and employee concurred,

> Our objective is not only a tourist one. It is to introduce the youth to their nation, and so the camp has a national dimension. Lebanon has suffered a lot with Israel. It has been attacked. Its citizens have been killed. Since Lebanon has suffered a lot from Israel, we of course would include these national symbols. There is a lot to be learned visiting Khiam and Qana, national symbols. ... In doing the camp, we wanted to let third and fourth generations know the way Lebanon has suffered, the way it bleeds ... and ... to know the deeds of Israel in Lebanon.

In organizing the emigrant youth camp, Lebanese government authorities have sought to deepen the identification of emigrants with the national homeland. This identification, however, entailed "the good, the bad, and the suffering of Lebanon." And "to know" how Lebanon suffered, tourists were taken to visit sites of past Israeli aggression.

But this tourism of turbulence has also been experienced by Arab Brazilian travelers in the day-to-day run of things, especially with omnipresent military checkpoints. Márcia, the second-generation woman mentioned at the beginning of this chapter, traveled to Lebanon with her uncle toward the end of civil strife in the late 1980s. During her stay, she was forced to pass through the checkpoints of varied military forces. "They would do those stops and ... they would ask you to open your bags, to see what you had. And you would drive a bit more. There was another [checkpoint]. And so you had to stop there again, show your passport and the like. It frightened you a bit." Márcia also explained that she had stayed with relatives in northern Lebanon and intended to visit her husband's family in the south. But neither relatives nor taxi drivers could take her to visit her in-laws. There were too many checkpoints from too many warring armies, including Syrian, Lebanese, and Israeli forces. "I ended up not going," she concluded. Touring the homeland has involved experiencing its past turbulence.

When he visited Lebanon in the mid-1990s, Said likewise recalled, his father's village in the south was still under Israeli occupation. He remembered well "the number of restrictions that you had because of the system that was there," including military checkpoints of Syria and Israel's proxy army, the SLA. While traveling south, Said pointed out, "I got to see combat with Israeli helicopters." Although he wanted to take pictures (and did so), his relatives made sure that their entourage quickly moved on. Intrigued, I asked Said whether he had become "enraged" by such "sights." He replied, "I was, of course. No one likes this kind of thing, but it's part of the context."[19] Armed conflict, in this light, was part of the de facto tourism of turbulence experienced by Said and others in Lebanon. Whether improvised or staged, such turbulence would have an impact on Arab Brazilians back in São Paulo.

INCONSISTENCY AND AMBIVALENCE IN AN INTENSIFIED ARAB BRAZILIAN IDENTITY

As witnesses to anti-Zionism in Syria and Lebanon, travelers were very open in speaking about Middle Eastern affairs on their return to Brazil. While some criticized the overt political agenda of Arab state and tourist entities, others expressed solidarity with them.[20] Reflecting on his experience in the "ghost town" of Quneitra, for instance, João reflected that he "could accept all of the [Syrians and Lebanese saying] 'shameless Jews,' 'Nazi Jews,'" but what bothered him most was that Syrian state authorities "could have reconstructed the city [of Quneitra] but resolved to leave it to show the world." Troubled by Syria's anti-Zionist agenda among emigrant tourists, he surmised that "no one wants peace. Peace doesn't interest anyone there. Neither for Arabs nor for Jews." A member of the Workers' Party in Brazil, João recalled that he tried to converse with relatives: "I asked my cousin in Lebanon, 'Why so much hate?' And she responded, 'Fifteen years of bombing changes the mentality of a people.' I never forgot what she told me." João was nonetheless critical of the nationalist fervor being "raised by the Syrian government" and expressed his preference to identify with a cosmopolitan ethos: "I consider myself no more Arab, Brazilian, white, black, or *asmar*.[21] I am a citizen of the world." This perspective, he concluded, can be attained through "travel."

Yet Nadia, a participant in the same excursion, articulated a different perspective about the guided tour of Quneitra. She reflected that travelers to Israel are frequently encouraged to visit museums and tourist sites dedicated to the Holocaust. If Israelis keep alive their memories, Nadia rhetorically asked, "Why can't Arabs preserve the memory of being victimized by Zionism with the area of Quneitra?" In addition to these opposed viewpoints, however, some travelers expressed a seemingly indifferent or ambivalent attitude. As a member of the same tourist excursion, Vanessa reflected:

Of course they [Arab state officials] pull toward the Arab side. But for me, I thought it was a tour, a cool tour. Everyone liked it. We saw new things, different customs, interesting foods. You know, we get indignant, but the trip was a cool tour in a land linked to my grandparents.

Aware of the politics of tourism, Vanessa still emphasized that her trip was just that: a trip. Ambivalent about anti-Zionism, she spoke of "a land linked to her grandparents."

The anti-Zionist tourist experience also provoked many to reflect on relations among Arabs and Jews in Brazil. After leaving the site of the destroyed United Nations complex in Qana, for instance, members of the Brazilian delegation on the bus entered into a discussion of their own relations with Jews. One girl told a story about an Arab friend's confrontation with a Jewish classmate back in São Paulo. In response to her friend's statement, "*Não gosto de yahud*, [I don't like (in Portuguese) Jews (in Arabic)]," the Jewish classmate asked why one would say such a racist thing. Surprised that the Jewish girl understood the word for "Jew" in Arabic, the friend replied, "It's because you want to finish off our [Arab] race." Having just witnessed the physical remnants of an Israeli attack on Lebanese civilians, no one debated the point. Although an anti-Zionist, and anti-Semitic, sentiment momentarily surfaced, it faded soon enough as the delegation arrived at the site where Jesus allegedly turned water into wine near Qana.

Back in São Paulo, tourist youth reflected on their experience in the Lebanese state-sponsored tourist excursion. Sandro, a second-generation high-school student, noted that the tours in al-Khiam and Qana in southern Lebanon were his favorite part of the camp. In his words, "I was happy to know that the mouse wasn't afraid of the cat, because ... the people would say, 'I am Lebanese. I am not afraid of countries that are judged to be superior to us.'" These sites, he continued, were part of the Lebanese government's desire "to show Arab descendants that they were sort of blindfolded, which were the majority, and that they weren't really inside of the situation to understand what was going on." Asking if he had a different way of being once he had returned to Brazil, Sandro replied, "For sure. Now I know who I am. I am Lebanese, and Lebanese do not bow to anyone. I am not inferior to anyone. ... I am Lebanese." Having come "to know" the situation in Lebanon, this youth developed an oppositional consciousness.

But many others took issue with the al-Khiam and Qana tours. After being shown the photographs of decapitated women and children at the memorial shrine in Qana, for instance, one Arab Brazilian youth commented to me in a very low voice, "*Isso é uma lavagem cerebral* [This is brainwashing]." The same remark was repeated by others during the tour, as several boys engaged in a self-reflective moment about the intention of state officials in taking them to the prison in southern Lebanon. A high-school student commented: "They [Lebanese state officials] want us to be angry at Israel." Several participants voiced the same sentiment during the trip and later on. When she saw the mural of a broken Star of David on the camp's wall, for instance, a young woman, Melissa, reflected that the camp organizers wanted youth to "get angry with Israel. ... [B]ut there's no use. There isn't this prejudice in Brazil." Likewise, Isabella, a high-school student, offered the following opinion back in Brazil:

> I found the political tours sort of revolting because, in my opinion, they intended to create in us hatred toward the Israelis. But in Brazil, our culture does not permit this kind of racism due to our miscegenation. They [Lebanese state officials] can show us the effects of war but not motivate us to hate a country or a culture.

Questioning the motives of state officials and politicized tourism, Isabella, along with Melissa, articulated critiques in the Brazilian nationalist language of racial democracy and mixture. Arab and Jewish interrelations in the alleged racially tolerant Brazil, each claimed, were not fraught with the "prejudice" and "racism" that severed the two groups in the Middle East. Nationalist precepts thus potentially counter the logics of exclusion that derive from them.

Although many Arab Brazilian youth rejected the anti-Zionism emitted in homeland tourism, the emigrant youth camp retained a positive significance in other seemingly personal, but equally intense, ways. Isabella, for instance, continued to reflect on how the camp related to her own lifestyle in Brazil and beyond. She explained:

> On the trip, I came to know the city where my great-grandfather ... was born and lived. It was a little sad because the city was completely destroyed by the war. But it's interesting to know that I am not simply Brazilian. I have another past in another country. I would really like to meet my relatives who still live there. ... My future project will be to try and find them and put together a genealogical tree of the family.

Notwithstanding her criticisms of its anti-Zionist agenda, the state-sponsored tourist program had an impact on the way that Isabella thought of herself: as not only Brazilian but also Lebanese. Planning to build a genealogical tree linking together these two branches of her background, Isabella articulated a Lebanese identity particular to Brazil.

Both overtly political and profoundly personal, this intensification of Arab Brazilian ethnicity was not limited to introspection. It was also put into practice. This can be illustrated in the case of Carlos, the third-generation Lebanese Brazilian boy mentioned earlier who was reunited with his great-uncle in the southern Lebanese village of Marjeyoun. When he returned to São Paulo,

Carlos decided to give a public presentation about his experience. The idea for the event came from Lebanese state officials, who repeatedly stressed the need to "publicize" the "good side" of Lebanon in "countries of emigration," such as Brazil.

Carlos's program was announced in a neighborhood newspaper and held at the local community center. He and his family set up a table lined with pamphlets about Lebanon's tourist sites, bills and coins of the national currency, and ethnic foods. They also taped to the walls maps of the region and displayed a large Lebanese flag. Relatives (second- and third-generation Lebanese and Italians) and a few locals made up the audience of fewer than twenty people. Carlos made a presentation of more than two hours about Lebanon and the emigrant youth camp that had taken him there. He spoke of Lebanon as a "crossroads" of civilization, as the land of the mythic Phoenicians, as a country beholding natural and cultural marvels. Carlos thus assumed the responsibility imparted to him by Lebanese state officials: He became an "ambassador" and "spokesperson" for Lebanon in his small, middle-class neighborhood in São Paulo.

Becoming a bit nervous at one point during the presentation, however, Carlos touched on what he called "the political aspect" of the country's history and the youth camp itself. Toward the end of the program, he explained, participants were taken to Lebanon's "liberated south." It was there, Carlos explained, that everyone visited the United Nations compound bombed by Israel in 1996, as well as al-Khiam prison, once overseen by the Israeli military. While recounting some of the former al-Khiam prisoners' stories, Carlos stated that they had seen "less than ten minutes of sun each day. They were whipped with the insides of tires. They were given only bread and water to eat." Though the details varied, the overall sentiment was conveyed: The Lebanese suffered at the hands of Israelis in Lebanon. Carlos thus fulfilled his role as ambassador of Lebanon in Brazil—or did he?

What caught my attention during this part of Carlos's talk was that which was not stated. Long before the public presentation, he confided to me (and to his family and friends) that, though he adored the emigrant youth camp and Lebanon, he felt troubled by the politicized tours in Qana and al-Khiam. Recalling his own sentiment immediately after visiting the sites, Carlos ironically pointed out that he, "who couldn't kill even a fly," came to feel resentment toward Israel. Like some of his fellow teenage travelers who reflected on this conscious-raising experience, Carlos concluded that these tourist sites were "pure politics to have us be angry at Israel." Notwithstanding this muffled criticism of the political intentions of Lebanese state officials, however, Carlos's presentation tacitly reproduced their anti-Zionist representations.

At 9:00 P.M., the presentation came to an end. The flag was brought down. The map was folded. The *kaffiyeh* worn by Carlos's younger brother was likewise removed, rolled up, and placed in a plastic bag. As the "emigrant" tourist, his family, and I made our way out of the local community center into the cool night's breeze, Carlos's mother volunteered, "Son [*Filhão*], I am very proud of you." Questions about whether Carlos had collaborated in the agenda of the Lebanese state and its anti-Zionist ideology, or whether he should have clarified his personal ambivalence about it, were not matters of great concern to Carlos or his family. He was a sixteen-year-old boy who had spoken eloquently about the country whence stemmed his paternal grandfather, and his family was proud of him. Indeed, the presentation was a visceral exercise of an intensified ethnicity that Carlos was still getting used to: being Lebanese in Brazil.

FAR FROM BEING an individual and idiosyncratic experience, Arab Brazilian homeland tourism has been targeted by airlines, travel agencies, as well as Arab state and business groups. Arab Brazilians' project to know their origins, in this light, has been recognized and targeted to increase Brazil–Middle East ticket sales and boost Syrian and Lebanese tourist economies. But Arab Brazilians have put to use travel practices in their own particular ways as well. João, Nadia, Vanessa, Sandro, Isabella, Carlos, and countless others expressed views of homeland tourism—violence and all—that were inconsistent and often ambivalent. These perspectives and practices illustrate the intensification of Arab ethnicity today in Brazil. Arab Brazilian tourists articulated multiple views regarding the homeland, the tourist sites through which they had come to know it, and the relations between Arabs and Jews in Brazil. Amid the increasing polarization between Arabs and Jews in the Middle East, their voices resound that there are culturally creative, and alternative, ways to defy these turbulent times.

CONCLUSION

~~~

In Secure Futures

Arabness, Neoliberalism, and Brazil

S YRIAN–LEBANESE DESCENDANTS today have celebrated their economic, political, and cultural contributions to the Brazilian nation.
Members of second and third generations have recurrently emphasized
Arabs' commercial prowess, ascent into political circles and liberal professions, masculine fame in familial regimes, and popularized forms of cuisine
and dance. This book has shown that such ethnic pride is not necessarily
unwarranted, but it needs to be understood in the Brazilian context of the "culture of neoliberalism" (Comaroff and Comaroff 2000: 304). Brazilians of
Syrian–Lebanese descent have been increasingly recognized in the export economy, transparent government, liberalized immigration policy, as well as com-
modity and consumer diversification. In such contexts, their alleged innate
ability to wheel and deal, purported proclivity toward endogamy, traditions
of cuisine and dance, and desires to tour Arab homelands have won increased
visibility. My goal has been to show how Arab ethnicity has gained greater
recognition in these ways during Brazil's neoliberal moment.

Theoretically, this book has aimed to push the study of ethnicity beyond
present-day parameters. Since the 1970s, scholarship has made path-breaking
inquires into the peripheral construction of ethnic difference from the colonial past through the national present (Friedlander 1975; Munasinghe 2001;
Stutzman 1981; Warren 1989 [1978]; Williams 1991). Seeking to use and move
beyond this historical framework, I have asked how the hierarchical relations
between ethnicity and the nation have shifted and reorganized during the
neoliberal moment of the world system. I have asserted that, while ethnicity

remains linked to nationalist hegemony today, its coordinates and references have gained greater privilege according to global cultural economic trends. Once solely rejected or coerced, ethnic subjects and substances have now become acknowledged as export partners, ethically accountable leaders, and market-niche consumers in the neoliberal nation. In this light, ethnicity has not been elevated beyond nationalist struggle. Rather, it has become privileged in unprecedented ways.

Framing Arab Brazilian currency in imagined political economy, the nationalist order, and the marketing of ethnic culture, I have sought to compose an ethnography without qualifiers. Each chapter in this book has moved between historical and current Arab self-understandings and institutional practices in São Paulo, changing models of the Brazilian nation and state, as well as world market flows and trends. I have used this approach to go beyond the critique of "writing culture"—not by calling for a return to past anthropological standards but, instead, by employing holism as a textual device. This has enabled me to present varied facets of Arab Brazilian livelihoods and lifestyles, including business, politics, liberal professions, family reproduction, country clubs, and tourism, as an interconnected whole without isolating them from the wider field of power relations. This book's holistic arrangement of the Arab experience in Brazil has endeavored to chart the many ways in which the hierarchical relations between ethnicity and nation have reorganized in the neoliberal world economy.

By way of "another arabesque," I have sought to convey the shifting place of Arabness in the Brazilian nation. As noted at the very beginning of this book, the "arabesque" in the title alludes to the public design of Arab ethnicity institutionalized by Brazilian executives, politicians, and socialites of Syrian–Lebanese descent. The adjective "another" refers to how Arab ethnicity was hidden or denigrated in earlier times, while it has been increasingly projected and recognized today as a unique resource that mirrors and makes up dominant neoliberal alliances and models in Brazil. Ultimately, my focus on this Arab formation in nationalist agendas and political-economic programs on the Brazilian periphery of the world system has sought to de-center or disrupt established ways of studying Arabness, exploring another arabesque that now circulates in the Americas.

OF COURSE, THESE BRAZILIAN contours of Arabness are not isolated from the increasingly insecure world order. Like their counterparts in the United States before and after the attacks on the World Trade Center on September 11, 2001, Brazilians of Middle Eastern descent—particularly Muslims—have become acquainted with the politics of insecurity and surveillance. The experiences of Dr. Nasser Rajab, a second-generation Arab Brazilian lawyer, illustrate expected and surprising outcomes between Arab ethnicity and the Brazilian nation in this still uncertain global order. On a sunny April afternoon in 2001, Dr. Rajab welcomed me into his law office in the "noble neighborhood" of Ibirapuera on the south side of São Paulo. Varied certificates, diplomas, and Orientalist paintings adorned the walls of his private office. On his antique desk was an old IBM desktop computer as well as a shiny new laptop. It comes in handy when Dr. Rajab jet-sets between his home base in São Paulo and his two other law offices in Brasília and Buenos Aires. Indeed, it took me several months to schedule a meeting with him between his frequent trips to the Brazilian and Argentine federal capitals.

As we sat down together in his São Paulo office, Dr. Rajab immediately addressed his appearance in the mainstream conservative newspaper *O Estado de S. Paulo* in December 2000.[1] He explained that his law firm had intended to legally confront the Agência Brasileira de Inteligência (Brazilian Agency of Intelligence). Although it is known as Abin, Dr. Rajab referred to the agency as the "Brazilian CIA." Based on leaked secret documents, the newsweekly *Veja* reported that Abin had spied on various political figures, their family members, and "Islamic ethnic groups."[2] Specifically, the *Veja* article reproduced an original Abin document that specified the need for special intelligence on "Islamic ethnic groups; identification and localization of groups in the country, [and] area of activity of Islamic groups."[3] Although the text of the magazine article focused on the more (in)famous cases wherein public figures and their families were spied on, it mentioned in passing the surveillance of "Islamic ethnic groups" as well. As the lawyer for the Sociedade Beneficente Muçulmana (Muslim Charity Society), founded by mostly Syrian–Lebanese immigrants in 1929, Dr. Rajab felt that it was his duty to look into the case and requested a copy of the documents in question.

Ultimately, Nasser decided to take Abin to court on "the crime of racism and the violation of the Administrative Privacy Law." In legal terms, he is using the 1988 Brazilian constitution's criminalization of racism. As the *O Estado de S. Paulo* article stated, "For the lawyer Nasser Rajab, [Abin] 'headed to the sinister field of ethnic and religious discrimination, in violation of legislation and already established principles in international treaties to which Brazil has adhered.'" Dr. Rajab is cited in the article as saying, "By generalizing the Islamic ethnic community as a target of surveillance, [Abin] committed a crime of racism." In our private conversation, however, he qualified that he does not think that anti-Arab and anti-Muslim racism is endemic to the entire Brazilian government. It is, rather, limited to some individuals within the intelligence agency itself. Nasser has thus sought to take only Abin to court.

When I remarked that "many Arabs speak of racial democracy," Nasser interjected: "But when there's a problem, no one wants to do anything." It remains to be seen whether this public revelation of anti-Arab and anti-Muslim racism can significantly alter Arab self-understandings in Brazil's alleged ethnic and racial democracy.

Nasser spoke at length about news reportage on the surveillance of so-called Islamic ethnic groups. Since Abin is a state agency for "national security," he pointed out, Muslim Arabs could now be viewed as a security threat. But he stressed that his court case against Abin is not just about the rights of Muslims to practice their religion without discrimination, but also about their right to gainful employment. "Imagine that you are going for a job interview in a business firm," he explained. "You arrive there for the interview and, unexpectedly, it comes up into conversation that you're Arab, that you're Muslim." Acknowledging this, Dr. Rajab hypothesized, might lead the potential employer to reject one's application for fear of becoming a target of surveillance as well. He concluded that Muslim Arabs' chances on the job market were threatened because of their representation as a national security risk. The court case against Abin was thus not just about religion or racism. It was also about defending Muslim Arab market mobility. That Dr. Rajab justified his implicit challenge to racial democracy in economistic terms is not surprising. As I mentioned in Chapter 3, the market has become a gauge to measure, defend, or contest race and ethnic relations in the nation.

Of course, this "controversy" carried personal consequences. Dr. Rajab explained that many friends and colleagues had remarked that it might draw undue media scrutiny or estrange potential clients. But he responded that his court action against Abin is nothing in comparison with the struggle of "our brothers" who are "taking a bullet in their chests each day in Palestine." The Arab Brazilian lawyer thus made sense of his court case in relation to a wider Arab struggle today. Much to his own surprise, however, Dr. Rajab noted that since the publication of the O Estado de S. Paulo article, he had received many letters and phone calls of solidarity from people throughout Brazil. In an alleged racial democracy, his denouncement of racism has drawn wide public support and encouragement.

One such phone call was made by the U.S. American vice-consul in São Paulo. Dr. Rajab explained that this vice-consul, who goes by the name Malcolm, expressed interest in meeting him and visiting his mosque. Initially, Dr. Rajab feared that this was a pretense for CIA surveillance. To his surprise, however, the vice-consul was personable, and, as Dr. Rajab exclaimed to me, "He was black!" In their conversation, Dr. Rajab clarified to the vice-consul the irony of an Islamic group becoming a target of racist surveillance. Islam, after all, is

known for racial tolerance and equality. "I'm sure you know," Dr. Rajab commented to the vice-consul, "that many blacks in the United States have converted to Islam for this reason specifically." The vice-consul replied, "It's not by
chance that my name is Malcolm." These cosmopolitan figures have since developed a collegial friendship. The vice-consul has visited Nasser's mosque and
joins him on jogs in Ibirapuera Park. Dr. Rajab and the vice-consul have even
been featured in the Arab community magazines *Chams* and *al-Urubat*. In one
issue, they were photographed sitting together at a table during an informal
luncheon after Friday prayer. Though Nasser rationalized his antiracist court
battle in terms of defending Muslim Arabs' market mobility, the Abin case has
earned him symbolic and social capital in, and beyond, the *colônia*.

This is not to demean Dr. Rajab's stand against anti-Arab and anti-Muslim
surveillance practices in Brazil. Rather, it is to contextualize Arabness in the
Brazilian dimension of an uncertain global order. No one else—whether Arab
or non-Arab Brazilian—had voiced public or private concern about Abin's
profiling of Muslim Arabs as a national security threat in Brazil. These sorts of
representations generally have been understood by middle- and upper-class
Brazilians of various origins as external effects of U.S. American influence and
foreign policy. That is, the image of "the Arab" as a security threat and a target
of surveillance has been categorically associated with U.S. American power by
middle- and upper-class Brazilians. As another second-generation Arab lawyer
commented to me, the image of Arabs as terrorists "is forced on [Brazil], but
it's not taking hold." That the image of "the Arab" as a security threat does not
translate easily into Brazil explains, in part, why its appearance in late 2000
failed to attract much public scrutiny, whether in support or opposition. Outside of Dr. Rajab's law office and Abin headquarters, the idea that Arabs are
security threats in need of surveillance does not resonate in Brazil.

THERE ARE LIMITS to the U.S. American globalizing encompassment of
Arabness, especially evident in media flows about "Middle Eastern terrorist rings" allegedly in the Brazilian city of Foz do Iguaçu and the triborder
region (briefly mentioned in the introduction). In October 2002, Jeffrey Goldberg, a reporter for the *New Yorker*, speculated that "Middle Eastern terrorist
groups"—including al-Qaeda—enjoyed organizational and financial bases in
and around Foz do Iguaçu.[4] Goldberg's article was unfounded and injurious,
but it nonetheless repositioned the triborder region within the U.S. American
"war on terror" spectacle. In the next few months of 2003, the rumor ballooned
in U.S. American and Brazilian media. Osama bin Laden himself, varied news
agencies claimed, had spent time in Foz do Iguaçu in the mid-1990s.[5] This was
ostensibly substantiated by the previous "discovery" of a photograph of the

Foz do Iguaçu waterfalls at an al-Qaeda training camp in Afghanistan. Of course, such suspicions of bin Laden's visit to a Brazilian city that borders Argentina and Paraguay had originated in U.S. American media.

In transnational circulation, this mass-mediated rumor had been picked up by a Brazilian advertising agency for tourism in Foz do Iguaçu by early 2004. The agency recruited bin Laden as a "poster boy" for national and international tourism in the region, placing his unmistakable brow on a sensationalist advertisement. "If bin Laden would have risked his neck to visit Foz do Iguaçu," reads the ad, "it's because it's worth it! … Foz, everybody wants to see it."[6] The publicity stunt mocks and capitalizes on U.S. American-derived suspicions that Foz do Iguaçu is a haven for terrorism. This suggests that the U.S. American "war on terror" can be subsumed by market logics, whereby the image of a terrorist enemy of the U.S. American government is remade into a poster boy for the Brazilian tourist industry. For now, the globalizing U.S. American-led structures of security and surveillance have been encompassed by the Brazilian culture of neoliberalism.[7]

In a more serious fashion, the U.S. American "war on terror" policy concerns were rebuked by Brazil, as well as the wider Latin American and Caribbean hemisphere at the annual assembly of the Organization of American States (OAS) in June 2003. The event convened foreign ministers and officials from the thirty-three member countries across North America, Latin America, and the Caribbean in Santiago del Chile. Predictably, the U.S. American representative, Secretary of State Colin Powell, tried to mend broken fences over the U.S. invasion of Iraq. Speaking of the threats of "tyrants, traffickers, and terrorists" ostensibly in the triborder zone of Argentina, Brazil, and Paraguay, Powell failed to convince his colleagues that questions of security and surveillance are not simply a U.S. American government concern but a hemispheric matter. Overwhelmingly, representatives from the other thirty-plus member countries emphasized instead that regional stability and democracy must be protected not by increasing security but by ensuring social and economic development.[8]

B RAZIL'S CURRENT POLITICAL-ECONOMIC moment thus continues. Engaging and moving beyond structural approaches to neoliberalism in Latin America (Babb 2001; Gwynne and Kay 1999; Kingstone 1999; Oxhorn and Ducantenzeiler 1998; Stokes 2001; Weyland 1996, 1998), this book's focus on export orientation, ethical accountability, and consumptive diversification has sought to capture the cultural embeddedness of neoliberalism in Brazil. In so doing, my intention has been not to show the purported advantages or benefits of the neoliberal experiment but, rather, to reveal its seductive and insidious power that captivates not just chief executives in export strategies, but also politicians and citizens in demands for ethical accountability, as well as consumers and advertisers in search of novel goods or different niches. The central argument of my book has been that Arab Brazilianness has gained greater recognition as an ethnic project in this "silent revolution" of political economy (Green 1995: 2).

Whether silent or strident, however, revolutions do not remain still. Although the Brazilian middle and upper classes welcomed *neoliberalismo* in the early 1990s and tacitly reapproved the political alliance, if not the economic model, in the 1994 election and 1998 reelection of President Fernando Henrique Cardoso, the public zenith of this experiment has wavered. By the mid-1990s, Cardoso and his cohorts had explicitly rejected the term *"neoliberalismo"* at the same time that they practiced its tenets by sealing or renewing accords with the IMF and the World Bank. Indeed, the disastrous effects of the free market on poor urban and rural Brazilians had become evident by that time. It was thus no surprise that José Serra, the candidate of Cardoso's political party, lost the 2002 presidential elections to the Workers' Party candidate Luiz Inácio "Lula" da Silva. The crucial question was whether Lula would be able to break with the structure and culture of neoliberalism.

As critically noted by the U.S. American sociologist James Petras, however, Lula's first two years as president saw a striking continuation of his predecessors' accords with "free market–IMF structural adjustment policies" (Petras and Veltmeyer 2003: 2).[9] Cynical pundits and lay observers in Brazil have likewise called Lula's presidency "the third mandate of Fernando Henrique [Cardoso]." Though there are potential signs of change, Lula has renewed Brazil's neoliberal experiment.[10] Aligned with Brazilian trade and industrial elites, Lula has emphasized the need to increase national exportation in the open economy and has pushed such necessary goals forward by taking ethical and political stands in national and transnational venues.[11] At the writing of this book, the continuity of neoliberalism seems evident.

Not surprising in this Lula-led Brazil, Arabness has maintained its intensity. In July 2003, for instance, Lula helped convene the "Planet Lebanon" conference. The meeting, which drew nearly 2,000 businesspeople to São Paulo and Foz do Iguaçu, was organized by the Lebanese Brazilian Chamber of Commerce, which is run by Brazilians of Syrian–Lebanese descent in São Paulo, and the Lebanese International Business Council, which is headed by a Lebanese expatriate in the United States. While receiving Lebanon's Prime Minister Rafiq Hariri, Lula trumpeted the conference as way to increase trade and commerce between Brazil and Lebanon.[12] In his speech inaugurating the conference, which was broadcast on Globo television's eight o'clock news program in early June 2003, he declared that his own life lies in Lebanese hands—that is, his personal physician is of Lebanese descent. At a later reception at the Mount Lebanon Athletic Club, he continued: "Lebanon is a land dear to Brazil due to the importance of the community of Lebanese origin in our country and due to the notable contribution given by the Lebanese immigrant to our development as a nation." While publicly celebrating the Lebanese presence in Brazil during this conference on trade and commerce, Lula announced his intention to visit Lebanon and the Arab world later that same year.

In early December 2003, Lula departed on a nine-day diplomatic and business mission to Syria, Lebanon, the United Arab Emirates, Egypt, and Libya. It was the first time that a Brazilian head of state had visited the Arab world since Emperor Dom Pedro II in the late nineteenth century. Not unlike the emperor's sizable entourage, Lula was "accompanied by fifty-six people, including four governors, five ministers, and seven federal deputies," in addition to roughly 150 Brazilian chief executives, including several from construction firms such as Odebrecht and Queiroz Galvão. The trip reflected Lula's goal to bring together South American and Arab countries in the transformation of what he called the "commercial geography of the world." In contrast with his predecessor's call to increase Brazilian exports to nontraditional markets abroad, Lula expressed market logics with a wider political (and populist) appeal. He declared to a few hundred executives in Lebanon: "It's about time for us to change the commercial geography of the world. If, alone, none of us can compete with rich countries, together we will have a lot of strength ... to make the rich countries bend their rules, so that we can compete in equal conditions." In the same speech, Lula remarked that contacts exist between Brazilian and Lebanese executives in view of the nearly 7 million Lebanese descendants in Brazil. He added, "I hope to God that Brazilian executives have learned the art of business with Lebanese executives."[13] In this sound bite, the inborn bargaining acumen historically imputed to Middle Easterners in Brazil was expressed in the struggles of South American and Arab "developing" countries with the "rich" North.

Acknowledged by media pundits and state officials, the mission also served to strengthen Brazil's place in the Arab world at a time when the Arab world's relations with the U.S. government had weakened in post–September 11 times. The nine-day excursion was replete with Lula's criticisms of Israeli and U.S. American occupations of Palestine, the Golan Heights, and Iraq; declarations of the Palestinian, Syrian, and Iraqi peoples' right to sovereignty; and the continued need to use and respect the United Nations. These ostensibly moral and political stands reflected President Lula's goal to make Brazil a protagonist—separate from, and opposed to, U.S. American foreign policy—in international affairs. But they were also part of a market-oriented mission. As one reporter noted, "In spite of this strong political and symbolic component of Lula's trip, the expectation of Brazilians is to increase the commercial flows of the country with this region. The president acted almost like a merchant."[14] In post–September 11 times, the Brazilian state combined anti-imperialist politics and market logics in the southern periphery of the global system.

One outcome of this diplomatic mission to the Arab world was the South America–Arab Nations Summit, held in Brasília in May 2005. In a historically unprecedented fashion, it brought together representatives from twelve South American countries and twenty-two Arab countries. In his opening speech, President Lula stated that the summit's purpose was to face the challenge of "designing a new international commercial and economic geography."[15] In such a task, he was well aware of the summit's inherently political signifi-cance: "What moves the leaders here today is the necessity to strengthen a political space for the construction of a world of peace, democracy, and social justice." Foreign Relations Minister Celso Amorim was even more explicit. "To create ... a new world economic geography," he explained, meant that, "to go from Brazil to Cairo, you won't need to pass through Washington and Paris."[16] Unsurprisingly ignored or dismissed by U.S. American media, the two-day summit included discussions on free trade and criticisms of U.S. American foreign policy.[17]

As he did during his official visit to the Arab world, President Lula refer-enced the Arab presence in Brazil and South America. At the opening of the summit, for instance, he reflected, "For Brazil and our continent, this summit has the taste of a reencounter: the reencounter of South Americans with a civ-ilization that first came to us by way of the Iberian heritage and, after, by way of immigration." Citing Brazil's "cultural and ethnic diversity as an example of democracy and tolerance" in his closing speech, President Lula likewise stated that "there are few countries that have the quantity of Arabs and Arab descendants who live in this country, who live in peace here, participate in pol-itics, share their religions. ... [T]hese people helped to build this country."[18] Arab Brazilian ethnicity was thus recognized during this largely symbolic encounter between South American and Arab political-economic elites.

In addition to such rhetorical flashes, the Arab presence in Brazil and South America gained a visual force in a photography exhibit organized by the Foreign Relations Ministry of the Brazilian government and co-sponsored by the Banco do Brasil Cultural Center specifically for the summit. Entitled "Amrik" in reference to the way "América" is thought to be pronounced in the Arabic language, the exhibit showcased two dimensions of "the Arab presence in South America:" the "immemorial legacy" of al-Andalus from the Iberian peninsula, which was "transmitted" to South Americans by the Spanish and Portuguese, and the mostly Syrian–Lebanese immigrants who likewise influenced and integrated into South American lifestyles.[19] The exhibit was replete with photographs of arabesque-style architecture of colonial South American churches, Moorish-inspired Gaucho cowboy gear, as well as Syrian and Lebanese elders and youth in scenes from their daily lives across South America. In relation to this Syrian–Lebanese immigrant dimension, the exhibit's pamphlet and website explain that, "the *primos* [cousins, in reference to Arab immigrants] brought culinary habits, such as *kibe*, tabouleh, tahini, *esfiha*, and the rich mixture of spices, to local recipes; their presence is also striking in commerce, in the storefronts, enterprises, and industries; in the clubs and charity associations; in literature, music, sport, medicine, and politics." "Amrik" was inaugurated in Brasília, and for the next several months, the exhibit toured Rio de Janeiro, São Paulo, and the southern city of Curitiba. Circulating in the Brazilian public sphere, this display of an "Arab América" was created for a summit that sought to map out "a new commercial geography of the world."

IN THIS LIGHT, it seems that Arabness in Brazil has continued to gain recognition through the culture of neoliberalism. This is meant not to deny the power of September 11 and its aftermath today but, rather, to avoid hasty predictions of a "new era" by paying attention to actual circumstances, if only anecdotally. At the Planet Lebanon conference in São Paulo in July 2003, during the Brazilian diplomatic mission to the Arab world in December 2003, and at the South America–Arab Nations Summit in Brasília in May 2005, Arab Brazilian ethnicity was recurrently referenced in the context of market logics and alliances between Brazil and the Arab world. This peculiar recognition is not new, but it forms part of another arabesque that has emerged in Brazil during the late twentieth and early twenty-first centuries, as I have tried to show throughout this book. In the future, I doubt whether the U.S. American equation between Arabness and insecurity will gain much resonance in the Brazilian national imagination. This, however, remains to be seen. What can be stated with more certainty is that the Arab ethnic project that gained force during the neoliberal experiment will continue in Brazil even after the eclipse of neoliberalism itself.

NOTES

INTRODUCTION: THE POLITICS OF PRIVILEGE

1. In 2002, São Paulo's Mayor Marta Suplicy signed an agreement with the World Bank to investigate corruption and ensure transparency in city government. Founded in the late 1990s, the World Bank's anticorruption program for political transparency was praised by U.S. Treasure Secretary Robert Rubin, who surmised that "multilateral banks of development are in a unique position in the fight against corruption": Carlos Eduardo Lins da Silva, "Wolfensohn é o ideólogo da mudança," *Folha de S. Paulo*, September 30, 1999; "Rubin propõe ataque do FMI à corrupção," editorial, *Folha de S. Paulo*, February 25, 1999.

2. Of course, the "structural violence" of neoliberal policies has had disastrous consequences for the majority of poor and working-class Latin Americans (Farmer 2003). My book does not address this dimension of the neoliberal moment (see Babb 1999; Sawyer 2001; Smith 2005; Smith-Nonini 1998). Given the already voluminous literature on this point, I feel that today it is more necessary to ask how neoliberalism has remained a dominant paradigm in Latin America despite its injurious effects on the majority of citizens. To move beyond neoliberalism, we must grasp how it has become embedded.

3. During his mandate as president from 2003 to 2005, Lula maintained accords with the IMF and the World Bank. In late March 2005, however, it was announced that Brazil would not renew one of the agreements with the IMF signed by his predecessor, Fernando Henrique Cardoso, despite the continuation of other accords with so-called multilateral global institutions.

4. Let it be noted that the actual term "racial democracy" was not coined by Freyre, though he was the first to celebrate Brazil's alleged "racial harmony" (see Guimarães 2005).

5. Syrian–Lebanese immigrants numbered roughly 130,000 in the United States from the 1870s until the 1930s (Suleiman 1999: 2), 107,000 in Brazil during the same period (Lesser 1999: 49), and 108,000 in Argentina from 1882 to 1950 (Jozami 1996: 28). Smaller numbers of Middle Easterners also immigrated to other Latin American and Caribbean countries.

6. In Buenos Aires, 53 percent of resident Arabs were said to have engaged in peddling or small-scale businesses (Klich 1992: 273). In New York City, over 50 percent of resident Arabs traded goods (Miller 1969 [1905]: 11, as cited in Khater 2001: 74).

7. A Tulsa, Oklahoma, blogger recently provided an interesting, and plausible, explanation for the character developed by Lynn Riggs: Immigrants from the southern Lebanese town of Marjeyoun had first come as peddlers during the Oklahoma land rush. They eventually established St. Anthony's Orthodox church in Tulsa. Sol Bayouth was one of the founders of the parish. He eventually became friends with Riggs, who used him as a "template for a character in his story 'Green Grow the Lilacs.'" See http://orthodox-okie.blogspot.com/2004_10_31 _orthodox-okie_archive (accessed on November 11, 2004).

8. This is my estimate based on discussions with immigration officials in São Paulo and with Arab Brazilian journalists. It also bears mentioning that the latter agree that the estimated number of immigrants has diminished greatly from the 1970s through the 1990s.

9. The numbers cited are always qualified with the adjective "estimated." The newspaper *Journal da Tarde* assessed that there are 6 million Lebanese and descendants "in all of Brazil": Tatiana Vicentini, "Colônia árabe teme retaliação dos EUA," *Journal da Tarde*, September 18, 2001, A24. *Folha de S. Paulo* proposed that there are 9 million Arab immigrants and descendants: "Brasil recebe árabes desde o século 19," *Folha de S. Paulo*, December 14, 1997, A29. Most recently, *Revista da Folha* stated that there are 7 million Lebanese and 3 million Syrian immigrants and descendants in Brazil: Débora Yuri, "O nosso lado árabe," November 23, 2001, 8. Referring to this source, the Memorial do Imigrante in São Paulo noted that there are 7 million Lebanese and 3 million Syrian descendants in Brazil.

10. Flávia Varella, "Patrícios, dinheiro, diploma e voto: A saga da imigração árabe," *Veja*, October 4, 2000, 122–29.

11. My colleagues often used the same calculations. In one memorable instance, Abdo, a well-to-do tourist industry executive, reflected that one of his colleagues once voiced skepticism about the population figures. "But these data," Abdo countered, "are collected by the consulates." I thus raised the question to a staff person in the Lebanese consulate in São Paulo. Upon hearing that 7 million Lebanese live in Brazil, I asked about the data's source. Disappearing for a few minutes, the employee returned with a book about the cuisine of immigrants in Brazil, titled *Correntes de imigrantes e invenções culinárias no 5º centenário do Brasil* (Roque 2000). Flipping to the chapter on "Lebanon," the employee pointed to two lines of text that gave the number 7 million "Lebanese descendents in Brazil" with no reference.

12. Anthropologists initially found that Brazilians moved between dozens of labels that made racial identification thoroughly inconsistent (Harris 1964; Kottack 1983; Wagley 1952). In contrast, Roger Sanjek noted that numerous designations of race does not indicate what Harris called the "maximization of ambiguity" (Harris 1970: 1; Sanjek 1971). My work asserts that there is a degree, and not "maximization," of ambiguity in racial and ethnic classification.

13. During this time period, these Middle Eastern sojourners included mostly Christians but also some Muslims and Magribi Jews. Lesser (1999: 45–47) noted that one of the first waves of Middle Easterners to Brazil were Jews from Morocco in the late nineteenth century.

14. In 1899, "Syria" was added as a place of origin on U.S. immigration censuses. "Lebanon" was added only in 1949.

15. Although *al-Urubat* is the magazine of the Sociedade Beneficente Muçulmana (Muslim Charity Society) in São Paulo, it calls itself Arab, broadly defined (though its main directors are Lebanese). In Arabic, *al-Urubat* means *O Arabismo* (Arabism, in Portuguese). *Al-Urubat* is written in both Portuguese and Arabic. The others are published in Portuguese.

16. *Carta do Líbano* means "Letter from Lebanon." Its editor-in-chief, Naime Fouad, is known to be somewhat partial to the Christian Lebanese cause. In framing the newspaper for an overwhelmingly Christian Lebanese audience, however, Naime does not counterpoise his politics to Arabness but seeks to claim a position within it.

17. "Argentina, Paraguay, Brazil Step up Search for 'Terrorists' in Tri-Border Area," BBC Monitoring Service, United Kingdom, September 15, 2001; Larry Rohter, "Terrorists Are Sought in Latin American Smugglers' Haven," *New York Times*, September 27, 2001. These and other

unsubstantiated reports were based on earlier U.S. American and European news coverage that conflated Arab communities with terrorist cells in the Foz do Iguaçu region.

18. For instance, see "Casa usada pela Al Qaeda tinha foto que seria das cataratas do Iguaçu," *Folha de S. Paulo*, November 16, 2001.

19. Rodrigo Dionisio, "Muçulmanos ganham destaque em 'O Clone,'" *Folha de S. Paulo*, September 23, 2001.

20. I do not mean to minimize the effects of September 11. But given the fact that both September 11 and *O Clone* were watched on television sets in Brazil, it should not seem surprising that a soap opera would have an equal effect on the lay public.

21. Despite their large concentration in the state of São Paulo, Arab immigrants' smaller presence in rural states, such as Mato Grosso and Goiás, was statistically significant because such regions received few immigrant waves (Diégues 1964). See also Gattaz 2001.

22. It was recently stated that "1 million immigrants and descendants live in the city of São Paulo": Ericka Sallum, "O que seria do nosso cardápio sem eles?" *Veja São Paulo*, February 5, 2003.

23. Of course, Middle Eastern descendants are not alone in the public construction of Arabness. As a researcher, I needed to speak with Brazilians of diverse backgrounds who consume or market Arabness in the public sphere and who interact with Arab Brazilians in commercial, marital, and leisure affairs.

24. Although immigrants who arrived in Brazil in the 1950s, '60s, '70s, and '80s spoke of family ties in relation to Syria and Lebanon, the descendants of earlier waves were more apt to reflect on family dispersion in North America and Latin America. A small but significant number of second- and third-generation Arab Brazilians recalled that distant relatives settled in varied countries throughout the Americas, but such family ties only effervesced in unexpected phone calls or letters and soon after dissipated into their own family narratives of immigration to Brazil.

25. The Arabic phrase "*Anah ibn 'arab*" means, literally, "I am the son of [an] Arab." It is a phrase that sounds strange to native speakers of Arabic (especially outside Lebanon), primarily because it is used by diasporans. However, the allegedly more correct grammatical construction, "*Anah min 'asl 'arabe*," or "I am of Arab origins," sounds technical to the ears of second or third generations who lack formal education in the mother tongue.

26. Let me add that my own third-generation status seemed to rest easy with second- and third-generation Arab Brazilians, though recent immigrants sometimes found me "more American." Such immigrants also voiced a desire to move to an allegedly "better life" in the United States.

27. Over beer toward the end of research, a second-generation friend pointed out that such self-positioning reinforced negative images of the United States. For him, I should have emphasized my Americanness to break down its domineering and whitened representation in Brazil. In my inebriated state, I fired back that this would merely have helped clean the image of empire. In retrospect, however, I am not sure.

28. I was not the only one who noticed. A colleague in the communications industry once pointed out that I needed to polish my appearance because of the expectations of influential business and liberal professionals.

ONE: PARIAHS TO PARTNERS IN THE EXPORT NATION

1. Notwithstanding its material basis in imported infrastructure, exportation has been viewed as ensuring the wealth of the nation in the global market. "For Brazil to import equipment and technology," explained a Brazilian exporter, "it needs to increase exportation … because you'll get more security." Of course, exports manufactured using imported equipment or technology may be seen as a disjunctive global flow, even "production fetishism" (Appadurai 1996).

Brazilian state and business elites clearly recognize the overlap, but they surmise that there is a chance to build a national economy in global times—through exportation.

2. See Clóvis Rossi, "Governo quer parceria com 'baleias,'" *Folha de S. Paulo*, November 13, 2001, B10; "Itamaraty aposta em exportações para emergentes," editorial, *Valor Econômico*, April 9, 2002, 6; Celso Lafer, "Parcerias no Oriente," *Folha de S. Paulo*, August 18, 2002, B2.

3. The "Orientals," in this text, were Maronite Christian Lebanese whose church service João do Rio observed. João do Rio was the pen name of Paulo Barreto, a well-known *ensaísta* (writer) in early twentieth-century Rio de Janeiro.

4. Lesser related that Ellis was a descendant of Confederate military men who fled the United States for Brazil on their defeat in the Civil War. He followed his father into Brazilian politics and became an essayist of the varied peoples who settled in São Paulo (Lesser 1999: 64).

5. Lesser sees this remark as evidence of the commentator's ability to discern ethnic differences among *turcos*. For me, it also shows how trade and commerce, signified by the "25 de Março street cocktail shaker," marked the meaning of *turco*, especially in São Paulo.

6. "Comércio atacadista desaparece da cadeia têxtil," *Gazeta Mercantil*, August 25, 2000.

7. "As ruas e sua história: A Rua Vinte e Cinco de Março," *A Nação*, October 9, 1963.

8. Gabriel Marques, "Rua Vinte e Cinco de Março: O rio das sete voltas," *Folha da Noite*, May 2, 1957; idem, "Rua Vinte e Cinco de Março: As chácras recuaram," *Folha da Noite*, May 3, 1957; idem, "Rua Vinte e Cinco de Março: O outro Harun Al-Rachid," *Folha da Noite*, May 6, 1957. See also Marques 1966.

9. Idem, "A velha rua do quibe cru. I," *O Estado de S. Paulo*, June 12, 1960; idem, "A velha rua do quibe cru. II," *O Estado de S. Paulo*, June 19, 1960. Raw kibe (or *kibi ni'yi*, in Arabic) is a mix of raw lamb meat and bulgur wheat that is best when eaten with fresh mint leaves and green onions. Not coincidentally, the best kibi that I was treated to in São Paulo was at a restaurant in the 25 de Março region.

10. "'Comandos' fiscais em ação na 25 de Março," *O Estado de S. Paulo*, June 28, 1960.

11. Atallah's father was the chamber's president for two terms from 1971 to 1974.

12. Although President Fernando Collor de Mello lifted the protectionist policies in 1991, the value of the national currency still did not allow Brazilian executives to import large amounts. With the stabilization of the monetary system in 1994, however, importation rates increased exponentially.

13. "Comércio atacadista desaparece da cadeia têxtil," *Gazeta Mercantil*, August 25, 2000. This is an overstatement but is nonetheless telling.

14. Wanise Ferreira, "25 de Março vira pólo de importados: Lojas de armarinhos e distribuidores de aviamentos importam a maioria dos produtos oferecidos," *O Estado de S. Paulo*, April 2, 1993. More recently, the 25 de Março region was labeled the prime place to obtain pirated garments, sunglasses, and tennis sneakers: Fátima Fernandes, "Piratas roubam mercado de empresas e U.S. \$10 bi do país," *Folha de S. Paulo*, September 3, 2000. See also Paulo Viera and Fernando Souza, "Piratas tomam a rua dos micreiros," *Veja São Paulo*, October 11, 2000.

15. This peculiar placement of the Arab past in São Paulo can be further highlighted through a comparison with Arab American history in New York City. Atlantic Avenue in Brooklyn, for instance, was once home to Syrian and Lebanese families whose livelihoods in the early twentith century were tied to small-scale textile businesses on Manhattan's Washington Street. From the 1970s onward, the Syrian and Lebanese families were replaced by Jordanian, Palestinian, and Yemeni immigrants (Orfalea 1988: 224–25). In this light, it seems that the contemporary Arabness of Atlantic Avenue in Brooklyn has been constructed by late twentieth-century immigrants, not by upwardly mobile second- and third-generation Arab Americans. Although recent immigrants, mostly from Lebanon, operate some small shops on Rua 25 de Março, the public display of Arabness in private museums and business meetings has been directed by second- and third-generation Arab Brazilians.

16. These numbers are cited by officials in the Secretariat of Regional Administrations (Administrações Regionais), sub-mayoral units of the São Paulo city government.

17. Michele Oliveira, "Bloqueio no Paraguai afeta negócios na Rua 25 de Março," *Gazeta Mercantil,* September 26, 2001. The article states that "the closing of the Friendship Bridge" that connects Foz do Iguaçu to Ciudad del Este in Paraguay "has had an impact in the region of Rua 25 de Março, in the city center. Known for imported products, the region faces shortages."

18. For a handful of instances covered by the press, see Alesandra Zapparoli, "Vaivém sem fim: Prefeitura faz nova tentativa de tirar os camelôs da região da 25 de Março," *Veja São Paulo,* August 11, 1999; Valéria Rossi, "Blitz anticamelô toma 25 de Março de madrugada: Para evitar a montagem das barracas, 350 fiscais e guardas civis chegaram à rua às 4 horas," *Jornal da Tarde,* June 30, 2000; Bárbara Souza, "Guardas e camelôs confrontam-se no centro: Ação na Ladeira Porto Geral deixou vários feridos por golpes de cassetete," *O Estado de S. Paulo,* October 7, 2000; José Gonçalves Neto, "Região da 25 de Março é alvo de blitz: Fiscalização atingiu comércio formal e também os ambulantes da região," *O Estado de S. Paulo,* October 12, 2000; Meire Furuno, "'Camelôdromo' da 25 segue intocável: Enquanto a Barão de Itapetininga está livre dos ambulantes, eles continuam ocupando a Rua 25 de Março," *Jornal da Tarde,* January 20, 2001; Liliana Ciardi, "Blitz tira camelôs da Rua 25 de Março," *Jornal da Tarde,* March 24, 2001.

19. The emphasis is Furlan's. Sadia is Brazil's largest poultry product company. Its exports make up nearly a third of the commerce with the Arab world, and Furlan is well acquainted with CCAB directors. Let it also be noted that Furlan was named Minister of Industry and Development in the Workers' Party–led federal government of President Lula.

20. In 1998, the Arabian Gulf accounted for $850 million of the total $1.7 billion of goods and services exported from Brazil to the Middle East region.

21. "Turismo em alta," *Câmara Árabe Notícias,* vol. 1, no. 2, 2001.

22. Tom Walsh, "Mideast's Future to Take Shape in Detroit," *Detroit Free Press,* September 25, 2003.

23. "Key Players in the U.S.–Arab Economic Forum," *Detroit Free Press,* September 29, 2003.

24. Tom Walsh, "Arab Leaders' Dialogue Is All about Power, Politics," *Detroit Free Press,* September 29, 2003.

25. "Seminário ensina a exportar para mercado árabe," *Gazeta Mercantil* (Santa Catarina), August 15, 2000; "Indústria cearense chama atenção de países do oriente," *Gazeta Mercantil* (Ceará), September 11, 2000; "Comércio exterior: Consórcio mineiro de confecções mira mercado árabe," *Gazeta Mercantil* (Minas Gerais), October 9, 2000; "ZF pode conquistar mercado árabe," *Gazeta Mercantil* (Amazonas), April 9, 2001; "Fiemt e Apex promovem encontro sobre exportação para os países árabes," *Gazeta Mercantil* (Mato Grosso), May 30, 2001; "Seminário discute perspectiva de comércio," *Gazeta Mercantil* (Goiás), June 20, 2001. These articles suggest how CCAB's spatial command is recognized by national business and media elites throughout Brazil. As the president of one commercial federation in the Amazon region remarked, "We have great opportunities in opening space with the Arab Chamber of Commerce abroad."

26. In addition to these seminars, the CCAB hosts monthly presentations at its São Paulo headquarters on diverse business topics for affiliates, executives, and government officials.

27. It must be added, however, that Pierre himself has reflected on the "lack" of Arabness in his own private life. As we took an elevator together one day, he nonchalantly asked about my ability to speak Arabic. "I speak, but not very well," was my response. Pierre answered, "At least you can speak." Continuing to voice regret, he noted: "I lost that aspect of culture." Despite such personal admissions, however, Pierre was represented (by himself and others) as a public expert in Arab culture during the "Exporting to the Arab World" seminars.

28. Since 1998, the CCAB has led about a dozen of these missions to the Arabian Gulf and North African regions. Co-sponsored by the Export Promotion Agency of the Brazilian

Ministry of International Relations from 2000 onward, these "commercial missions" are said "to provide the executive with the opportunity to directly meet with the buyer and/or distributor of their products. The CCAB takes care of the logistics and you, your business." The "logistics" of the commercial missions are worked out with affiliated Arab chambers of commerce and Brazilian embassies. Advertising in local business magazines and newspapers, as well as distributing booklets of the "profiles" of Brazilian companies, the CCAB works to ensure that Arab executives participate in several "trade fairs" and other related events.

29. There are several customs and habits "to keep in mind," instructs the CCAB pamphlet, when negotiating business deals with Arab executives. The heels of one's shoes, for instance, cannot be shown because it is an offensive gesture in the Gulf region. Also, the left hand can never be used, since it is seen as polluted. And, of consequence for female participants in the mission, women must wear head scarves in public at all times.

30. "Câmara Árabe comemora seu cinquentenário," *Câmara Árabe Notícias*, vol. 2, no. 7, 2002, 3.

31. "O Jantar dos 50 Anos," *Chams*, vol. 11, no. 120, September 2002.

32. "Bate-Papo com Dorthéa Werneck: Projeto CCAB–APEX e exportações brasileiras," *Câmara Árabe Notícias*, vol. 1, no. 4, 2001, 8.

33. "Discurso do … Secretário-Geral das Relações Exteriores, Embaixador Osmar Chohfi," A Palavra Internacional do Brasil (accessed on May 2, 2002).

TWO: ETH(N)ICS AND TRANSPARENT STATE REFORM

1. Curiously, the significant Arab presence in mid-twentieth-century Brazilian politics was reiterated by a political pundit nearly fifty years later in the newspaper *Folha de S. Paulo*. In 1999, Ricardo Ricupero recalled that in 1961 or 1962, he had "heard from the late Emílio Carlos [Kryillos, a Syrian–Lebanese politician] that there were more than fifty members of what he called the 'block of the United Arab Republic' in the [Brazilian] National Congress": Ricardo Ricupero, "Patrícios, mascates, e deputados," *Folha de S. Paulo*, August 29, 1999. Acclaiming the political ascent of Syrian–Lebanese *patrícios* (countrymen), Ricupero's comments came at a fortuitous time. On the same day, the newspaper ran articles on a "mafia" popularly associated with Arabs: Otavio Cabral, "Escândalos perseguem vereadores pela cidade"; "Vereadores paulistanos são vistos com desconfiança após escândalos"; and "Desgaste não evita nova candidatura," all in *Folha de S. Paulo*, August 29, 1999. Constructed in early twentieth-century Brazil, Arabs' reputation for economic cleverness was increasingly conflated with political corruption in the late 1990s.

2. Many attest to the rightist political tendency of the *colônia*. I discerned that Syrian–Lebanese politicians garner diverse affiliations on the right and left, though rightist elements seem to be most successful in culling the community's electoral and financial support.

3. The symbol of Jânio Quadros's campaign was the *vassourinha* (little broom). He would use it to "sweep out" the corruption supposedly endemic to the political establishment in São Paulo. Although Quadros won the election and served his term, he was stripped of political rights with the onset of the military dictatorship in 1964.

4. In the words of the principal investigator on the City Council, the *máfia de propinas* permitted councilpersons to "suggest the name of a political client who he want[ed] to see appointed and, in exchange, take on the responsibility of 'supporting' the mayor, 'approving' the bills that are addressed to the legislative [body]" (Cardozo 2000: 34). Interestingly, Cardozo received the most votes of any City Council candidate in the 2000 municipal elections. He has since become a federal deputy (after his victory in the 2002 round of elections).

5. Rebecca Reichmann (1999: 17) makes a brief comment on Paulo Maluf's support of São Paulo's first black mayor, Celso Pitta. Let me add that for a time in the press, political cartoons satirized Maluf, a *turco*, as the "father" of Pitta, a black Brazilian.

6. "A intenção de voto para a CPI das regionais," *Folha de S. Paulo*, February 9, 1999; "Quem votou contra a CPI," *Folha de S. Paulo*, February 24, 1999; "Veja como votaram os 'mandantes' das regionais," *Folha de S. Paulo*, February 25, 1999; "Como devem votar os vereadores na CPI da oposição," *Folha de S. Paulo*, March 2, 1999; "Veja como seu vereador deve votar," *Folha de S. Paulo*, May 18, 1999; "Veja como seu vereador deve votar," *Folha de S. Paulo*, May 20, 1999; "Como votaram os vereadores de São Paulo," *Folha de S. Paulo*, May 21, 1999; "Como votaram os vereadores de São Paulo," *Folha de S. Paulo*, May 27, 1999; "Como votaram os vereadores de São Paulo," *Folha de S. Paulo*, May 28, 1999; "Os vereadores que enterraram a CPI," *Folha de S. Paulo*, May 29, 1999; "Como votaram os vereadores de São Paulo," *Folha de S. Paulo*, June 4, 1999; "Como votaram os vereadores na prorrogação da CPI por apenas três dias," *Folha de S. Paulo*, June 5, 1999; "Como votaram os vereadores de São Paulo," *Folha de S. Paulo*, June 9, 1999.

7. "Brasil é 45° no ranking mundial da corrupção," *Folha de S. Paulo*, October 27, 1999.

8. "Brasil melhorou pouco desde 1995," *Folha de S. Paulo*, October 27, 1999.

9. "Mudança de discurso," *Folha de S. Paulo*, February 3, 1999.

10. Interestingly, Jews were not present in this "mix." Also important to note was Simon's differentiation between Arabs and Lebanese, despite Athie's tendency to conflate the labels.

11. As stated in the introduction, race mixture has been a lightning rod of Brazilian nationalism ever since the publication of Gilberto Freyre's *Casa grande e senzala* (1977 [1933]). Curiously, Arab families were suspected of marital endogamy in early twentieth-century Brazil and, hence, were peripheral to nationalist ideology. Today, Christian Arabs stress their "mixture" even though they often marry in the *colônia*. This will be discussed in Chapter 4.

12. "Fiscais passam por novo rodízio," *Folha de S. Paulo*, January 27, 1999.

13. Gonzalo Navarrete, "Governistas resistem a CPI," *Folha de S. Paulo*, February 9, 1999.

14. Lilian Christofoletti, "Prefeito afasta administrador que não foi indiciado," *Folha de S. Paulo*, March 6, 1999.

15. "Pitta era refém de esquema malufista, afirma advogado," *Folha de S. Paulo*, April 5, 1999.

16. Fábio Zanini and Sílvia Corrêa, "'Sim, a dona Marta é do PT', diz eleita," *Folha de S. Paulo*, October 30, 2000.

17. Frei Betto, "A rebelião ética," *Folha de S. Paulo*, November 5, 2000. As part of the Catholic church (though not ordained a priest), Betto was involved in helping dissidents flee Brazil during the early years of the country's dictatorship. He was imprisoned in 1969 for approximately four years and had a hand in the formulation of Liberation Theology, the Unified Workers' Confederation (CUT), and the Workers' Party (PT).

18. Thomas Traumann, "Prefeita eleita Marta Suplicy recebe oferta de pesquisa do Banco Mundial," *Folha de S. Paulo*, November 16, 2000; João Batista Natali, "Bird quer programa anticorrupção: Instituição estuda financiar projeto de transparência na prefeitura," *Folha de S. Paulo*, November 12, 2000; "Parceria contra corrupção," *Jornal da Tarde*, March 17, 2001; Maurício Moraes, "Marta quer parceria com o Bird para combater corrupção em São Paulo," *O Estado de S. Paulo*, March 16, 2001. Curiously, the Workers' Party (to which Marta Suplicy belongs) has conventionally eschewed relations with neoliberal organizations such as the World Bank.

19. Marcus Lopes, "Bird vai mapear focos de corrupção em SP," *O Estado de S. Paulo*. March 17, 2001.

20. "Pesquisa sobre corrupção vai ouvir servidor," *Folha de S. Paulo*, May 8, 2002.

21. "Prefeita diz que fez convênio para combater a corrupção," *Folha de S. Paulo*, March 13, 2002.

22. "Rubin propõe ataque do FMI à corrupção," editorial, *Folha de S. Paulo*, February 25, 1999; Marcio Aith, "FMI propõe humanizar a globalização," *Folha de S. Paulo*, September 29, 1999; Carlos Eduardo Lins da Silva, "Wolfensohn é o ideólogo da mudança," *Folha de S. Paulo*, September 30, 1999.

23. Marketed as a *franquia de comida árabe*, the Arab food chain Habib's, as well as the growing popularity of "Middle Eastern cuisine," is discussed in Chapter 5. Suffice it to say that

the actual label "*árabe* [Arab]" is used when referring to what would be called "Middle Eastern" cuisine in the United States. The ubiquitous presence of *comida árabe* in the present-day Brazilian market may explain why food—and not other markers of ethnicity, such as clothes or language—was used to associate Arabness with corruption.

24. Bustavo Ioschpe, "Aos vencedores as batatas: Os piores de 1998," *Folha de S. Paulo*, January 11, 1999.

25. Barbara Gancia, "BEM FEITO," *Folha de S. Paulo*, April 25, 1999.

26. Early in his political career, Pitta refused to identify as black (perhaps due to his disaffection for the black movement on the left). But he later assumed his blackness as his administration drew increased criticism.

27. Another political commentator employed the wordplay on the pizza expression in relation to Maluf, remarking that, "though everything here ends in pizza, the senhor ... of this (mis)governed municipality will be the indigestible and authoritarian *kibe*": Celso Luiz Prudente, "Casa Grande x Senzala," *Folha de S. Paulo*, September 13, 2000.

28. "Protesto troca pizza por esfiha," *O Estado de S. Paulo*, June 21, 2000.

29. José Simão, "Uêba! Melô a CPI e fiquemos sem Grana Garib!" *Folha de S. Paulo*, June 11, 1999.

30. Idem, "Buemba! Buemba! Na Globo abunda Pita," *Folha de S. Paulo*, March 16, 2000.

31. At the time, Garib had already left the City Council (attempting to escape scrutiny) and taken his place in the São Paulo State Assembly, to which he had been elected in 2000. Hence, Wadih Helou substituted Garib in the State Assembly: idem, "Grana Garib! Turcocircuito em Sampa!" *Folha de S. Paulo*, July 1, 1999.

32. An accomplished writer and public figure, Jabor appears weekly on Globo's eight o'clock nightly news program. He has also participated in cable-television programs, such as *Manhattan Connection*, aired on a Globo-related television station. He is widely watched by middle and upper classes.

33. Arnaldo Jabor, "Temos de beber desta lama luminosa e vital," *Folha de S. Paulo*, April 4, 2000; idem, "Corrupção global vai do angu até o FBI," *Folha de S. Paulo*, May 2, 2000.

34. Such metaphors of racial and ethnic difference underlie Prudente's article mentioned earlier, "Casa Grande x Senzala," *Folha de S. Paulo*, September 13, 2000.

35. Arnaldo Jabor, "Pitta ficou com os lábios roxos e a boca seca," *Folha de S. Paulo*, March 21, 2000.

36. "A data celebrada na Câmara Municipal de São Paulo" and "Palavras de Myryam Athie," *Chams*, vol. 10, no. 100, January 2001; "Câmara Municipal de São Paulo homenageia descendentes libaneses: A vereadora Myryam Athiê organiza e discursa para 300 convidados," *Carta do Libano*, vol. 6, no. 55, November 2000.

37. Curiously, the cover in Portuguese used not the common expression "*descendentes libaneses*" but, rather, "*líbano-descendentes* [Lebanon descendants]," specifically with a hyphen.

38. "Líbano, 57 anos de Independência," *Jornal do Brás*, November 25–December 15, 2000.

39. A handful of instances specifically concerning the *colônia árabe* include Lei Número 11.889, 28 de setembro de 1995. "Institui o 'Dia da República Árabe Síria' no âmbito do Município de São Paulo." Projeto de Decreto Legislativo 0071, Ano 1997. "Dispõe sobre a outorga da Medalha Anchieta ao Presidente da República Libanesa, Exmo. Sr. Elias Hraoui." Projeto de Lei Número: 0696, Ano 1997. "Declaram Cidades-Irmãs Amman e São Paulo." Lei Número 116/1998. "Institui no calendário oficial do Municipio de São Paulo, o 'Dia da Rua Vinte e Cinco de Março e Adjacências." Projeto de Lei Número: 0188, Ano 1998. "Declaram Cidades-Irmãs Tel Aviv e São Paulo."

40. Diário Oficial do Município. Lei Número 11.741, 6 de abril de 1995. São Paulo: São Paulo.

41. "Monte Líbano," *Chams*, vol. 7, no. 64, January 1998.

42. Projeto de Lei Número 00543, Ano 1999 "Institui no âmbito do município de São Paulo, o dia 22 de novembro como sendo o dia comemorativo da independência do Líbano." Diário Oficial do Município. Lei Número 13.000, 7 de junho de 2000. São Paulo: São Paulo.

43. A handful of instances include: Projeto de Lei Número: 00193, Ano 2001. "Denomina Rua Moacir Facundes, o logradouro … no bairro Fazenda Aricanduva, Distrito da Cidade Líder." Projeto de Lei Número: 00345, Ano 2000. "Altera denominação de praça pública. …" Projeto de Lei Número: 00396, Ano 2001. "Altera denominação da Avenida Indianópolis para Républica Árabe Síria." Projeto de Lei Número: 00454, Ano 1998. "Altera denominação da Rua Valdemar … para Rua Giuseppe Garibaldi."

44. Projeto de Lei Número: 00368, Ano 2000. "Declara 'Cidade Irmãs' Monte San Giacomo e São Paulo…"

45. Projeto de Lei Número: 00424, Ano 1998 "Institui no âmbito do município de São Paulo, o dia 6 de junho como sendo o dia da mulher progressista." Projeto de Lei Número: 00543, Ano 1999. "Institui no âmbito do município de São Paulo, o dia 22 de novembro como sendo o dia comemorativo da independência do Líbano." Resolução Número 00001, Ano 2000. "Institui … a comemoração annual do "dia internacional da mulher."

46. A friend active in political circles once remarked that Myryam Athie is known for her clientelism. He even reached into his pocket in a jesting enactment of such politics. In this light, a group of men who helped finance Athie's successful reelection campaign in October 2000 were honored as "pioneers" at the Lebanese independence day event in November 2001.

47. Projeto de Lei No: 0894, Ano 1995. "Denomina Praça do Islã no Bairro do Paraíso." Lei No: 12239, 28 de março de 1996. "Denomina Praça Salim Abeid … no Bairro do Paraíso." Projeto de Lei No: 0158, Ano 1996. "Declara 'Cidades Irmãs' Beirute e São Paulo."Lei No: 13.029, 18 de julho de 2000. "Denomina Praça Marjeyoun … no Bairro de Paraíso." Lei No: 12.886, 7 de outubro de 1999. "Declara 'Cidades-Irmãs' Damasco e São Paulo."

48. See the Secretaria Municipal de Relações Internacionais website at http://www2.prefeitura.sp.gov.br/secretarias/relacoes_internacionais/organizacao/0001.

49. Marcus Lopes, "Marta: Prioridade para publicidade," *Jornal da Tarde*, March 27, 2002, C3.

50. See http://ww2.prefeitura.sp.gov.br//milpovosespecial/index_especial.htm. Boasting that "there are more than forty municipal laws decreeing cities as partners of São Paulo," an online article explains the mayor's intent in such acts of "international cooperation." It reads: "The mayor treats this subject with care, making priority agreements … that attend to the mutual interests of the involved parties. In this respect, the communities of foreign origin can become important allies in the sense of establishing and maintaining the dynamic of these processes of cooperation. One of the criteria to identify potential partners ('sister cities') … is the possibility of involving the communities of descendants" within the city of São Paulo.

THREE: TURCOS IN THE MARKET MODEL OF RACIAL DEMOCRACY

1. Of course, these inequalities are very real. What needs to be qualified is that material disparities do not necessarily mean that "racial democracy" can be dismissed as some sort of smoke screen. John Burdick (1998) has deftly observed that, although black women have experienced racial discrimination in the workplace, they were not dismissive of the ideal of racial democracy. In this chapter, though, my point is that economic statistics used to question racial democracy should be themselves understood as a "sociocultural" fact.

2. Reflecting on similar findings, Truzzi (1997) and Knowlton (1961) took note of the impressive entrance of *sírio-libaneses* into several distinguished law schools in São Paulo through the 1960s as well.

3. Though significant throughout the twentieth century, the recent decrease in the percentage of Middle Eastern graduates from the school may be due to any number of factors. On the one hand, there are several postsecondary institutions that offer medical degrees. On the other hand, established practitioners note that the "prestige" and "attraction" of being a medical doctor has decreased in recent years. This is discussed in the third section of this chapter.

4. There is, of course, a dynamic of change in the professional trajectories of women with college educations. Yet, as was suggested at the Lebanese independence day event (and at another event mentioned later), women have rarely received the spotlight for their achievements in business or liberal professions.

5. In the colloquial expression, colleagues frequently referred to the Turk as a poor *mascate*, the Syrian as a "remediated" or "middle-class" store owner, and the Lebanese as a rich magnet of high society. The popular expression has been cited, in one form or another, in a variety of academic works—hence, the title of Mintaha Alcury Campos's 1987 book *Turco pobre, sírio remediado, libanês rico* (Poor Turk, Remediated Syrian, Rich Lebanese).

6. This compendium organized by Betty Greiber, Lina Maluf, and Vera Mattar (1998) contains roughly two dozen edited interviews with immigrant and second-generation Syrian–Lebanese in Brazil. The excerpts included in this paragraph are from that compendium.

7. Since there are a limited number of appointments on each level of the "tenure" system in Brazilian universities, open competitions are periodically held for qualified candidates.

8. The neoliberal opening of the economy has not yet significantly altered the field of law, though negotiations are currently under way between the Brazilian government and the World Trade Organization. Analogous to the American Bar Association, the Ordem dos Advogados do Brasil has expressed fears of opening the juridical sector of the economy to foreign law offices: see "Advogados temem abertura de mercado," *Gazeta Mercantil*, August 30, 2002.

9. Varella, "Patrícios, dinheiro, diploma e voto," 126.

10. In Portuguese, Jô asked, "Então, será por isso que fica regateando na cirugia, tira um pouco menos do pulmão, menos do coração … e tal."

11. In Portuguese, Riad replied (with no accent), "Não, na verdade, devido à origem, devo tirar mais, mais do pulmão, mais do coração, mais …"

12. This doctor also recounted his wife's experience during a short visit to Goiás in the central-western region of Brazil. After picking up a taxi at the airport, the doctor's wife saw several street signs with Lebanese names in the city. She asked the driver whether there were Lebanese around town. Somewhat puzzled, the driver responded that there were no "*libaneses*" in the region. Perceptively, the woman then asked if there were *turcos* in the city, and the driver answered, "*Ufa! O que mais tem aqui é turco!* [Agh! What there's most of here are Turks!]."

FOUR: MIXING CHRISTIANS, CLONING MUSLIMS

1. See Lesser (1994, 1999); Jorge Safady (1972b); and Wadih Safady (1966). Christian Arabs belong to the Eastern Rites of the Roman Catholic church—namely, the Maronite and Melkite branches—as well as to the Syrian Orthodox church of the Patriarchate of Antioch. Muslim Arabs belong to Sunni, Shia, Alawi, and Druze branches of Islam.

2. Sales and Salles (2002: 11) briefly mention the statute law for foreigners as part of the "national security" concerns of the military dictatorship during the democratic opening. I suggest that it was also part of the then emergent neoliberal moment.

3. This point historically builds on Louise Cainkar's (1994) research in the contemporary Palestinian Arab community in Chicago. She showed that whereas men have easily chosen between Arab and non-Arab partners, this freedom of choice has been rarely afforded to Palestinian women. They must either marry Palestinian men or remain single.

4. Second-generation women also had varying views of immigrant men, who were not necessarily "good catches." Lena, a woman in her early fifties, explained that her parents had encouraged her to marry an older immigrant. Although the man was hardworking, Lena noted, he lacked "refinement." The suitor did not frequent the cinema but only worked in his garment business on 25 de Março. Fearing that he would expect the same of his wife at home, Lena ended up marrying a second-generation Lebanese man in Brazil.

5. Although Wadih Safady did not specifically say that Arab Muslims were marrying Arab or Brazilian Christians, he later added that there were also "various cases" of "miscegenation" between Arab Muslims and non-Arab Christians (Safady 1966: 225). This suggests that his first statement was meant to imply interreligious marriage among Arabs themselves.

6. Referred to as "Oriental" or Eastern Rites, the Maronite and Melkite branches both are part of the Roman Catholic church. Although not specified by Diégues, Orthodox Christians were also very numerous in early twentieth-century immigration waves from the Middle East.

7. It was assumed that white workers were more economically productive than the national variety (Andrews 1991; Skidmore 1974).

8. Freyre's *Casa grande e senzala* was indicative not only of racial mixture, but also of a sexual relationship—namely, between privileged white men and women of color (Needle 1995: 69). Stamped with nationalist approval, the exercise of male virility and sexual prowess was seen as a central instrument in the making of the Brazilian people.

9. In contrast, the historian Akram Khater (2001) noted that, although immigration waves from Mount Lebanon were overwhelmingly made up of young men, they were often married before they departed the region.

10. Read against the grain, this finding not only indicates that immigrant men exercised greater liberty than women in choosing spouses. It also suggests that male immigrants attained a putatively higher level of exogamy because they were marrying Brazilian-born daughters of Arab immigrant parents (categorized as "Brazilian"). Indeed, Arab women showed a high rate of endogamy (63.05 percent). Let it be stressed, however, that Guimarães's article shows that women from all immigrant groups showed strikingly high degrees of endogamy.

11. It bears mentioning that the character of Mister Nacib was modified in Barreto's film. Played by Marcelo Mastroianni, Nacib turned out to be a mixed figure. During one scene, Nacib specified his background to a customer who called him *turco*. Nacib explained that his father was Syrian and his mother, a "Neapolitana [*sic*]." In spite of this mixed heritage, however, Nacib was portrayed with a heavy "Arabic" accent and retold various stories from "Syria." This cinematic version suggests that there were two competing images of Arab men by the early 1980s. On the one hand, they were mixed, but on the other, they could still be recognized as ethnics.

12. Curiously, a Japanese Brazilian man once remarked that his grandfather used to joke, *O árabe tem armamento grande* (Arab men carry a large weapon) and *O árabe tem pistola grande* (Arab men have a big gun). He explained that his grandfather was accustomed to seeing big and hairy Arab men carrying large trunks and eating heavy foods, such as pistachios, sesame-seed paste, and raw meat. The grandfather thus imagined Arab men in the way they were represented cinematically.

13. Exercising less freedom in choosing marital partners (especially vis-à-vis their male counterparts), Arab women experienced a different fate. In the Brazilian nationalist ideology of mixture, male sexuality was central to the "racially mixed" Brazilian people, but (whitened) women's sexuality was synonymous with honor and morality, protected by male family members and the Brazilian state itself (Caufield 2000). Arab women were thus left out of the celebrated mixture of "Arabs" in Brazilian nationalism. In this regard, Lena, a second-generation Lebanese woman, remarked, "It became known that Arab men were good fathers and took good

care of their wives." When I queried, "What about Arab women?" she responded, "The prestige was of the Arab man. In relation to the woman, you didn't speak about [her]."

14. Less surprisingly, executives also stem from Argentina and Mexico. But they often work for multinational corporations based in the United States or Europe.

15. That the great majority of interviewees frequented social and religious associations in the *colônia* might account for why the percentage of mixed marriages is significantly lower than that of endogamous ones.

16. One interviewee who had married a second-generation Italian woman went so far as to stress that the ethnic background of a spouse does not matter as much as whether she comes from a good family. "In the present-day," he began, "the descent of the wife doesn't matter much. It matters much more, in my opinion, if the family is good, who they are. It doesn't matter if they're German, Spanish, or Syrian–Lebanese." Despite such claims to color blindness, Arab Brazilian marriage patterns show a marked tendency in terms of race.

17. Asking about the tendency not to marry Afro- or Asian Brazilians, interviewees stressed that their family or friends do not marry *negros* (blacks) or *japoneses* (Japanese). Although this suggests that Christian Arabness is being whitened, its subjects in mixed marital arrangements did not refer to their ethnicity in such terms. This "unmarked" process of racialization is a classic mark of whiteness.

18. Indeed, interracial couples were rarely seen in Syrian–Lebanese social circles. One of the few stories I came across was that of a second-generation Lebanese woman who had secretly dated, and eventually married, a black Brazilian man. Her father refused to attend the wedding ceremony, and the woman was somewhat ostracized from her family. After the estranged father fell ill, though, he was cared for by the daughter and her husband.

19. Of course, this mixed model of ethnicity in the private sphere also relates to public images. Take, for instance, the marriage between the daughter of a middle-class Lebanese immigrant family and a man of "Portuguese descent." Nothing marked ethnicity in the wedding ceremony and reception. But the thank-you card sent to guests later included a photograph of the Lebanese bride as a belly dancer and the groom as a "typical Portuguese" (with a flat-top hat and tweed vest). As the brother of the bride later related, the couple had wanted to "do something different" with the wedding picture and opted for the ethnic parody. As discussed later, the soap opera *The Clone*, which featured belly dancing, had started a couple months earlier. In the circulation of this picture among the newlyweds and guests, the Arab ethnicity created in a mixed marriage engaged with its representation in the Brazilian public sphere.

20. Let it be added that the two female spouses were permitted to immigrate to Brazil in the early 1980s and early 1990s, respectively. At the time, the "family reunification" clause was not in place de jure, but as an immigration bureaucrat remarked, the justification for it was already being used de facto.

21. Glória Perez, as cited in Cristian Klein, "Islamismo chega ao horário nobre," *Folha de S. Paulo*, July 1, 2001.

22. Against her parents' wishes, Samira, the daughter of Mohammed and Latiffa, began to date a Brazilian boy, Zé Roberto. To marry his Muslim sweetheart, however, Zé Roberto ultimately converted to Islam.

23. As related by André Gattaz (2001: 207–209), the most polarized relations existed between Shia Muslims and Maronite Catholics, while Sunni Muslims, Orthodox Christians, and Melkite Catholics fell into the middle of the continuum. Yet most of my informants claimed to not hold "prejudice" toward other religious groups. One Maronite man stressed that Christians and Muslims get along well in Brazil. "You must learn to get along," related Jean, "because if you invite me and I don't show up, tomorrow I'll invite you and you won't show up, either. You'll say, 'He ignored me, so I'll ignore him [*Fez pouco caso de mim, então vou fazer pouco caso dele*].'" Where politico-religious tensions meet invidious high society, Christians and Muslims profess to get along well in Brazil.

FIVE: ETHNIC REAPPROPRIATION IN
THE COUNTRY CLUB CIRCUIT

1. My attention to this market of Arabisms stands in contrast to a recent prognosis made by the historian André Gattaz, who has reflected that the present "tendency" for Middle Eastern entities established in the 1920s and '30s "is to disappear amidst the total neglect of descendents, [who are] totally integrated in Brazilian life and not interested in maintaining a foreign ethnic identity" (Gattaz 2001: 240). Against this monolithic observation, my work understands ethnic associations as hybrid spaces of leisure for mostly second- and third-generation Arab Brazilians. Amid the mélange of ballroom and belly dances, "Italian" and "Arab" cultural nights, as well as musical staples from Frank Sinatra and Fairuz, though, there has been a conscientious selection of cultural forms perceived to connect socialites with Arab authenticity. Far from disappearing today, ethnicity has been self-consciously recognized in *colônia* clubs.

2. Incessantly struggling for greater "Lebanese" visibility in the theretofore labeled *colônia síria* (then sometimes spelled "*syria*"), Basílio Jafet also lay behind the name change of the Hospital Sírio, which became Hospital SírioLibanês.

3. Chukri al-Khuri gained infamy as a Lebanese nationalist through several Middle Eastern newspapers (in Arabic) in early twentieth-century São Paulo. When "Lebanon" became a distinct geopolitical entity under French colonialism in the late 1920s, he became the diplomatic representative of Lebanon in Brazil.

4. These sport and social clubs were frequented by entire families, but were (and are) exclusively operated by men. In some contrast, Middle Eastern women founded and operated charity leagues, including the Liga das Damas Sírias in 1912 and the Cedro do Líbano in 1947. Even in these philanthropic associations, however, men were usually in charge of finances and patrimony. Both are still run by Syrian and Lebanese women.

5. *Taulé* (lit., table, in Arabic) is the term used for backgammon (or *gamão*, in Portuguese).

6. Similar soccer matches today between Esporte Clube Sírio and Monte Líbano continue to represent what one mother has called "Homerian struggles."

7. There were precedents. Truzzi related that a bill in the City Council of São José do Rio Preto in 1906 proposed that "all *turcos*" caught speaking "the *turco* language near a Brazilian" would exact a sizable fine (Truzzi 1997: 75). Lesser (1999: 52) explained that the bill was thought to be "'so violent and absurd' that it was never discussed."

8. Consequently, the Club Germânico (Germany Club) changed its name to Club Pinheiros (Pine Club). Likewise, the Palestra Itália (Italian Palestra club) changed its name to Palmeiras (Palm Tree club). Today, Palmeiras operates a professional soccer team, but its club is still considered somewhat elite, especially in relation to the popular Corinthians (the team of the *povão*, or masses).

9. Arabs' linguistic difference was mocked by national elites as well. Wadih Safady reflected that the heavy Arab accent in Portuguese was "ridiculed" and "the motive for a theater piece in São Paulo for the past thirty years" (Safady 1966: 200–201; see also Truzzi 1997: 75). Called *Arabatache* (which means "fourteen" in Arabic), the play "mocked" Arabic speakers' difficulty in pronouncing the "p," "v," and "g" in Portuguese. The play was based on a short story by the São Paulo writer Cornélio Pires (2002 [1923]). The second-generation Lebanese Abdo likewise noted that Middle Eastern peddlers' enunciation of numbers in Arabic, such as *arabatache*, was ridiculed by non-Arabs. "*Arabatache* sounded like '*rouba o tacho*' [steal the pot] to Brazilian ears," he recounted, so when a peddler said "fourteen," Brazilians thought that he was planning to steal a pot or kettle. Language thus marked Arabs' marginal status in Brazil in the first half of the twentieth century.

10. Gabriel Marques, "A velha rua do quibe cru I." *O Estado de S. Paulo*, June 12, 1960.

11. *Ventre* literally means "womb" in Portuguese. But the term *dança do ventre* figuratively means "belly dance."

12. Guilherme de Almeida, "Cosmopolis: O oriente mais próximo," *O Estado de S. Paulo*, May 19, 1929. See also Lesser (1999).

13. Annual "cultural marathons" include art, dance, choir, theater, and music competitions. Since Monte Líbano's entrance into the association ten years ago, directors have noted with pleasure the increase in cultural production among club members. In ACESC competitions, their performances reflect not only Brazilian styles—the MPB music genre, for instance—but also European or U.S. American tastes: Frank Sinatra, Andrea Bocelli, or Tony Bennett. This "culturally creative environment"—to use the words of an ACESC official—has been a space for Brazilian elites to consume national and international genres of music, theater, and art.

14. One such tension arose during a musical competition between ACESC members at the Clube Hebraica. As it was later described to me, several Lebanese socialites went to the highbrow Jewish club to cheer for contestants from their own club. Having arrived early, one Lebanese woman sat next to a group of Jewish Brazilians. As her other Arab colleagues arrived later looking for places to sit, one member of the Jewish entourage offered a seat and unsuspectingly muttered to the Lebanese woman, "It doesn't hurt to be polite." The woman did not openly voice her indignation but stated to me, "How snobby!"

15. This marketing scheme began when the founder and chief executive, Dr. Alberto Saraiva (who is a Portuguese immigrant), met with an advertising executive who proposed the Habib's model, along with three others. Saraiva, who learned the art of Arab cuisine from the now deceased chef Paulo Aboud found most appealing the Habib's motif.

16. Roberto de Oliveira, Mariliz Pereira Jorge, and Paulo Sampaio, "O nosso lado árabe," *Revista da Folha*, in *Folha de S. Paulo*, September 23, 2001, 8.

17. In the documentary *Tales from Arab Detroit*, the same remark is made by the Lebanese owner of a "Mediterranean" restaurant in Detroit, Michigan. I do not think it is an overstatement to say that an "Arab restaurant" would be shunned by much of the U.S. American public today.

18. In the popular *Seinfeld*-like sitcom *Os Normais*, aired on the Globo television network, there was once a scene in which a character named Ruy arrived at the house of his fiancée, Ivonné. When Ivonné opened the door in her underwear, Ruy acted surprised, asking "*Ué?!* You're not ready? I told you to be ready to go out tonight." Ivonné defended herself by saying that they had not agreed on where to go. Ruy then asked, "Aren't we going to an Arab restaurant?" Ivonné repeated, "*Restaurante árabe?*" She agreed but beckoned Ruy to wait while she prepared herself to go to a "*restaurante árabe.*" Although they never did go to a *restaurante árabe*, this small exchange between two Brazilian yuppies on a popular sitcom points to the commonness of the so-called Arab restaurant today in Brazil.

19. Samir uses the term "*sírio-libanesa*" in reference to the cuisine served. In one of our meetings, he reflected that "Arab" is simply too general, especially given the number of "Arab fast-food" chains today. Most importantly, Samir stressed that the recipes used at his restaurant had been handed down from his Lebanese grandfather, who ran a small restaurant in turn-of-the-century Rio de Janeiro. Ethnic terminology reflected claims of cultural authenticity.

20. That said, Arab eating establishments represented just one of the many ethnic varieties that opened their doors from the 1990s onward. Especially during my research in 2000–2001, for instance, the city of São Paulo witnessed an explosion in Japanese sushi bars, takeouts, and restaurants. This striking visibility of Arab and Asian foods did not go unnoticed by other restaurateurs. As I was once passing a friend's Italian restaurant that had not been faring well, the friend complained, "The time of the Italian restaurant has passed. Now it's the time of the Japanese [restaurant] and the Arab [restaurant]." Like *comida árabe*, Japanese cuisine has become a familiar, and desired, object of consumption in the Brazilian market.

21. Other examples of Melo's reviews include "Novo árabe reúne elegância e boa comida," *Folha de S. Paulo*, September 15, 2000; "Árabes são como jóias brutas do oriente," *Folha de S. Paulo*, June 25, 2000; "Árabes podem ser refinados no Líbano e também em São Paulo," *Folha*

de S. Paulo, November 26, 2000. "Esqueça o medo e vá comer no árabe," *Folha de S. Paulo*, September 23, 2001.

22. Paloma Cotes, "Novela aumenta procura por cursos de dança do ventre," *Folha de S. Paulo*, October 28, 2001, C8.

23. One non-Arab female instructor, Priscilla, explained that belly dancing "is an exercise adapted to the woman's body because the benefits ... far beyond any cultural context ... are physiological." A non-Arab man who sells belly dancing supplies at his small store pointed out that the dance has attracted students because of its "intimate relation with the female body." While the samba, merengue, and lambada may come and go as passing fads, he reflected, belly dancing will continue to gain popularity because of its inherent relationship with the woman's body. Belly dancing now forms part of a commodified genre of dance in Brazil.

24. "Notícias," *Diário Popular*, September 8, 2001. It remains unclear whether Globo outsourced the selling of the sandals and bracelets (the CD was released under Globo's label). One thing remains very clear, however: The "Moroccan" wrist bracelets that connect to the finger were being worn by girls and women soon after the soap opera began.

25. Shortly after I interviewed him, the proud owner of the chain made news in the *Gazeta Mercantil*, a mainstream Brazilian business newspaper that is similar to the U.S. *Wall Street Journal*. See "Khan el Khalili: Casa de chá abre franquia de bazar egípcio," *Gazeta Mercantil*, August 22, 2001; "Bazar egípcio da Vila Mariana abre primeira franquia," *Gazeta Mercantil*, September 3, 2001; "Khan El Khalili abre loja em Itu," *Gazeta Mercantil*, September 3, 2001.

26. While I was speaking with Sérgio about my research in the *colônia árabe*, he expressed much interest and entered into a discussion of Jorge Amado's *Tocaia grande*. Stressing the ubiquitous presence of Arabs throughout the rural and urban spaces of Brazil, Sérgio also volunteered some commentary on his own European ethnic heritage. "I'm German on my father's side," he reflected, "and Portuguese and Italian on my mother's." Expressing his whiteness in a nationalist idiom, Sérgio quipped, "*É uma mistura!* [It's a mixture!]."

27. *Shuf* literally means "see" in Lebanese Arabic. The label derives from a wordplay by way of Brazil's most popular magazine, *Veja*, which literally means "see." As Monte Líbano members say tongue in cheek, "'*Shuf*' is our *Veja*."

28. Ethnic cuisine produced by the hands of *nordestino* labor can also be seen at the sushi restaurants around São Paulo. In fact, many sushi men today are migrant workers from the northeastern state of Ceará (Jeffrey Lesser, personal communication).

29. The majority of his students in Arabic language instruction at Club Homs, for instance, were not Middle Eastern descendants or even club members. Many were college students and young professionals seeking to learn a language besides English and Spanish. One student, Rogério, a computer technician in his late twenties, reflected that he already speaks Spanish and Italian and wanted to study another language. In the teacher's words, the growing interest in the Arabic language has to do with "globalization."

30. Men seemed to be enjoying themselves, but most women stayed in their place, clapping their hands and smiling. This was a space where men could exercise their sexuality, admire dancers' bodies, and interact with them. Female spectators, in contrast, clapped their hands and danced in place, but the majority vacillated between inspecting the aesthetics of the belly dancers' bodies and keeping a watch on their husbands, sons, or boyfriends.

31. Club Homs, "Resgate Cultural," *Homs*, vol. 2, no. 6, December 1998, 18–20.

SIX: AIR TURBULENCE IN HOMELAND TOURISM

1. Only a handful of more than eighty interviewees had not partaken in tourism abroad.

2. Airline tickets and tour packages to the Middle East frequently appeared in the weekly tourism sections of *Folha de S. Paulo* and *O Estado de S. Paulo* in 2000 and early 2001. Special four-page focuses on Lebanon appeared in *Folha de S. Paulo* on December 2, 1996, January 1,

1999, and February 14, 2001. The media depictions related archaeological and natural marvels. They also listed the prices of airline tickets, as well as the names of tourist agencies and descriptions of their full packages.

3. I do not mean to confuse the Zionist State of Israel and Jewishness. However, Arab Brazilians themselves used "Israel" and "Jews" as synonyms. This conflation of Zionism and Judaism is not dealt with here.

4. Giving a speech about the family reunion at the closing ceremony of the emigrant youth camp, Carlos recounted how the camp enabled him to renew family ties that had almost been lost. He made news on radio stations and in newspapers and became a poster boy for the state-sponsored emigrant youth program to the public sphere in Lebanon.

5. As I met with Oswaldo in the meeting room of KLM's branch in São Paulo, there was a white board in the corner of the room on which was written "Sales and Marketing," followed by a list of different target groups and commercial strategies. These included "Real, Commercial, Incentives, Targets, Student, Ethnic, Groups." The word "ethnic" was written not in its Portuguese form, *étnica* or *etnicidade*, but in English.

6. The four largest airline companies transporting people between Brazil and the Middle East (except Israel) are Varig, Air France, Alitalia, and KLM Royal Dutch Airlines. All four companies were well aware of each other's passenger totals.

7. The statement stems from an advertisement of AMET in several member media enterprises.

8. In the Arab Brazilian community, the three magazines chosen were *Al-Urubat*, *Chams*, and *Orient Express*.

9. Meeting with the president of AMET, who is the editor-in-chief of a popular Jewish community magazine, I raised the possibility that many Jewish Brazilians were from Arab cities and nations (and, implicitly, Arab as well as Jewish). But the magazine editor replied that Jewish Brazilians were Jewish, not Arab, *ponto final* (period).

10. Indeed, the winning entry in Air France's "Your Dream Trip" contest stemmed from the *Chams* magazine.

11. After asking whether he could keep the magazine in which the Air France advertisement had appeared, Wilson recalled that Alitalia used to be the *dono do pedaço* (king of the hill) in relation to the Brazil–Middle East segment of the airline industry. "You can be certain," concluded Wilson, "that someone in Rome took a look at the numbers and decided that there were more profitable connections" than South America–Middle East flights.

12. Fearab stands for Federation of Arab Entities in the Americas. The organization was founded in Argentina by mostly Brazilians and Argentines of Arab descent in 1973, but it retains significant links to the Arab Republic of Syria. Today the federation has national entities across Latin America and North America, as well as the Caribbean. Although its Honduran contingent was injuriously called "fanatical" by outsiders in González's account (González 1992), Fearab is a well-respected, if symbolic, force in the São Paulo *colônia* (see Hajjar 1985).

13. "Viagem ao passado: Jovens sócios do Club Homs conhecem a terra de seus ancestrais e convivem com uma cultura milenar," *Homs*, no. 3, 1997. Participants in excursions recalled that Syrian state officials had treated them like "diplomats." Excursions to Syria also meant tourist dollars for its economy. The magazine article noted that passengers embarked with fifty-four pieces of luggage and returned with 147.

14. "Tourism: Wide Ranging Opportunities for Investment," *World Links*, July–August 2002.

15. The Lebanese government's Ministry of Emigrant Affairs was instituted by decree no. 4859 in 1993. By 2000, it had been incorporated as a department into the Ministry of Foreign Affairs.

16. A small number of Arab Brazilians have also traveled to Palestine and Israel. A second-generation Armenian Palestinian named Sahak explained that he had traveled to visit his mother's relatives in Jerusalem in 1997. He remembered being surprised when his aunt told him

that they could not speak Arabic while walking on the city's busy streets. "In the old city, we can speak Arabic," he explained, "but in the bus, in the streets of Jerusalem, no way. My aunt said that the Jews [*judeus*] do not like to even hear Arabic spoken." Sahak repeated, "They [the Israelis] are stepping on them [the Palestinians]."

17. It was also said that tourists were shown the water-rich territory just south of Quneitra occupied by Israel in 1973. "Seeing" the rich pastures, one participant reflected that Israel will never return the land because of its fertility.

18. After more than one hour of hearing terrifying tales of torture in the prison, emigrant youth were escorted back toward the buses. Perhaps inadvertently, many of us ended up passing by a few small stands selling "souvenirs." A large yellow and green sign read, "Site Where Donations for the Islamic Resistance Are Accepted." The souvenirs sold included Hezbollah flags in three sizes; Hezbollah baseball caps; postcards of Hezbollah's leader, Hassan Nasrallah; video cassettes of bombing raids and the homecoming of displaced families after liberation; key chains with Hezbollah insignia; and coloring books that recounted Hezbollah's and Lebanon's struggle, as well as dozens of other items. Like sightseeing at any other tourist site, this "tour" had its own souvenirs. Let it be noted, however, that our tour guide beckoned us to hide these symbols of Hezbollah when officially meeting with Lebanese government officials.

19. War-torn Beirut also made an impression on him: "One thing that marked me a lot was this contrast between some really beautiful things and, at the same time, really ugly things right beside [them]. Buildings destroyed by bombs. This part is really sad." Postwar reconstruction in Lebanon likewise caught the attention of second-generation Abdo, who has made three trips. Abdo reflected: "I went after the war in '96, when the marks of destruction were still in Beirut, and … I went in 2000. I got really excited because Beirut is being restored, it's becoming a beautiful city, but I got really worried with the country's poverty. It's a country without much [*pause*], much future in the matter of jobs and the economy."

20. Experiencing spaces of past Israeli aggression in Syria and Lebanon, Arab Brazilians reflected on the irony of witnessing the near absence of street crime, which is an ever present aspect of their middle- to upper-class lives in São Paulo. Said reflected, "I felt safer than here because there wasn't theft, mugging. You could stop the car with the door open. Here I stopped and locked the car. They broke in and stole one of the interior panels. Here you go around with a better car, you can't stop at a light without looking on all sides. So on this point, here is much more violent than there. … The day-to-day war that you have here is really much more violent than the one there." Others expressed amazement at how gold sellers in the *suk* (open market, in Arabic) in Syria left their stores unlocked. "As much in Syria as in Lebanon," stated Vanessa, "the streets were tranquil and safe."

21. João, interestingly enough, used the Arabic term of difference, *asmar*, instead of its analogue in Brazilian Portuguese, *moreno*.

CONCLUSION: IN SECURE FUTURES

1. Fausto Macedo, "Muçulmanos pedem inquérito contra a Abin: Sociedade sediada em São Paulo alega estar sendo vítima de espionagem," *O Estado de S. Paulo*, December 17, 2000.

2. "Espionagem no Planalto: Bastante ativos, os agentes secretos da Abin espionam o que não devem e vigiam até os passos do governador Itamar Franco," *Veja*, November 15, 2000, 38–45. For a follow-up article, see Policarpo Júnior, "O documento secreto da espionagem: Dossiê sigiloso mostra que a Abin se interessa por uma gama de assuntos muito mais ampla do que costuma admitir," *Veja*, November 22, 2000, 42–47.

3. This citation stems from Abin documents reprinted by *Veja*. The excerpt reads, "Grupos étnicos islâmicos; identificação e localização de grupos no País, área de atuação dos grupos islamicos [Islamic ethnic groups; identification and localization of groups in the country, area of activity of Islamic groups]."

4. Jeffrey Goldberg, "In the Party of God," *New Yorker*, October 28, 2002, 75–80.

5. For a few instances, see "Bin Laden Reportedly Spent Time in Brazil in '95," *Washington Post*, March 18, 2003, A24; "Bin Laden esteve em Foz do Iguaçu e até deu palestra em mesquita," *O Estado de S. Paulo*, March 16, 2003; Policarpo Júnior, "Ele esteve no Brasil," *Veja*, March 19, 2003.

6. Maristella do Valle, "Bin Laden vira garoto-propaganda de Foz," *Folha de S. Paulo*, March 24, 2003, F2.

7. I am indebted to Paul Amar for his provocative suggestion that post–September 11 military-industrial globalization is competing with and possibly overtaking neoliberal globalization: Paul Amar, "Police and Polis in the Transnational Middle East: Security, Sexuality, and Militarized Urban Regimes in Cairo, Rio de Janeiro, and Baghdad," Lecture given at the Center for Middle Eastern Studies, University of California, Berkeley, 2005.

8. Larry Rohter, "Latin Lands Don't Share Powell's Priorities," *New York Times*, June 9, 2003.

9. As Petras also notes, Lula had actually increased debt payments to the IMF by "nearly 14 percent" by early 2003.

10. Though recurrently denouncing his predecessor's ostensible neoliberalism, Lula and his left-center alliance recently showed signs of a potential break with the status quo. In March 2005, the government announced that it would not be renewing its contract with the IMF, which had been in place since 1998. This decision, however, seemed to have more to do with the impending 2006 presidential elections in Brazil.

11. Mentioned briefly in Chapter 2, the nongovernmental organization Transparency International asked Lula and his opponent, José Serra, to sign an "anticorruption commitment" during the 2002 presidential race. The "commitment" included several measures to strengthen the institutional safeguards against corruption that each candidate promised to implement if elected president.

12. Paula Santa Maria, "Primeiro-ministro do Líbano visita Lula," *Gazeta Mercantil*, June 4, 2003, A5; Gabriela Valente, "Lula e Hariri criam comissão bilateral," *Gazeta Mercantil*, June 10, 2003, A8

13. Fernando Rodrigues and Alan Marques, "No Líbano, Lula defende uma nova 'geografia comercial,'" *Folha de S. Paulo*, December 6, 2003, A4.

14. Fernando Rodrigues, "Lula 'vende' Brasil na Síria e defende Estado palestino," *Folha de S. Paulo*, December 4, 2003, A4.

15. "Discurso do presidente da República, Luiz Inácio Lula da Silva, na sessão de abertura da Cúpula América do Sul–Países Árabes," Centro de Convenções Ulysses Guimarães, May 10, 2005.

16. Eliane Cantanhêde, "Democracia é algo que existe também no Sul, diz ministro," *Folha de S. Paulo*, May 16, 2005, A14.

17. The *New York Times* published one article: Larry Rohter, "Little Common Ground at Arab–South American Summit Talks," *New York Times*, May 11, 2005. As to be expected, the correspondent dismissed the summit as being irreconcilably divided. The Brazilian press also commented on this U.S. American and European "lapse" in reporting on the event. See Fábio Maisonnave, "Governo dos EUA e analistas ignoram evento," *Folha de S. Paulo*, May 12, 2005, A6.

18. Eliane Cantanhêde and Cláudia Dianni, "No final, Lula diz que falta de democracia é ameaça global," *Folha de S. Paulo*, May 12, 2005, A4.

19. See the exhibit's official website at http://www.amrik.com.br.

REFERENCES

NEWSPAPERS, MAGAZINES, AND BULLETINS

al-Nur
al-Urubat
A Nação
Carta do Líbano
Câmara Árabe Notícias
Chams
Correio Paulistano
Diário Popular

Folha de S. Paulo
Folha da Noite
Gazeta Mercantil
Homs
Isto É
Jornal da Tarde
Jornal do Brás
O Estado de S. Paulo
O Oriente

Oriente, Encanto e Magia
Orient Express
Revista Sírio
Shuf
Univinco
Valor Econômico
Veja
Veja São Paulo

BOOKS, ARTICLES, THESES

Abraham, Nabeel and Andrew Shryock, eds. 2000. *Arab Detroit: From Margin to Mainstream.* Detroit: Wayne State University Press.

Abraham, Sameer, and Nabeel Abraham, eds. 1983. *Arabs in the New World: Studies on Arab-American Communities.* Detroit: Wayne State University Press.

Abu-Lughod, Leila. 2005. *Dramas of Nationhood: The Politics of Television in Egypt.* Chicago: University of Chicago Press.

Akmir, Abdeluahed. 1991. *La inmigración arabe en Argentina (1880–1980).* Madrid: Universidad Complutense de Madrid.

Alonso, Ana Maria. 1994. "Politics of Space, Time, and Substance: State Formation, Nationalism, and Ethnicity." *Annual Review of Anthropology* 23: 379–405.

Amado, Jorge. 1945. *São Jorge de Ilhéus.* Rio de Janeiro: Olympus.

———. 1981. *Tocaia grande: A face obscura.* Rio de Janeiro: Editora Record.

———. 1991. *A descoberta da América pelos turcos.* Rio de Janeiro: Editora Record.

———. 1998 (1958). *Gabriela, cravo e canela.* 79th ed. Rio de Janeiro: Editora Record.

Amaral, Roberto. 2002. "Mass Media in Brazil: Modernization to Prevent Change." Pp. 38–46 in *Latin Politics, Global Media,* ed. Elizabeth Fox and Silvio R. Waisbord. Austin: University of Texas Press.

Anderson, Benedict. 1991 (1983). *Imagined Communities: Reflections on the Origin and Spread of Nationalism.* New York: Verso.
———. 1994. "Exodus." *Cultural Inquiry* 20: 324–25.
Andrews, George Reid. 1991. *Blacks and Whites in São Paulo, Brazil: 1888–1988.* Madison: University of Wisconsin Press.
Antonius, George. 1965 (1939). *The Arab Awakening: The Story of the Arab National Movement.* New York: Capricorn Books.
Aoun, Farid. 1979. *Do cedro ao mandacaru.* Recife: Editora Pernambucana.
Appadurai, Arjun. 1996. *Modernity at Large: Cultural Dimensions of Globalization.* Minneapolis: University of Minnesota Press.
Appelbaum, Nancy P., Anne S. Macpherson, and Karin Alejandra Rosemblatt. 2003. "Racial Nations. Pp. 1–31 in *Race and Nation in Modern Latin America*, ed. Nancy P. Appelbaum, Anne S. Macpherson, and Karin Alejandra Rosemblatt. Chapel Hill: University of North Carolina Press.
Araújo, Oscar Egidio de. 1940. "Enquistamentos étnicos." *Revista do Arquivo Municipal* 6, no. 65: 227–46.
Associação dos Antigos Alunos da Faculdade de Medicina da Universidade de São Paulo (AAAF-MUSP). 1995. *Médicos da Faculdade de Medicina da Universidade de São Paulo.* São Paulo: AAAFMUSP.
Assrauy, Nagib. 1967. *O Druzismo.* Belo Horizonte: Editora São Vicente.
Aswad, Barbara, ed. 1974. *Arabic Speaking Communities in American Cities.* New York: Center for Migration Studies.
Azevedo, Thales. 1951. *As elites de côr: Um estudo de ascenção.* São Paulo: Companhia Editora Nacional.
Babb, Florence. 2001. *After Revolution: Mapping Gender and Cultural Politics in Neoliberal Nicaragua.* Austin: University of Texas Press.
Bacelar, Jeferson. 2001. *A hierarquia das raças: Negros e brancos em Salvador.* Rio de Janeiro: Pallas.
Baer, Werner. 1995. *The Brazilian Economy: Growth and Development*, 4th ed. Westport, Conn.: Praeger.
Baringer, Sandra. 1998. "*Oklahoma!* and Assimilation." *Proceedings of the Modern Language Association* 113, no. 3: 452–53.
Barth, Frederik. 1969. "Introduction." Pp. 9–38 in *Ethnic Groups and Boundaries: The Social Organization of Culture Difference.* London: George Allen and Unwin.
Basch, Linda, Nina Glick-Schiller, and Cristina Szanton-Blanc. 1994. *Nations Unbound: Transnational Projects, Postcolonial Predicaments, and Deterritorialized Nation-States.* Langhorne: Gordon and Breach.
Bastani, Jorge Tanus. 1945. *O Líbano e os libaneses no Brasil.* Rio de Janeiro: C. Mendes Junior.
Bastide, Roger. 1964. *Brasil: Terra de contrastes.* Rio de Janeiro: Companhia Editora Nacional.
Bastide, Roger, and Florestan Fernandes. 1971. *Brancos e negros em São Paulo*, 3rd ed. São Paulo: Companhia Editora Nacional.
Bergsman, Joel. 1970. *Brazil: Industrialization and Trade Policies.* New York: Oxford University Press.
Bezerra, Marcos Otávio. 1995. *Corrupção: Um estudo sobre poder público e relações pessoais no Brasil.* Rio de Janeiro: Relume-Dumará.
Bilate, Anver. 1966. *Zé Felipe: O libanês.* Rio de Janeiro: C. Mendes Júnior.
Bourdieu, Pierre. 1977. *Outline of a Theory of Practice.* Cambridge: Cambridge University Press.
———. 1984. *Distinction: A Social Critique of the Judgment of Taste.* Cambridge, Mass.: Harvard University Press.
———. 1991. *Language and Symbolic Power.* Cambridge, Mass.: Harvard University Press.

Bourdieu, Pierre, and Louis Wacquant. 1999. "On the Cunning of Imperialist Reason." *Theory, Culture and Society* 16, no. 1: 41–58.

Browning, Barbara. 1995. *Samba: Resistance in Motion.* Bloomington: Indiana University Press.

Bruner, Edward. 1996. "Tourism in Ghana: The Representation of Slavery and the Return of the Black Diaspora." *American Anthropologist* 98, no. 2: 290–304.

Buechler, Simone. 2002. "Enacting the Global Economy in São Paulo, Brazil: The Impact of Labor Market Restructuring on Low-Income Women." Ph.D. diss., Columbia University, New York.

Burdick, John. 1998. *Blessed Anastácia: Women, Race, and Popular Christianity in Brazil.* New York: Routledge.

Cainkar, Louise. 1994. "The Palestinian Community in Chicago." Pp. 85–106 in *The Development of Arab-American Identity,* ed. Ernest McCarus. Ann Arbor: University of Michigan Press.

Câmara de Comércio Árabe Brasileira. 1989. *Almanaque.* São Paulo: CCAB.

———. 1998. *Câmara de Comércio Árabe Brasileira.* São Paulo: CCAB.

Campos, Mintaha Alcuri. 1987. *Turco pobre, sírio remediado, libanês rico: A trajetória do imigrante libanês no Espírito Santo.* Vitória: Instituto Jones dos Santos Neves.

Cardoso, Fernando Henrique, and Octávio Ianni. 1960. *Côr e mobilidade social em Florianopolis.* São Paulo: Companhia Editora Nacional.

Cardozo, José Eduardo. 2000 *A máfia das propinas: Investigando a corrupção em São Paulo.* São Paulo: Editora Fundação Perseu Abramo.

Carrillo, Luis Ramirez. 1994. *Secretos de familia: Libaneses y elites empresariales en Yucatan.* Mexico City: Consejo Nacional para la Cultura y las Artes.

Carvalho, A. Dardeau. 1976. *Situação jurídica do estrangeiro no Brasil.* São Paulo: Sugestões Literárias.

Carvalho, Hernani de. 1951. *Sociologia da vida rural.* Rio de Janeiro: Editora Civilização Brasileira.

Carvalho, Rejane Vasconcelos Accioly de. 1999. *Transição democrática brasileira e padrão midiático publicitário da política.* Campinas: Pontes.

Caufield, Sueann. 2000. *In Defense of Honor: Sexual Morality, Modernity, and Nation in Early-Twentieth Century Brazil.* Durham, N.C.: Duke University Press.

Cavarzere, Thelma Thais. 1991. "Direito internacional da pessoa humana: A circulação internacional de pessoas." Ph.D. diss., Universidade de São Paulo.

Chase, Jacquelyn, ed. 2002. *The Spaces of Neoliberalism: Land, Place and Family in Latin America.* Bloomfield, Conn.: Kumarian Press.

Chavez, Antonio. 1950. *As normas nacionalizadoras no direito brasileiro.* São Paulo: Saraiva.

Chatterjee, Partha. 1993. *The Nation and Its Fragments.* Princeton, N.J.: Princeton University Press.

Cheah, Pheng, and Bruce Robbins, eds. 1998. *Cosmopolitics: Thinking and Feeling beyond the Nation.* Minneapolis: University of Minnesota Press.

Clifford, James. 1994. "Diaspora." *Cultural Anthropology* 9, no. 3: 302–38.

———. 1997. *Routes: Travel and Translation in the Late Twentieth Century.* Cambridge, Mass.: Harvard University Press.

———. 1998. "Mixed Feelings." Pp. 362–70 in *Cosmopolitics: Thinking and Feeling beyond the Nation,* ed. Pheng Cheah and Bruce Robbins. Minneapolis: University of Minnesota Press.

Clifford, James, and George Marcus, eds. 1986. *Writing Culture: The Poetics and Politics of Ethnography.* Berkeley: University of California Press.

Colloredo-Mansfeld, Rudy. 2002. "An Ethnography of Neoliberalism: Understanding Competition in Artisan Economies." *Current Anthropology* 43: 113–37.

Comaroff, Jean, and John Comaroff. 1992 (1982). "Of Totemism and Ethnicity." Pp. 49–68 in *Ethnography and the Historical Imagination.* Boulder, Colo.: Westview Press.

———. 2000. "Millennial Capitalism: First Thoughts on a Second Coming." *Public Culture* 12, no. 2: 291–343.

Comaroff, John. 1996. "Ethnicity, Nationalism and the Politics of Difference in an Age of Revolution." Pp. 162–83 in *The Politics of Difference: Ethnic Premises in a World of Power*, ed. Patrick MacAllister and Edwin Wilmsen. Chicago: University of Chicago Press.

Conselho de Imigração e Colonização. 1943. *Ante-projeto de lei sobre imigração e colonização*. Rio de Janeiro: Imprensa Nacional.

Cutait, Daher Elias. 2000. *Um médico, uma vida*. São Paulo: Editora Mandarim.

DaMatta, Roberto. 1991. *Carnivals, Rogues, and Heroes*. South Bend, Ind.: University of Notre Dame Press.

———. 1995. "For an Anthropology of the Brazilian Tradition or 'A Virtude está no Meio.'" Pp. 270–91 in *The Brazilian Puzzle: Culture on the Borderlands of the Western World*, ed. David Hess and Roberto DaMatta. New York: Columbia University Press.

Davies, Charlotte Aull. 1999. *Reflexive Ethnography: A Guide to Researching Selves and Others*. New York: Routledge.

Dávila, Arlene. 1999. "El Kiosko Budweiser: The Making of a 'National' Television Show in Puerto Rico." *American Ethnologist* 25, no. 3: 452–70.

———. 2001. *Latinos Inc.: The Marketing and Making of a People*. Berkeley: University of California Press.

Dean, Warren. 1969. *The Industrialization of São Paulo, 1880–1945*. Austin: University of Texas Press.

Degler, Carl. 1986 (1971). *Neither Black nor White: Slavery and Race Relations in Brazil and the United States*. Madison: University of Wisconsin Press.

De la Torre, Carlos. 1999. "Neopopulism in Contemporary Ecuador: The Case of Bucaram's Use of the Mass Media." *International Journal of Politics, Culture, and Society* 12, no. 4: 555–71.

Departamento Estadual da Estatística. 1947. *Catálogo das indústrias do Município da Capital, 1945*. São Paulo: Rothschild Loureiro e Cia.

Diégues, Manuel. 1964. *Imigração, urbanização e industrialização*. Rio de Janeiro: Instituto de Estudos Pedagológicos.

———. 1976 (1952). *Etnias e culturas no Brasil*. Rio de Janeiro: Civilização Brasileira.

Dilley, Roy. 1990. "Contesting Markets: A General Introduction to Market Ideology, Imagery, and Discourse." Pp. 1–28 in *Contesting Markets: Analyses of Ideology, Discourse, and Practice*, ed. Roy Dilley. London: Edinburgh University Press.

Duany, Jorge. 2002. *The Puerto Rican Nation on the Move: Identities on the Island and in the United States*. Chapel Hill: University of North Carolina Press.

Duoun, Taufik. 1944. *A emigração sirio-libanesa ás terras de promissão*. São Paulo: Tipografia Editora Árabe.

Ellis, Alfredo, Jr. 1934. *Populações paulistas*. São Paulo: Companhia Editora Nacional.

Estatuto do Estrangeiro, Lei No. 6.815 de 19-8-80. 2000. 26th ed. São Paulo: Editora Atlas.

Euraque, Darío. 1994. "Formacíon nacional, mestizaje, y la inmigración arabe palestina a Honduras." *Estudios Migratórios Latinoamericanos* 9, no. 26: 47–66.

Evans, Peter. 1979. *Dependent Development: The Alliance of Multinational, State, and Local Capital in Brazil*. Princeton, N.J.: Princeton University Press.

Fanon, Frantz. 1965. *Black Skin, White Masks*. New York: Grove Press.

Farhat, Emil. 1987. *Dinheiro na estrada: Uma saga de imigrantes*. São Paulo: T. A. Queiroz.

Farmer, Paul. 2003. *Pathologies of Power: Health, Human Rights, and the New War on the Poor*. Berkeley: University of California Press.

Fausto, Boris. 1993. "Um balanço da historiografia da imigração para o Estado de São Paulo." *Estudios Migratórios Latinoamericanos* 8, no. 25: 415–40.

Fausto, Boris, ed. 1999. *Fazer a América: A imigração em massa para a América Latina*. São Paulo: Editora da Universidade de São Paulo.

Fausto, Boris, Oswaldo Truzzi, Roberto Grün, and Célia Sakurai. 1995. *Imigração e política em São Paulo*. São Paulo: Editora IDESP/Sumaré.

Fawaz, Leila. 1983. *Merchants and Migrants in Nineteenth Century Beirut*. Cambridge, Mass.: Harvard University Press.

Federação de Entidades Árabes do Brasil (Fearab). 1974. *II congresso panamericano árabe: São Paulo—Brasil*. São Paulo: Fearab.

Ferguson, James, and Akhil Gupta. 2003. "Spatializing States: Toward an Ethnography of Neoliberal Governmentality." *American Ethnologist* 29, no. 4: 981–1002.

Fernandes, Florestan. 1969. *The Negro in Brazilian Society*. New York: Columbia University Press.

Firro, Kais. 1988. "Silk and Socio-Economic Changes in Lebanon, 1860–1919." Pp. 20–50 in *Essays on the Economic History of the Middle East*, ed. Elie Kedourie and Sylvia Haim. London: Frank Cass.

Fontaine, Pierre, ed. 1985. *Race, Class, and Power in Brazil*. Berkeley: University of California Press.

Foster, Robert. 1991. "Making National Cultures in the Global Ecumene." *Annual Review of Anthropology* 20: 235–60.

———. 2002. *Materializing the Nation: Commodities, Consumption, and Media in Papua New Guinea*. Bloomington: University of Indiana Press.

Foucault, Michel. 1980. *Power/Knowledge*. New York: Pantheon Books.

French, John. 1991. *The Brazilian Workers' ABC*. Chapel Hill: University of North Carolina Press.

Freyre, Gilberto. 1977 (1933). *Casa grande e senzala*. Rio de Janeiro: José Olympio Editora.

Friedlander, Judith. 1975. *Being Indian in Hueyapan: A Study of Forced Identity in Contemporary Mexico*. New York: St. Martin's Press.

Fry, Peter. 1982. *Para inglês ver*. Rio de Janeiro: Zahar Editores.

———. 1995. "O que a cindarela negra tem a dizer sobre a 'política racial' no Brasil." *Revista USP* 28: 122–35.

Galleti, Roseli. 1996. "Migrantes estrangeiros no centro de São Paulo: Coreanos e bolivianos." Pp. 133–43 in *Emigração e imigração internacionais no Brasil contemporâneo*, 2nd ed., coord. Neide Lopes Patarra. São Paulo: Fundo de População das Nações Unidas.

Gattaz, André Castanheira. 2001. "História oral da imigração libanesa para o Brasil—1880–2000." Ph.D. diss., Universidade de São Paulo.

Geertz, Clifford. 1973. *The Interpretation of Cultures*. New York: HarperCollins.

Ghanem, Sadalla Amin. 1936. *Impressões de viagem (Libano-Brasil)*. Montevideo: Graphica Brasil.

Gilroy Paul. 1993. *The Black Atlantic: Modernity and Double Consciousness*. Cambridge, Mass.: Harvard University Press.

Glick-Schiller, Nina. 2001. *Georges Woke Up Laughing: Long-Distance Nationalism and the Search for Home*. Durham, N.C.: Duke University Press.

Glick-Schiller, Nina, Linda Basch, and Cristina Blanc-Szanton, eds. 1992. *Towards a Transnational Perspective on Migration: Race, Class, Ethnicity, and Nationalism Reconsidered*. New York: New York Academy of Sciences.

Gois, Chico de. 2000. *Segredos da máfia: Os bastidores do escândalo que abalou São Paulo*. São Paulo: Publisher Brasil.

Goldstein, Donna. 2003. *Laughter Out of Place: Race, Class, Violence, and Sexuality in a Rio Shantytown*. Berkeley: University of California Press.

González, Nancie. 1992. *Dollar, Dove, and Eagle: One Hundred Years of Palestinian Migration to Honduras*. Ann Arbor: University of Michigan Press.

Goulart, José Alípio. 1967. *O mascate no Brasil*. Rio de Janeiro: Conquista.

Green, Duncan. 1995. *Silent Revolution: The Rise of Market Economics in Latin America*. London: Cassell.

Greiber, Betty, Lina Maluf, and Vera Mattar. 1998. *Memórias de imigração: Libaneses e sírios em São Paulo*. São Paulo: Discurso Editorial.

Gros, Denise. 2004. "Institutos liberais, neoliberalismo e políticas públicas na Nova República." *Revista Brasileira de Ciências Sociais* 19, no. 54: 143–60.

Grün, Roberto. 1999. "Construindo um lugar ao sol: Os judeus no Brasil." Pp. 353–81 in *Fazer a América: A imigração em massa para a América Latina*, ed. Boris Fausto. São Paulo: Editora da Universidade de São Paulo.

Guillermoprieto, Alma. 1990. *Samba*. New York: Alfred A. Knopf.

Guimarães, Antônio Sérgio Alfredo. 2005. "Racial Democracy." Pp. 119–40 in *Imagining Brazil*, ed. Jessé Souza and Valter Sinder. New York: Lexington Books.

Guimarães, Caio de Freitas. 1952. "A assimilação dos principais grupos estrangeiros, através das estatísticas dos casamentos e nascimentos, na população do Município de São Paulo 1940–46." *Boletim do departmento de estatística do Estado de São Paulo* 14, no. 2: 81–114.

Guimarães, César, and Roberto Amaral. 1998. "Brazilian Television: A Rapid Conversion to the New Order." Pp. 51–70 in *Media and Politics in Latin America: The Struggle for Democracy*, ed. Elizabeth Fox. London: Sage Publications.

Gulick, John. 1955. *Social Structure and Culture Change in a Lebanese Village*. New York: Wenner Gren.

Gupta, Akhil. 1995. "Blurred Boundaries: The Discourse of Corruption, the Culture of Politics, and the Imagined State." *American Ethnologist* 22, no. 2: 375–402.

———. 1997. "The Song of the Nonaligned World: Transnational Identities and the Reinscription of Space in Late Capitalism." Pp. 179–99 in *Culture, Power, Place: Explorations in Critical Anthropology*, ed. Akhil Gupta and James Ferguson. Durham, N.C.: Duke University Press.

Gupta, Akhil, and James Ferguson, eds. 1997. *Anthropological Locations: Boundaries and Grounds of a Field Science*. Berkeley: University of California Press.

Gwynne, Robert. 1999. "Globalization, Neoliberalism and Economic Change in South America and Mexico." Pp. 68–97 in *Latin America Transformed: Globalization and Modernity*, ed. Robert Gwynne and Cristóbal Kay. New York: Arnold and Oxford University Press.

Gwynne, Robert, and Cristóbal Kay. 1999. "Latin America Transformed: Changing Paradigms, Debates and Alternatives." Pp. 2–29 in *Latin America Transformed: Globalization and Modernity*, ed. Robert Gwynne and Cristóbal Kay. New York: Arnold and Oxford University Press.

Habermas, Jürgen. 1989. *The Structural Transformation of the Public Sphere: An Inquiry into a Category of Bourgeois Society*. Cambridge: MIT Press.

———. 1992. "Further Reflections on the Public Sphere." Pp. 421–61 in *Habermas and the Public Sphere*, ed. Craig Calhoun. Cambridge, Mass.: MIT Press.

———. 2001. "Why Europe Needs a Constitution." *New Left Review* 2, no. 11: 12–23.

Hajjar, Claude. 1985. *Imigração árabe: Cem anos de reflexão*. São Paulo: Ícone Editora.

Hale, Charles. 1997. "Cultural Politics of Identity in Latin America." *Annual Review of Anthropology* 26: 567–90.

———. 2002. "Does Multiculturalism Menace? Governance, Cultural Rights, and the Politics of Identity in Guatemala." *Journal of Latin American Studies* 34, no. 3: 485–524.

———. 2005. "Neoliberal Multiculturalism: The Remaking of Cultural Rights and Racial Dominance in Central America." *PoLAR: Political and Legal Anthropology Review* 28, no. 1: 10–19."

Hall, Michael. 1979. "Italianos em São Paulo (1880–1920)." *Anais (Museu Paulista)* 29: 201–15.

Hall, Stuart. 1997 (1991). "The Local and the Global: Globalization and Ethnicity." Pp. 173–187 in *Dangerous Liasons: Gender, Nation, and Postcolonial Perspectives*, ed. Anne McClintock, Aamir Mufti, and Ella Shohat. Minneapolis: University of Minnesota Press.

Hanchard, Michael. 1994. *Orpheus and Power: The Movimento Negro of Rio de Janeiro and São Paulo, Brazil, 1945–1988*. Princeton, N.J.: Princeton University Press.

Hannerz, Ulf. 1996. *Transnational Connections: Culture, People, Places*. New York: Routledge Press.

Harris, Marvin. 1964. *Patterns of Race in the Americas*. New York: Walker.

————. 1970. "Referential Ambiguity in the Calculus of Brazilian Racial Identity." *Southwestern Journal of Anthropology* 14, no. 4: 1–14.

Hasenbalg, Carlos. 1979. *Discriminação e desigualdades racias no Brasil*. Rio de Janeiro: Graal.

————. 1988. *Estrutura social, mobilidade e raça*. São Paulo: Vertiço.

Hasenbalg, Carlos, and Nelson do Valle Silva. 1992. *Relações raciais no Brasil*. Rio de Janeiro: Rio Fundo Editora.

Hatoum, Milton. 1989. *Relato de um certo oriente*. São Paulo: Companhia das Letras.

————. 2000. *Dois irmãos*. São Paulo: Companhia das Letras.

Helayel, Munir. 1961. "A emigração libanesa para o Brasil." *Anuário Brasileiro de Imigração e Colonização*, vol. 2: 172–73.

Heras, Maria Cruz. 1991. *La emigración libanesa en Costa Rica*. Madrid: Editorial Cantárabia.

Hess, David, and Roberto DaMatta, eds. 1995. *The Brazilian Puzzle: Culture on the Borderlands of the Western World*. New York: Columbia University Press.

Himadeh, Sa'id. 1936. *The Economic Organization of Syria and Lebanon*. Beirut.

Hobsbawm, Eric, and Terence Ranger, eds. 1983. *The Invention of Tradition*. Cambridge: Cambridge University Press.

Holloway, Thomas. 1980. *Immigrants on Land: Coffee and Society in São Paulo, 1886–1930*. New York: Routledge Press.

Hourani, Albert, and Nadim Shehadi, eds. 1992. *The Lebanese in the World: A Century of Emigration*. London: I. B. Tauris.

Howell, Sally, and Andrew Shryock. 2004. "Cracking Down on Diaspora: Arab Detroit and America's War on Terror." *Anthropological Quarterly* 76, no. 3: 443–62.

Instituto Brasileiro de Geografia e Estatística (IBGE). 1981. *Censo demográfico*. Rio de Janeiro: IBGE.

————. 1991. *Censo demográfico*. Rio de Janeiro: IBGE.

Issawi, Charles, ed. 1966. *The Economic History of the Middle East 1800–1914*. Chicago: University of Chicago Press.

Jafet, Basílio. 1935. *A supremâcia reconhecida*. São Paulo: Editora Esphinge.

Jafet, Nami. 1947. *Ensaios e discursos*. São Paulo: Editora SA.

Jorge, Salomão. 1948. *Álbum da colônia sírio-libanesa no Brasil*. São Paulo: Sociedade Impressora Brasileira.

Jousiffe, Ann. 1998. *Lonely Planet: Lebanon*. Victoria, Australia: Lonely Planet Publications.

————. 2001. *Lonely Planet: Lebanon*. Victoria, Australia: Lonely Planet Publications.

Jozami, Gladys. 1996. "The Return of the '*Turks*' in 1990s Argentina." *Patterns of Prejudice* 30: 16–35.

Junior, Amarilio. 1935. *As vantagens da imigração syria no Brasil*. Rio de Janeiro.

Kadi, Joana, ed. 1994. *Food for Our Grandmothers: Writings by Arab-American and Arab-Canadian Feminists*. Boston: South End.

Karam, John Tofik. 2004. "A Cultural Politics of Entrepreneurship in Nation-Making: Phoenicians, Turks, and the Arab Commercial Essence in Brazil." *Journal of Latin American Anthropology* 9, no. 2: 319–51.

Karpat, Kemal. 1985. "The Ottoman Emigration to America." *International Journal of Middle East Studies* 17: 175–209.

Kashmeri, Zuhair. 1991. *The Gulf Within: Canadian Arabs, Racism and the Gulf War*. Toronto: James Lorimer.

Kay, Cristóbal. 1989. *Latin American Theories of Development and Underdevelopment*. New York: Routledge.

Kayal, Philip and Kathleen Benson, eds. 2002. *A Community of Many Worlds: Arab Americans in New York City*. New York: Syracuse University Press.

Keynes, John Maynard. 1974 (1936). *The General Theory of Employment, Interest, and Money*. Cambridge: Cambridge University Press.

Khater, Akram. 2001. *Inventing Home: Emigration, Gender, and the Middle Class in Lebanon, 1870–1920.* Berkeley: University of California Press.

Kingstone, Peter. 1999. *Crafting Coalitions for Reform: Business Preferences, Political Institutions, and Neoliberal Reform in Brazil.* University Park: Pennsylvania State University Press.

Klich, Ignácio. 1992. "*Criollos* and Arabic Speakers in Argentina: An Uneasy *Pas de Deux*, 1888–1914." Pp. 243–83 in *The Lebanese in the World: A Century of Emigration*, ed. Albert Hourani and Nadim Shehadi. London: I. B Tauris.

———. 1998. "Arab–Jewish Coexistence in the First Half of the 1900s' Argentina: Overcoming Self-Imposed Amnesia." Pp. 1–37 in *Arab and Jewish Immigrants in Latin America: Images and Realities*, ed. Ignácio Klich and Jeffrey Lesser. London: Frank Cass.

Klich, Ignácio, and Jeffrey Lesser, eds. 1998. *Arab and Jewish Immigrants in Latin America: Images and Realities.* London: Frank Cass.

Knowlton, Charles. 1961. *Sírios e libaneses em São Paulo.* São Paulo: Editora Anhembi.

———. 1992. "The Social and Spatial Mobility of the Syrian and Lebanese Community in São Paulo." Pp. 285–312 in *The Lebanese in the World: A Century of Emigration*, ed. Albert Hourani and Nadim Shehadi. London: I. B. Tauris.

Kofes, Suely, et al. 1996. "Gênero e raça em revista: Debate com os editores da revista Raça Brasil." *Cadernos Pagu* 6–7: 241–96.

Kondo, Dorinne. 1990. *Crafting Selves: Power, Gender, and Discourses of Identity in a Japanese Workplace.* Chicago: University of Chicago Press.

Kottack, Conrad. 1983. *Assault on Paradise: Social Change in a Brazilian Village.* New York: Random House.

Kurban, Taufik. 1933. *Os syrios e libaneses no Brasil.* São Paulo: Sociedade Impressora Paulista.

Kwong, Peter. 1997. "Manufacturing Ethnicity." *Critique of Anthropology* 17, no. 4: 365–87.

Lacaz, Carlos da Silva. 1977. *Vultos da medicina brasileira*, 4 vols. São Paulo: Almed.

———. 1982. *Médicos sírios e libaneses do passado: Trajetória em busca de uma nova pátria.* São Paulo: Almed.

Leopoldi, Maria Antoineta. 2000. *Política e interesses na industrialização brasileira: As associações industriais, a política econômica e o Estado.* São Paulo: Paz e Terra.

Lesser, Jeffrey. 1992. "From Pedlars to Proprietors: Lebanese, Syrian, and Jewish Immigrants in Brazil." Pp. 393–410 in *The Lebanese in the World: A Century of Emigration*, ed. Albert Hourani and Nadim Shehadi. London: I. B. Tauris.

———. 1994. "Immigration and Shifting Concepts of National Identity in Brazil during the Vargas Era." *Luso-Brazilian Review* 31, no. 2: 23–44.

———. 1995. *Welcoming the Undesirables: Brazil and the Jewish Question.* Berkeley: University of California Press.

———. 1996. "(Re)Creating Ethnicity: Middle Eastern Immigration to Brazil." *Americas* 53, no. 1: 45–65.

———. 1998. "'Jews Are Turks Who Sell on Credit': Elite Images of Arabs and Jews in Brazil." Pp. 38–56 in *Arab and Jewish Immigrants in Latin America: Images and Realities*, ed. Ignácio Klich and Jeffrey Lesser. London: Frank Cass.

———. 1999. *Negotiating National Identity: Immigrants, Minorities, and the Struggle for Ethnicity in Brazil.* Durham, N.C.: Duke University Press.

Lewis, J. Lowell. 1999. "Sex and Violence in Brazil: Carnival, Capoeira, and the Problem of Everyday Life." *American Ethnologist* 26, no. 3: 717–32.

Linger, Daniel. 2001. *No One Home.* Stanford, Calif.: Stanford University Press.

Luxner, Larry. 2000. "Esfihas to Go." *Saudi Aramco World* 51, no. 6: 34–37.

MacCannell, Dean. 1976. *The Tourist: A New Theory of the Leisure Class.* New York: Schocken Books.

Machado Jr., Armando Marcondes. 1998. *Centro Acadêmico XI de Agosto: Faculdade de Direito de São Paulo, 1961–1998*, 4 vols. São Paulo: Mageart.

Mankekar, Purnima. 1999. *Screening Culture, Viewing Politics: An Ethnography of Television, Womanhood, and Nation in Postcolonial India.* Durham, N.C.: Duke University Press.

Marcus, George. 1995. "Ethnography in/of the World System: The Emergence of Multi-Sited Ethnography." *Annual Review of Anthropology* 24: 95–117.

————. 2000. *Ethnography through Thick and Thin.* New York: Routledge.

Marcus, George, and Michael Fischer. 1986. *Anthropology as Cultural Critique: An Experimental Moment in the Human Sciences.* Chicago: University of Chicago Press.

Marques, Gabriel. 1966. *Ruas e tradicões de São Paulo: Uma história em cada rua.* São Paulo: Conselho Estadual de Cultura.

Martins, José de Souza. 1989. "A imigração espanhola para o Brasil e a formação da força-de-trabalho na economia cafeeira: 1880–1930." *Revista de História* 121: 5–26.

Masao, Miyoshi. 1993. "A Borderless World? From Colonialism to Transnationalism and the Decline of the Nation-State." *Critical Inquiry* 19: 726–51.

Massad, Joseph. 1993. "Palestinians and the Limits of Racialized Discourse." *Social Text* 11, no. 1: 90–112.

McCarus, Ernest, ed. 1994. *The Development of Arab-American Identity.* Ann Arbor: University of Michigan Press.

Miller, Lucius Hopkins. 1969 (1905). *Our Syrian Population: A Study of the Syrian Communities of Greater New York.* San Francisco: Reed.

Mintz, Sidney. 1985. *Sweetness and Power: The Place of Sugar in Modern History.* New York: Penguin Books.

Miranda, Ana. 1997. *Amrik: Romance.* São Paulo: Companhia das Letras.

Mita, Chiyoko. 1995. "Ochenta años de inmigracíon japonesa en el Brasil." *Estudios Migratorios Latinoamericanos* 10, no. 30: 431–52.

Mott, Maria Lúcia. 2000. "Imigração árabe, um certo oriente no Brasil." Pp. 181–95 in *Brasil: 500 Anos de Povoamento.* Rio de Janeiro: IBGE.

Mouffe, Chantal. 1979. "Hegemony and Ideology in Gramsci." Pp. 168–204 in *Gramsci and Marxist Theory,* ed. Chantal Mouffe. London: Routledge and Kegan Paul.

Munasinghe, Viranjini. 2001. *Callaloo or Tossed Salad? East Indians and the Cultural Politics of Identity in Trinidad.* Ithaca, N.Y.: Cornell University Press.

Naber, Nadine. 2000. "Ambiguous Insiders: An Investigation of Arab American Invisibility." *Ethnic and Racial Studies* 23: 37–61.

Nader, Laura. 1972. "Up the Anthropologist—Perspectives Gained from Studying Up." Pp. 284–311 in *Reinventing Anthropology,* ed. Dell Hymes. New York: Pantheon Books.

Narayan, Kirin. 1993. "How Native Is a 'Native' Anthropologist?" *American Anthropologist* 95: 671–86.

Nassar, Raduan. 1975. *Lavoura arcaica.* Rio de Janeiro: Editora Record.

Needle, Jeffrey. 1995. "Identity, Race, Gender and Modernity in the Origins of Gilberto Freyre's *Oeuvre.*" *American Historical Review* 100, no. 1: 55–82.

Neiva, Artur Hehl. 1945. *O problema imigratório brasileiro.* Rio de Janeiro: Imprensa Nacional.

Nunes, Heliane Prudente. 1993. "A imigração árabe em Goiás." Ph.D. diss., Universidade de São Paulo.

Nylen, William. 1993. "Selling Neoliberalism: Brazil's *Instituto Liberal.*" *Journal of Latin American Studies* 25: 301–11.

O'Dougherty, Maureen. 2002. *Consumption Intensified: The Politics of Middle-Class Daily Life in Brazil.* Durham, N.C.: Duke University Press.

Olguin Tenorio, Myriam. 1990. *La inmigración arabe en Chile.* Santiago: Ediciones Instituto Chileno Arabe de Cultura.

Omi, Michael, and Howard Winant. 1986. *Racial Formation in the United States: From the 1960s to the 1980s.* New York: Routledge.

Ong, Aihwa. 1999. *Flexible Citizenship: The Cultural Logics of Transnationality.* Durham, N.C.: Duke University Press.

Ong, Aihwa, and Donald Nonini, eds. 1997. *Ungrounded Empires: The Cultural Politics of Modern Chinese Transnationalism.* New York: Routledge.

Orfalea, Gregory. 1988. *Before the Flames: A Quest for the History of Arab Americans.* Austin: University of Texas Press.

Ortiz, Renato. 1988. *A moderna tradição brasileira: Cultura brasileira e indústria cultural.* São Paulo: Editora Brasiliense.

Osman, Samira Adel. 1998. "Caminhos da imigração árabe em São Paulo: História oral de vida familiar." M.A. thesis, Universidade de São Paulo.

Owensby, Brian. 1999. *Intimate Ironies: Modernity and the Making of Middle-Class Lives in Brazil.* Stanford, Calif.: Stanford University Press.

Oxhorn, Philip, and Graciela Ducantenzeiler, eds. 1998. *What Kind of Democracy? What Kind of Market? Latin America in the Age of Neoliberalism.* University Park: Pennsylvania State University Press.

Pardue, Derek. 2004. "Blackness and Periphery: A Retelling of Hip-Hop Culture of São Paulo, Brazil." Ph.D. diss., University of Illinois, Urbana-Champaign.

Parker, Richard. 1991. *Bodies, Pleasures, and Passions: Sexual Culture in Contemporary Brazil.* Boston: Beacon Press.

———. 1999. *Beneath the Equator: Cultures of Desire, Male Homosexuality, and Emerging Gay Communities in Brazil.* New York: Routledge.

Petras, James, and Henry Veltmeyer. 2003. "Whither Lula's Brazil? Neoliberalism and 'Third Way' Ideology." *Journal of Peasant Studies* 31, no. 1: 1–44.

Pierson, Donald. 1942. *Negroes in Brazil: A Study of Race Contact at Bahia.* Chicago: University of Chicago Press.

Pires, Cornélio. 2002 (1923). *Patacoadas.* São Paulo: Ottoni Editora.

Puls, Mauricio. 2000. *Folha Explica: O Malufismo.* São Paulo: Folha de São Paulo.

Queiroz, Maria Isaura Pereira de. 1985. "The Samba Schools of Rio de Janeiro, or the Domestication of an Urban Mass." *Diogenes* 129: 1–32.

Reich, Robert. 1992. *The Work of Nations.* New York: Doubleday.

Reichl, Christopher. 1995. "Stages in the Historical Process of Ethnicity: The Japanese in Brazil." *Ethnohistory* 42, no. 8: 31–62.

Reichman, Rebecca, ed. 1999. *Race in Contemporary Brazil.* University Park: Pennsylvania State University Press.

Ribeiro, Paula. 1999. "Saara: Uma pequena ONU no Rio de Janeiro." *Travessia* 12, no. 34: 35–38.

Ricardo, David. 1951 (1815). *The Works and Correspondence of David Ricardo,* 11 vol., ed. M. H Dobb and Piero Sraffa. Cambridge: Cambridge University Press.

Riggs, Lynn. 1931. *Green Grow the Lilacs.* New York: Samuel French.

Rio, João do (Paulo Barreto). 1928. *As religiões do Rio.* Rio de Janeiro: Editora Companhia Nacional.

Robbins, Bruce. 1998. "Actually Existing Cosmopolitanism." Pp. 1–19 in *Cosmopolitics: Thinking and Feeling beyond the Nation,* ed. Pheng Cheah and Bruce Robbins. Minneapolis: University of Minnesota Press.

Roberts, Lois J. 2000. *The Lebanese in Ecuador: A History of Emerging Leadership.* Boulder, Colo.: Westview Press.

Roque, Carlos. 2000. "Líbano." Pp. 155–64, in *Correntes de imigrantes e invenções culinárias no 5º centenário do Brasil.* São Paulo.

Roquette-Pinto, Edgar. 1935. *Rondônia,* 3rd ed. Rio de Janeiro: Editora Companhia Nacional.

Rosa, Zita de Paula. 1983. "Imigração: um tema controvertido na voz dos plenipotenciários da oligarquia cafeeira." *Revista de História* 15: 15–31.

Rowe, Peter, and Hashim Sarkis. 1998. *Projecting Beirut: Episodes in the Construction and Reconstruction of a Modern City.* New York: Prestel.

Said, Edward. 1978. *Orientalism.* New York: Praeger.

———. 1979. "Zionism from the Standpoint of Its Victims." *Social Text* 1: 7–58.

Safady, Jamil. 1972a. *Panorama da imigração árabe.* São Paulo: Editora Comercial Safady.

———. 1972b. *O café e o mascate.* São Paulo: Editora Comercial Safady.

Safady, Jorge. 1972a. *Antologia árabe do Brasil.* Editora Comercial Safady.

———. 1972b. "A imigração árabe no Brasil (1880–1971)." Ph.D. diss., Universidade de São Paulo.

Safady, Wadih. 1966. *Cenas e cenários dos caminhos da minha vida.* São Paulo: Penna Editora.

Sales, Teresa, and Maria do Rosário R. Salles. 2002. *Políticas migratórias: América latina, Brasil e brasileiros no exterior.* São Carlos: Editora UFSC.

Saliba, Therese. 1999. "Resisting Invisibility: Arab Americans in Academia and Activism." Pp. 304–19 in *Arabs in America: Building a New Future,* ed. Michael Suleiman. Philadelphia: Temple University Press.

Salibi, Kamal. 1988. *A House of Many Mansions: The History of Lebanon Reconsidered.* Berkeley: University of California Press.

Samhan, Helen Hatab. 1999. "Not Quite White: Race Classification and the Arab-American Experience." Pp. 209–26 in *Arabs in America: Building a New Future,* ed. Michael Suleiman. Philadelphia: Temple University Press.

Sanders, Todd, and Harry G. West. 2003. "Power Revealed and Concealed in the New World Order." Pp. 1–35 in *Transparency and Conspiracy: Ethnographies of Suspicion in the New World Order,* ed. Harry G. West and Todd Sanders. Durham, N.C.: Duke University Press.

Sanjek, Roger. 1971. "Brazilian Racial Terms: Some Aspects of Meaning and Learning." *American Anthropologist* 73: 1126–43.

Sansone, Lívio. 2003. *Blackness without Ethnicity: Constructing Race in Brazil.* New York: Palgrave Macmillan

Sassen, Saskia. 1998. *Globalization and Its Discontents.* New York: New Press.

———. 2001. "Spatialities and Temporalities of the Global: Elements for a Theorization." Pp. 260–78 in *Globalization,* ed. Arjun Appadurai. Durham, N.C.: Duke University Press.

Sawyer, Suzana. 2001. "Fictions of Sovereignty: Of Prosthetic Petro-Capitalism, Neoliberal States, and Phantom-Like Citizens in Ecuador." *Journal of Latin American Anthropology* 6, no. 1: 156–97.

Schein, Louisa. 1998. "Importing Miao Brethren to Hmong America: A Not-So-Stateless Transnationalism." Pp. 163–91 in *Cosmopolitics: Thinking and Feeling beyond the Nation,* ed. Pheng Cheah and Bruce Robbins. Minneapolis: University of Minnesota Press.

———. 2001. *Minority Rules: The Miao and the Feminine in China's Cultural Politics.* Durham, N.C.: Duke University Press.

Schopmeyer, Kim. 2000. "A Demographic Portrait of Arab Detroit." Pp. 61–92 in *Arab Detroit: From Margin to Mainstream,* ed. Nabeel Abraham and Andrew Shryock. Detroit: Wayne State University Press.

Scott, James. 1998. *Seeing Like a State: How Certain Schemes to Improve the Human Condition Have Failed.* New Haven, Conn.: Yale University Press.

Seyferth, Giralda. 1990. *Imigração e cultura no Brasil.* Brasília: Editora UnB.

———. 1995. "La inmigración alemana y la politica Brasileña de colonización." *Estudios Migratórios Latinoamericanos* 10, no. 29: 53–75.

Shaheen, Jack. 1984. *The T.V. Arab.* Madison: Bowling Green State University Press.

Sheriff, Robin. 1999. "The Theft of Carnaval: National Spectacle and Racial Politics in Rio de Janeiro." *Cultural Anthropology* 14, no. 1: 3–28.

———. 2001. *Dreaming Equality: Color, Race, and Racism in Urban Brazil.* New Brunswick, N.J.: Rutgers University Press.

Shryock, Andrew. 2002. "New Images of Arab Detroit: Seeing Otherness and Identity through the Lens of September 11." *American Anthropologist* 104: 917–22.

———. 2000. "Public Culture in Arab Detroit: Creating Arab/American Identities in a Transnational Domain." Pp. 32–60 in *Mass Mediations: New Approaches to Popular Culture in the Middle East and Beyond*, ed. Walter Armbrust. Berkeley: University of California Press.

Simpson, Amelia. 1993. *Xuxa: The Mega-Marketing of Gender, Race, and Modernity*. Philadelphia: Temple University Press.

Skidmore, Thomas. 1967. *Politics in Brazil, 1930–1964: An Experiment in Democracy*. New York: Oxford University Press.

———. 1974. *Black into White: Race and Nationality in Brazilian Thought*. New York: Oxford University Press.

———. 1993. "Bi-racial U.S.A vs. Multi-racial Brazil: Is the Contrast Still Valid?" *Journal of Latin American Studies* 25: 373–86.

Smilianskaya, I. M. 1966. "From Subsistence to Market Economy, 1850s." Pp. 226–47 in *The Economic History of the Middle East 1800–1914*, ed. Charles Issawi. Chicago: University of Chicago Press.

Smith, Adam. 1976 (1776). *An Inquiry into the Nature and Causes of the Wealth of Nations*, ed. Edwin Cannan. Chicago: University of Chicago Press.

Smith, Anthony. 1994. "The Politics of Culture: Ethnicity and Nationalism." Pp. 706–33 in *Companion Encyclopedia of Anthropology*, ed. Tim Ingold. New York: Routledge.

Smith, James. 2001. "Of Spirit Possession and Structural Adjustment Programs." *Journal of Religion in Africa* 31, no. 4: 427–56.

———. 2005. "Buying a Better Witch Doctor: Witch-finding, Neoliberalism, and the Development Imagination in the Taita Hills, Kenya." *American Ethnologist* 32, no. 1: 141–58.

Smith-Nonini, Sandy. 1998. "Health 'Anti-Reform' in El Salvador: Community Health NGOs and the State in the Neoliberal Era." *Political and Legal Anthropology Review* 21, no. 1: 99–113.

Sociedade Nacional de Agricultura. 1926. *Immigração: Inquérito promovido pela Sociedade Nacional de Agricultura*. Rio de Janeiro: Villani e Barbero.

Souza, Rafael Paula. 1937. "Contribuição á etnologia paulista." *Revista do Arquivo Municipal* 3, no. 3: 95–105.

Stein, Stanley. 1957. *The Brazilian Cotton Manufacture: Textile Enterprise in an Underdeveloped Area, 1850–1950*. Cambridge, Mass.: Harvard University Press.

Stepan, Nancy Leys. 1991. *The Hour of Eugenics: Race, Gender, and Nation in Latin America*. Ithaca, N.Y.: Cornell University Press.

Stokes, Susan Carol. 2001. *Mandates and Democracy: Neoliberalism by Surprise in Latin America*. New York: Cambridge University Press.

Stolcke, Verena. 1988. *Coffee Planters, Workers, and Wives: Class Conflict and Gender Relations on São Paulo Plantations, 1850–1980*. New York: St. Martin's Press.

Stutzman, Ronald. 1981. "*El Mestizaje*: An All-Inclusive Ideology of Exclusion." Pp. 45–94 in *Cultural Transformations and Ethnicity in Modern Ecuador*, ed. Norman Whitten. Urbana: University of Illinois Press.

Suleiman, Michael, ed. 1999. *Arabs in America: Building a New Future*. Philadelphia: Temple University Press.

Tannenbaum, Frank. 1947. *Slave and Citizen: The Negro in the Americas*. New York: Vintage.

Tasso, Alberto. 1988. *Aventura, trabajo y poder: Sirios e libaneses en Santiago del Estero, 1880–1980*. Buenos Aires: Ediciones Indice.

Truzzi, Oswaldo. 1992. *De mascates a doutores: Sirios e libaneses em São Paulo*. São Paulo: Editora Sumaré.

———. 1995. "Sírios e libaneses em São Paulo: A anatomia da sobre-representação." Pp. 27–69 in *Imigração e política em São Paulo*, ed. Boris Fausto. São Paulo: Editora IDESP/Sumaré.

———. 1997. *Patrícios: Sírios e libaneses em São Paulo*. São Paulo: Editora Hucitec.

Tsing, Anne. 2001a. "The Global Situation." *Cultural Anthropology* 15, no. 3: 327–60.

———. 2001b. "Inside the Economy of Appearances." Pp. 155–88 in *Globalization*, ed. Arjun Appadurai. Durham, N.C.: Duke University Press.

Twine, France Winddance. 1998. *Racism in a Racial Democracy: The Maintenance of White Supremacy in Brazil.* New Brunswick, N.J.: Rutgers University Press.

Varella, Flávia. 2000. "Patrícios, dinheiro, diploma e voto: A saga da imigração árabe." *Veja*, October 4, 122–29.

Varella-Garcia, Marileila. 1976. "Demographic Studies in a Brazilian Population of Arabian Origin." *Social Biology* 23, no. 2: 162–67.

Vasconcellos, Mayra Moreira. 2000. *Dança do ventre—Dança do coração.* São Paulo: Radhu.

Velben, Thorstein. 1996 (1899). *The Theory of the Leisure Class.* New York: Prometheus.

Viana, Oliveira. 1932. *Raça e assimilação.* São Paulo: Companhia Editora Nacional.

Viva O Centro. 1994. *Camelôs: Subsídios para o equacionamento do problema do comércio informal de rua e sua solução.* São Paulo: Associação Viva o Centro.

Wade, Peter. 1997. *Race and Ethnicity in Latin America.* London: Pluto Press.

Wagley, Charles, ed. 1952. *Race and Class in Rural Brazil.* Paris: United Nations Educational, Scientific and Cultural Organization.

Wallerstein, Immanuel. 1974. *The Modern World-System: Capitalist Agriculture and the Origins of the European World-Economy in the Sixteenth Century.* New York: Academic Press.

Warren, Kay. 1998. *Indigenous Movements and Their Critics: Pan-Maya Activism in Guatemala.* Princeton, N.J.: Princeton University Press.

———. 1989 (1978). *The Symbolism of Subordination: Indian Identity in a Guatemalan Town.* Austin: University of Texas Press.

Weinstein, Barbara. 1983. *The Amazon Rubber Boom.* Cambridge, Mass.: Harvard University Press.

———. 1995. *For Social Peace in Brazil: Industrialists and the Remaking of the Working Class in São Paulo, 1920–1964.* Chapel Hill: University of North Carolina Press.

Weyland, Kurt. 1996. *Growth without Equity: Failures of Reform in Brazil.* Pittsburgh: University of Pittsburgh Press.

———. 1998. "Swallowing the Bitter Pill: Sources of Popular Support for Neoliberal Reform in Latin America." *Comparative Political Studies* 31, no. 5: 539–68.

Wilk, Richard. 1993. "'It's Destroying a Whole Generation': Television and Moral Discourse in Belize." *Visual Anthropology* 5: 229–44.

———. 1995. "Learning to Be Local in Belize: Global Systems of Common Difference." Pp. 110–33 in *Worlds Apart: Modernity through the Prism of the Local*, ed. Daniel Miller. New Brunswick, N.J.: Routledge.

Wilkie, Mary. 1973. "The Lebanese in Montevideo, Uruguay: A Study of an Entrepreneurial Ethnic Minority." Ph.D. diss., University of Wisconsin, Madison.

Williams, Brackette. 1989. "A Class Act: Anthropology and the Race to Nation across Ethnic Terrain." *Annual Review of Anthropology* 18: 401–44.

———. 1991. *Stains on My Name, War in My Veins: Guyana and the Politics of Cultural Struggle.* Durham, N.C.: Duke University Press.

Williams, Judith. 1968. *The Youth of Haouch El Harimi, a Lebanese Village.* Cambridge, Mass.: Harvard University Press.

Williamson, John. 1990. "What Washington Means by Policy Reform." Pp. 5–20 in *Latin American Adjustment: How Much Has Happened*, ed. John Williamson. Washington, D.C.: Institute of International Economics.

———. 1993. "Democracy and the 'Washington Consensus.'" *World Development* 21, no. 8: 1329–36.

Winant, Howard. 1994. *Racial Conditions: Politics, Theory, Comparisons.* Minneapolis: University of Minnesota Press.

Wolf, Eric. 1980. *Europe and the People without History*. Berkeley: University of California Press.

Wolfe, Joel. 1994. "'Father of the Poor' or 'Mother of the Rich'? Getúlio Vargas, Industrial Workers, and Constructions of Class, Gender, and Populism in São Paulo, 1930–1954." *Radical History Review* 58: 76–94.

Yúdice, George. 1995. "Civil Society, Consumption, and Governmentality in an Age of Global Restructuring." *Social Text* 45: 1–25.

———. 1999. "The Privatization of Culture." *Social Text* 59: 17–34.

Yuri, Débora. 2001. "O nosso lado árabe." *Revista da Folha*, September 23, 8.

Zogby, John. 1990. *Arab America Today: A Demographic Profile of Arab Americans*. Washington, D.C.: Zogby International.

INDEX

JOHN TOFIK KARAM is Assistant Professor in the Latin American and Latino Studies Program at DePaul University.